Lanier Golf Guides have set the standard for the industry. . .

Golf Resorts—The Complete Guide™ *Golf Courses—The Complete Guide*™
Golf Resorts International

"I'm amazed at the number of golf resorts that have developed recently, and I'm delighted to see a reference guide of this scope and quality."—**Fuzzy Zoeller**

"*The Complete Guide to Golf Resorts* is a wonderful golf destination guide. It points out the championship golf courses around the country and lists the various LPGA and PGA competitions held on them. But more than that, the Guide is a well-researched multi-purpose book with a special-interest index highlighting diversions such as shopping areas and suggestions for family entertainment near the resorts. This work is a comprehensive travel guide for anyone interested in planning a trip around the exhilarating sport of golf."—**LPGA**

"If Golf is your game, more to your liking will be *Golf Resorts*. Just reading the description of more than 400 golf resorts is likely to persuade duffer and expert alike to head for the fairway."—**Washington Times**

"The Guide is most impressive and well done. You should be congratulated on your fine effort in putting together this guide."—**Stephen F. Mona,**
Executive Director,
Georgia State Golf Association

"Executives who enjoy golf vacations may appreciate a new guidebook: *Golf Resorts,* by Pamela Lanier . . . details on 400 golf resorts, special facilities and the 'special challenge' of each course."—**Industry Week**

"I loved reading *Golf Resorts*—it's about practicing the sport in style! If you're lucky to get older and a bit wiser, you learn that part of the fun is the actual physical environment."—**Peter A. Georgescu, President,**
Young & Rubicam Advertising

"The first comprehensive guide to the more than 400 resorts nationwide. Rates, facilities and courses are described in detail."—**Denver Post**

"For planning a personal 'escape holiday' or business conference detailing resort amenities and approximate rates, written by seasoned author, Pamela Lanier."—**Travelore Report**

"There is much I don't know about golf, but there is nothing Pamela doesn't know about golf resorts."—**Franklin Mieuli, part-owner, San Francisco Forty-Niners**

"At last—a guide to the resorts with details for the conference planner as well as those contemplating a vacation. The narrative's refreshing, with titillating tidbits of history, local lore and useful info, such as courses that still have caddies, and where Babe Ruth might have birdied a few holes."—**Benjamin Taber,**
President, Phillips Screw
Company

"Seven million Americans spent $8 million on golf-related trips last year. U.S. golfers even have their own guidebook to courses. Earlier this year, accommodations and travel author Pamela Lanier produced *Golf Resorts*, a nationwide listing of 400 resorts and 1800 public courses."—**The Trend Letter (John Naisbitt)**

"Don't leave home without it."—**Barry McDermott, golf writer, Southern Links**

"A guide to 400 golf resorts nationwide. Lists rates, special facilities, the course challenge. Available in bookstores."—**Travel Age**

"I'd like to play more golf, but it always rains on my day off—now this guide lists everything you need to know, but does it tell how to hit the ball?"—**Meat Loaf**

"All the information you could want for the ideal golf vacation could be found in *Golf Resorts—The Complete Guide.*"—**Golden Years Magazine**

"This book is terrific—it'll do everything for my golf game except straighten out my slice."—**Perry Butler**

"The sub-title pretty much says it all. The best places, state by state, to stay and shoot a few holes, are listed in this guide. Information on the courses, fees, room rates, reservation policies, seasons and other amenities is provided." —**University of Arizona Library**

"A unique travel book for golfers that goes beyond information on rooms, rates and restaurants. History and vital statistics are provided for golf resorts. With over 400 resort listings from Alabama to Wyoming, Lanier's book should suit most golfing travelers."—**Booklist**

"I love this game, and what a far out book."—**Michael Amato, Motley Crue**

"This unique guide lists over 400 golf resorts throughout the United States, catering to golfers."—**Book Passage**

"Now for the sports section, I offer Pamela Lanier's *Golf Resorts*—the first comprehensive guide to more than 400 golf resorts, public golf courses nationwide, plus information about nearby restaurants, shopping, and other sporting activities." —**Arts in Review WCFLN Philadelphia, Pennsylvania**

"Now there is a brand new 'hands on' guide to golf resorts in the U.S. Everything the golfer needs to know about resort rates and special facilities, such as health spas, tennis programs or gourmet dining is included. For you spouses, boyfriends or girlfriends who don't golf but get dragged along on a golf vacation, there is information for you too: local attractions, recommended restaurants and shopping opportunities. Also, information on tennis, swimming pools and health clubs, as well as special notes on children's activities. You should be able to find a copy of *Golf Resorts* in any good bookstore."—**Travel briefs (Jack McGuire**
WXEZ, Chicago, Illinois)

Other books from Lanier Guides:

**Golf Resorts—
The Complete Guide**™

**Golf Courses—
The Complete Guide**™

**Condo Vacations—
The Complete Guide**™

Elegant Small Hotels™

All Suite Hotel Guide™

22 Days In Alaska

**The Complete Guide to Bed &
Breakfasts, Inns & Guesthouses in
the United States and Canada**™

Bed & Breakfast Cookbook

Lanier Publishing
International, Ltd.

John Muir Publications

Running Press

To Contact the Guide, please write:

Golf Resorts International
P.O.Box 20429
Oakland, CA 94620

Dedication

This book is dedicated to the protection of our environment.

Greenspaces such as golf courses are important for the environment and enhance the quality of life.

No greenspace is as important to us all as the rain forest.

The rain forests are being destroyed at an alarming—no, terrifying— rate. We urge all of you who have learned to love nature to find out how you can help save the rain forests from destruction.

Rain Forest Action Network
301 Broadway, Suite A
San Francisco, CA 94133
415-398-4404

Golf
RESORTS

INTERNATIONAL

Over 150 of the finest
Golf Resorts in the World

Pamela Lanier

Introduction by
John Stirling

NATIONAL GOLF FOUNDATION

SPONSOR MEMBER

A *Lanier* Guide

Cover Photo of the Turnberry Hotel,
Strathclyde, Scotland courtesy of Venice
Simplan Orient Express, Inc.

Cover Design—Ken Scott

Book Design—Bob Ross, John Richards,
J. C. Wright

Senior Golf Editor—Sarah Morse

Acknowledgements: I wish to acknowledge
and thank the following individuals for
their help with this Guide: Peter Morse,
Tony Morse, Carol and Don Gwaltney,
Monnie Tiffany, John Fite, Golf Pro at the
Claremont Country Club, Martin Calfee,
Steve Cox, Barry Terjesen, David Bohn,
Margaret Bollenbacher, Margaret Callahan,
Marianne Barth, Mary Ellen Callahan,
Tobie Vale, Lauren Elliot, Venetia Young,
Seifu Haile, John Richards, Lauren
Childress, John Smeck, Dona Turner,
Karen Hunter, Hal Hershey, George Young,
Al Heeg, Phil Wood, Michael Hendrickson,
Todd Nolan, Stephen Starbuck, Brad
Bunin, Doug McClelland, Liz Susman,
Elizabeth Hart, George Kelley, Tucky
Pogue, Tina Bell, Elizabeth Bell, Corinne
Rednour, Julianne Dalena and Peter Balas.

I especially want to thank Jack Elliot,
President of the Northern California Golf
Association for his assistance. The United
States Golf Association, the National Golf
Foundation, the Golf Course Architects
Association, each of the states' individual
golf associations and Departments of
Tourism. To the various countries'
departments of tourism and golf
associations we are indebted and also to
our friends at the American Hotel Motel
Association and the International Hotel
Association.

Library of Congress Cataloging-in-Publication Data

Lanier, Pamela
    Golf Resorts International / Pamela Lanier
        p.   cm.
    ISBN 0-89815-335-2   : $19.95
    1. Golf resorts.   2. Golf resorts—Directories.   I. Title.
GV962.L34   1989
796.352'06'8—dc20
                                                          89-29356
                                                          CIP

ISBN No. 0-89815-335-2

Published by
Lanier Publishing International, Ltd.,
P.O. Box 20429
Oakland, CA 94620

Distributed by
Ten Speed Press
P.O. Box 7123
Berkeley, CA 94707.

Printed in the
United States of America

The information in this book was supplied in
large part by the golf resorts themselves and is
subject to change without notice. We strongly
recommend that you call ahead and always
verify the information in this book before
making final plans or reservations. The author
and publisher of this directory make no repre-
sentation that it is absolutely accurate or
complete. Errors and omissions, whether typo-
graphical, clerical, or otherwise, do sometimes
occur and may occur anywhere within the body
of this publication. The author and the publisher do not assume and hereby disclaim any liabil-
ity to any party for any loss or damage by errors
or omissions in this book whether such errors
or omissions result from negligence, accident or
any other cause.

Table of Contents

Introduction

This guide to international golf resorts represents a journey to many courses on which I've played and given clinics, on behalf of the British PGA. Beyond resort descriptions, the listings are an invitation to links, oceanside, desert, meadowland, and mountain courses offering constant challenge and beauty for the beginner and expert alike.

Naturally, I'll tout the courses where the game originated, whether it's the blistery approach to St. Andrews's 17th green, the natural amphitheaters of Waterville's links, or the watery grave on the Brabazon's 18th, where we retained the Ryder Cup in '89. Stop by and see me at the Meon Valley Golf and Country Club near Southampton—perhaps I'll give you a few tips! I hope this comprehensive book inspires you to play the courses, and that you'll get as much fun out of the game as I have.

—John Stirling
  Captain, British PGA, 1989–1990
  National Coach, English Golf Union

A Good Golf Course (What Is It?)

How does one define what a "good" golf course really is? It means different things to different people. One definition might be that a "good", or successful, golf course is one that creates a desire in the golfer to return and play it again and again. He might not be able to explain why the attraction exists—it just feels good!

A good golf course is one that the real estate developer, municipality, daily fee operator, resort, or private club can afford to maintain. A golf course might be very dramatic, picturesque, and striking in its visual effect, but if it is too difficult to play, the average golfer, after playing it once of twice, will decide that he is not enjoying it and will never go back again. Income from green fees will diminish and the quality of maintenance will suffer. Poor maintenance will cause a further reduction in rounds of golf played. Also, because of excessively steep mounding and other design features, maintenance costs may be higher than usual. Can this be called a "good" golf course since it is not producing the results expected of it? Anticipated costs of maintenance *must* be considered during the design phase of the facility.

The design relationship between the parking area, the pro shop, the practice tee and green, the first and 10th tees, and the 9th and 18th greens is very important. This involves walking from the automobile to the pro shop, reaching the practice areas, starting and completing the 18 holes, and returning to the automobile. First and last impressions of the facility are developed during this process.

The design of a good 18-hole golf course first involves the development of a routing plan which takes advantage of existing topography. The goal is to have an interesting rotation of par for the course in which each hole would be followed by one of a different par, such as 4-5-4-3-4-5-4-3-4 for each nine holes. This example is not often possible because of topography and property boundary restrictions (I think it has happened to me twice in the last thirty years!), but an attempt must be made to achieve as much as possible in this regard.

Taking advantage of existing topography means using all the interesting features existing on the land in our design. Where nature has not provided interesting contours or other features, we must attempt to match nature's theme and make it appear that only clearing, floating, and planting was required to develop the golf course.

A good golf course is interesting and challenging, but not impossible or unfair, for all types of golfers, including low, middle, and high handicapper and, very importantly, the ladies. This is done mostly by having multiple tee locations, and positioning hazards so that the longer hitter is faced with the need for accuracy, while the others are provided with much more space at their drive landing area. In short, the farther one hits the ball, the more accurate he must be.

The practice fairway should face toward the north, with a southerly direction being the second choice. The first several holes on the first nine should not require hitting toward the rising sun, and the final holes on the back nine should not aim toward the west.

Each individual hole should be a complete picture within itself, with each area of the hole being a unified part of the total effect. Tee design, contouring throughout the entire length of the hole; mowing patterns at tee, fairway, and green; tree types and location; water courses and lakes; and perhaps the most important part of the whole picture, the individual design of each green, together with locations of those seemingly necessary, but on, so troublesome cart paths; all are part of the picture to be developed.

If possible, each hole should be aimed in a somewhat different direction than the previous hole, to prevent monotony of the view from the several holes as play progresses. If it is necessary at times to have a succession of parallel holes, they should individually be of different lengths and character.

This is only a short summary of some of the items involved in designing and developing a "good" golf course. The profession of Golf Course Architecture, created out of necessity as a result of the development of the game in Scotland, requires a lifetime of study and practice. It overlaps, and require knowledge of other fields, such as agronomy, hydrology, land surveying, civil engineering, landscape architecture, arboriculture, site planning, golf course maintenance, heavy equipment operation, and others.

The education process never ends.

—Arthur Jack Snyder
  Former President
  Golf Course Architects Association

Guide Notes

Much of the challenge and excitement of golf is in exploring the beauty and infinite variety of new courses. While traditions and customs vary from country to country, many unforgettable experiences await traveling golfers who are familiar with some of the basic. In many places you won't find motorized carts, so plan to walk the often hilly layout. Carry proof of your current handicap and a letter of introduction from your pro, as some courses require it. Many clubs in Europe and South America are designed primarily for the golfer; don't expect to find restaurants, bars and extensive lines of clothing. And, most important, be sure to bring an ample supply of golf balls! Players in Australia carry little buckets of seed and sand to repair divots, while in Asia female caddies and greenskeepers are the norm. A round of golf isn't as casual in Switzerland as in the tropics, so don't count on just showing up and expect to play. Remember to carry cash for caddies and incidentals, as credit cards aren't always accepted in some of the more remote areas. And be sure to verify (in writing) rates, starting times, and exactly what equipment you'll need to make your golfing vacation the best ever.

In this guide we will acquaint you with the ever-expanding world of golf resorts—those special havens striving to give the traveler a memorable eighteen holes and then some. Many of these resorts are newcomers, and others are from another generation and well-established, but all have one thing in common—great golf and plenty of it!

Our descriptions are brief—just enough to tempt you. If you're interested in learning more, write or call the resort for brochures, and be sure to inquire about golf packages, as these often include extras such as clinics, airport transfers, sightseeing excursions, and usually represent substantial savings. Our price code is based on the most current rate available for double occupancy. Of course, prices are always subject to change, and vary with season, so make it a point to confirm the rate when you book. Generally, prices are:

under $100 = $	$150—$199 = $$$
$100—$149 = $$	$200+ = $$$$

We have indicated when a hotel will not accept pets, or when pets are accepted under special conditions. Children are accepted when accompanied by their parents except as otherwise noted.

Most hotels have at lease some rooms designed to accommodate the handicapped, and should you have special personal requirements, be sure to indicate when you make your reservations. International resorts are dedicated to providing guests with the finest and most comprehensive sports facilities imaginable, and we give you information on everything from jogging trails to tennis courts, marlin fishing to polo.

Nobody can golf all the time, so we have included information on a host of other diversions in the proximity of each resort, whether you fancy historic gardens and houses, the top fly fishing school, or championship shopping; it's all there for you.

Golf resorts are extremely popular, especially during high seasons, and tee times are often booked far in advance. We suggest you book your starting times with the pro shop or the front desk when you make your room reservation. Descriptions of the courses and the challenge they represent are at the heart of this guide. The total course length is expressed in yardage (measured from the men's white tees) on U.S. courses, and in many other parts of the world, length is measured in meters. In Europe and other countries, the concept of "par" and Standard Scratch Score are synonymous.

Consider the pro shop personnel your best friends. They'll help you rent clubs, replenish your supply of tees, tell you whether the greens are fast, and be happy to sell you a shirt with a good-looking logo.

Every attempt has been made to provide current and complete information. Some information has been provided by the hotels' management, and their policies may change. If you feel anything in this book is even slightly inaccurate, please let us know on the reader response form in the back. This book is as complete as we can make it, but even as we go to press, information on new resorts is pouring in. If you know of a golf resort we've missed, please let us know! Here's hoping you hit 'em straight!

—Pamela Lanier
San Francisco
November 1989

Golf Resorts

Listings by Country

Sheraton Mirage Port Douglas

Address: Davidson Street, Port Douglas, Queensland 4871

Phone: 070-985-888 008-222229

Innkeeper: Mark Kissner

No. rooms: 294

Rates: $$$, Credit Cards: AmEx, Visa, MC, Other CC

Services: Gift shops, Doctor, Car Rental, Babysitting, Children's Day Care, Room Safes, Concierge Service

Restaurant: Macrossans, Coffee Shop

Bar: Daintree Lounge

Business Fac.: FAX 070 985 885

Sports Fac.: Pool, Tennis, Sailing, Bicycling, Spa

Location: North Queensland

Attractions: Great Barrier Reef, Crocodile Farms, Mossman Gorge

Course: Mirage Country Club GC

Distance: 6261m, Par: 72

Rating: 70.0, No. of holes: 18

Phone Club-House: 070-99-3388

Pro's name: Peter Knight

Queensland, land of the orange-earthen outback, wallaby and dingo, surfies, ruddy-faced men tending sheep on Texas-size farms, cosmopolitan Brisbane, and traditional values, is on the threshold of a colossal tourist boom. Here on the northeastern tip of the state with the fewest taxes, twenty miles north of Cairns is where you'll find a tropical Xanadu on the edge of that biological extravaganza, the Great Barrier Reef. Alongside Four Mile Beach, not far from the virgin rainforests of the famous Daintree region, Mirage (as in Mirage Princeville and Gold Coast Resort) has created a sophisticated paradise of condominiums, hotel, 300-berth marina, sporting facilities and shops. The effect is low rise, open structures that are "floating" in water under cloudless skies surrounded by mature tropical landscaping, alabaster sand and designer greens. Everything seems ultra-civilized, chic, and tasteful. One gets the feeling that expense wasn't a problem.

The hotel is large, exquisitely appointed and offers virtually every conceivable amenity, from a wide range of restaurants and bars to some thought-provoking excursions. Who can resist a heart-stopping railroad ride inland to Atherton Tableland which passes over 40 bridges en route to the thundering Barron Falls? At the resort, you'll find tournament-quality tennis, a myriad of daily activities, pools, shops, a spa, helipad, a children's day care center and more. The real drawing card is proximity to the reef. Here on this living phenomena that's a national park, guests can explore the mysterious underwater plant life and thousands of species of colorful fish. Between September and December, game fishermen congregate to hunt for the huge black marlin cruising these clear waters.

The eighteen holes are made up of two very different nines, which were ready for play in the spring of 1988, yet because of the fast tropical growth, they are lush and mature. The Reef nine has sweeping views of the Coral Sea with a few tees surrounded by rainforest. Mountain nine, offers holes under the shadows of the Atherton Tablelands and has greens set on islands in lagoons. You can play year round here, and survey it all from a cart.

Seehotel Werzer-Astoria

There are a thousand good reasons to vacation here in southern Austria, frolicking under jagged snow-capped mountains on one of Carinthia's larger lakes, the Worthersee. This smart summertime resort in a pristine setting offers a touch of romantic luxury amid lovely gardens, coves, and expansive lawns. Hand-in-hand with excellent sports facilities goes a combination of antiques and Old Word refinements such as damask linens, crystal and silver. Sitting right on the sandy shores, guests will find two indoor tennis courts and two squash courts, plus eight outdoor courts, a relaxation center with sauna, fitness room, solarium, massage and beauty parlor. Riding, archery, hiking and tours are easily accessible. Family activities are stressed, and there are water sports for everyone. The shining star here is the cuisine. The food is quite sophisticated, the wine list impressive, and with the restaurant perched above the serene blue waters, you can count on a most beguiling culinary experience.

If you prefer, you can have a caddie on these 18 holes, some of which border the lake. Its a rolling course, not overly hilly, with many water hazards and exhilarating views, wildflowers and always that invigorating mountain air.

Address: Portschach am Worthersee, Karnten A-9210

Phone: 061 04272-2231

Rates: $$$$

Services: Beauty Parlor, Massage, Hairdresser, Sauna, Vapor Bath, Solarium

Restrictions: No dogs allowed on the beach

Restaurant: Lake Terrace

Bar: Piano Bar

Business Fac.: FAX 04272 2251

Sports Fac.: Riding, Archery, Tennis, Squash, Hiking

Attractions: Lake and water sports, Tour Program

Course: Moosburg

Distance: 6230m, Par: 72, No. of holes: 18

Phone Club-House: 04272

Schloss Ernegg

Address: A-3261, Steinakirchen am Forst, Niederosterreich

Phone: 061 07488-214 800-221-4980

Innkeeper: Countess Auersperg Lee

No. rooms: 21

Rates: $, Credit Cards: Visa, Other CC

Restaurant: Schloss

Bar: Medival Knights'

Sports Fac.: Billards, Table Tennis, Riding

Location: Otscherland

Attractions: Danube Valley, Wachau Vineyards, Castles, Vienna

Course: Schloss Ernegg

Distance: 5585m, Par: 72

Rating: 70.0, No. of holes: 27

Phone Club-House: 07488/214

Pro's name: Peter Kreier

If you've dreamed of roaming around a romantic private castle—the kind with family heirlooms, suits of armor, trophies, stables, drawing rooms and creaking floors from centuries past, then this is a retreat you should consider. Owned by successive generations of the Counts of Auersperg for over 300 years, this 12th century castle lies secluded among the forests in the foothills of the Alps, between Vienna and Salzburg. The current Countess manages the 20 room hotel, where guests find the ineffable charm of the views of rising Alps and verdant Danube Valley, plus true comfort in a house-party atmosphere. Our favorite suite, lifted from the 16th century, is complete with stained glass windows, a vaulted ceiling and a stone column gracing the center of the room. We found the bathtub behind a screen, and the toilet was inside an outside wall!

The restaurant is reason enough to stay in this colonnaded hostelry with its warmly familial dining room whose menus boast game, trout and local favorites supported by the castle's farm. The cellar, well-stocked and impressive, includes a fine sampling of local vintages, such as the light Veltliner we tried from the nearby Wachau vineyards.

There's excellent trout fishing in the area, as well as historic castle ruins, fortresses and monasteries, and narrow gauge railway followers will want to check out the one nearby. The castle maintains stables with horses available for guest' use, and an early morning ride through the nearby hills and forests might be the perfect warmup before you tee off.

Adjacent to the castle is a nine hole course that twists and winds and has no shortage of trees, and across the road is another 18 holes. Peter Kreier, the congenial golf pro, is ready to give you tips on how to play the 27 holes, and it's up to you to stay out of the meandering river and lakes that shimmer under an Alpine summer sun.

Schloss Fuschl

Set on a peninsula on Lake Fuschl, and surrounded by 37 acres of lush parkland, this 15th century chateau of the Archbishops of Salzburg, has been admirably restored. Interiors are exquisite, with 84 rooms and 23 suites of varying size. Details are important here, from the finely frescoed ceilings to the antique chests and chairs. Many rooms have breathtaking views over park and lake. Naturally, the beach is private, and if sailing appeals to you, the lake is all yours. Four conference rooms can accommodate from 10 to 250 people, should you be looking for a luxurious retreat near Salzburg. The Schloss Restaurant's chef produces a level of cuisine to match the impressive setting, and as it boasts fish from its own fisheries and game specialties from its grounds, diners can enjoy a repast such as pan-fried fillet of fera on Pernod basil noodles, followed by warm apricot dumplings with butter-bread crumbs. An excellent selection of Austrian wines is stashed in the castle's cellar.

If you can bear to leave the tranquility, there are mountain bike tours, a museum with the world's biggest pipe collection, and the summer music festivals for which Salzburg is renowned. If you're adventuresome, visit one of the Salzbergwerkes (salt mines). Kids will love wearing miner's clothing and sliding down passages in the dark.

You can tee off just 2 kilometers from where the Archbishops lived it up. Its nine holes of pure pleasure, and the Standard Scratch Score is 61. You'll have some great vistas of the lake, but basically this is a forested course. Fairways are wide, and there are a couple of uphill holes.

Address: A-5322, Hof Bei, Salzburg A-5322

Phone: 061 06229-22530 800-223-6800

Innkeeper: Uwe Zeilerbauer

No. rooms: 84

Rates: $$$, Credit Cards: Visa, Other CC

Services: Full Health Spa

Restaurant: Schloss

Bar: Bar

Business Fac.: Sec. Serv. FAX

Sports Fac.: Swimming, Tennis Handball, Riding, Polo

Attractions: Salzburg, Salt mine, Mountain Bike Tours

Course: Golf Club Fuschl

Distance: 3694m, Par: 62

Rating: 61.0, No. of holes: 9

Hotel Panhans

Address: A-2680 Semmering, Hochstrasse 32 Semmering

Phone: 02664/8181

Innkeeper: Eduard Aberham

No. rooms: 66

Rates: Credit Cards: Visa, Other CC

Services: Child Care, Gift Shop, Spa, Casino, Beauty Care & Massage, Children's Activities

Restaurant: Kaiser Karl

Bar: Tanz-u.Cocktailbar

Business Fac.: Sec. Svc., Translators

Sports Fac.: Swimming, Tennis, Skiing, Cross Country

Attractions: Vienna, Guided Hiking Tours with Picnics

Course: Semmering

Distance: 3860m, Par: 62, No. of holes: 9

Phone Club-House: 02664/8154

Pro's name: Harald Blaschek

This legend in Austrian hotel history was saved from demolition a decade ago, and after a complete facelift, the splendor of the "Belle Epoch" has been recaptured. To ensure accuracy in the revitalization, stage designer Gottfried Neumann-Spallart was entrusted with the design. Arriving here, where wealthy Europeans came to "take the air," is a three-star adventure, if you take the train from Gloggnitz to the top, three thousand feet up from the valley floor. Rooms reek of Art Nouveau, interiors stress the elegance of the period, the air is pure, and the food worthy of a Gault Millau toque. Most rooms have postcard views of the forests, mountain gorges and snow-capped peaks. Seminars, meetings and small conventions can be handled with ease, and guests can literally waltz the night away in the large ballroom. There are bridge tournaments regularly, poetry readings, and an air of tranquil gentility here. Try your hand at the baccarat table, or order a Courvoisier and simply be seen. There's a spa, indoor swimming pool, gift shop, and table tennis, and some of the best mountain hiking anywhere.

The nine hole golf course opened in 1926, and has aged gracefully. Its only two kilometers from the hotel, and meanders around the base of the Pinkenkogel. While it isn't a perfectly manicured layout, the splendor of the alpine setting made up for the four balls we lost in the lupin.

Cotton Bay Club

This outlying Bahamian island, whose name in Greek means "freedom," was settled by a group of pioneers who sailed south from Bermuda in the seventeenth century. Crowds and highrises you'll not find, rather, small picturesque settlements dot the island, and mostly its a glorious excuse to enjoy the indolent life of sailing, beach roaming, biking, great food, and one of the Caribbean's best golf courses. Seventy-seven air conditioned guest rooms and cottages are nestled amid palms bordered by a 2 mile-long crescent-shaped beach. The atmosphere is casual, with coats preferred for gentlemen at dinner, with a tinge of refinement in the air, no doubt from the days when Henry Luce and his pals visited. The dining room, a tropical out-door/indoor creation overlooks the ocean, and serves exceptional Bahamian dishes in addition to the old standbys. Don't pass up the flambeed bananas, with lime juice, freshly ground allspice and good rum.

Tennis buffs will find four courts, and the others can snorkel, swim in the pool, windsurf or see what fishing the staff can arrange.

Golfers can have it all on the Robert Trent Jones 18 hole gem that is a visual treat with its oceanview holes. The par-5 16th hole skirts a rocky inlet as it stretches to 508 yards. Beautifully maintained, the course, sitting on a bluff affords some knockout views.

Address: Rock Sound, P.O. Box 28, Eleuthera

Phone: 809-334-6101 800-225-4255

No. rooms: 77

Rates: $$$$, Credit Cards: AmEx, Visa, MC,

Restaurant: Restaurant

Bar: Bar

Business Fac.: FAX 305-667-5609

Sports Fac.: Swimming, Tennis, Bicycles

Location: Bahama Out Islands

Attractions: Lighthouse Point, Deepsea Fishing, Scuba Diving

Course: Cotton Bay Club

Distance: Par: 72

No. of holes: 18

Guest policy: Green fee included for hotel guest,

Divi Bahamas Beach Resort & Country Club

Address: P.O. Box N-8191, Nassau

Phone: 809-326-4391 800-367-3484

No. rooms: 120

Rates: $, Credit Cards: AmEx, Other CC

Services: Shutte, Fresh Flowers Daily, Safe deposit boxes, Gift shop, boutique.

Restaurant: Papagayo

Bar: Flamingo Club

Business Fac.: FAX 809-326-4728

Sports Fac.: Driving Range, Tennis, Swim

Attractions: Nassau, Casinos, 30 Scuba Diving Sites

Course: Divi Bahamas Country Club
Distance: 6800, Par: 72
No. of holes: 18

This is a secluded part of the other side of Nassau—180 acres and a long white sandy beach on the southwestern shore, formerly the South Ocean Beach Hotel. Everything has been refurbished and spruced up, including 120 rooms and the elegant Papagayo restaurant. You can play tennis day or night, windsurf, snorkel, sunbathe around the pool, linger over lunch on the terrace, or shop till you drop. But possibly the most incredible sights are beneath the clear water, and the Peter Hughes Dive South Ocean can take you to more than 30 scuba diving sites. Hop on the complimentary shuttle into Nassau for shopping, entertainment and the bright lights of the casinos.

The 18 hole championship Joe Lee golf course, playing 6,800 yards from the back tees, is right outside the door. You'll drive across rolling fairways to well-trapped greens bordered by dazzling flora, small lakes and views to crow about. Stop by the pro shop and the driving range, they're staffed by friendly people eager to help you enjoy your game.

Paradise Island Resort & Casino

There's about as much fun-in-the-sun here as one could pack into any vacation or business trip,(but I could play a little golf.) This is Resorts International's extravaganza encompassing Britannia Towers, Paradise Towers and the Paradise Island Casino, and a smorgasbord of over a thousand guest rooms and suites, and nearly every facility known to man. Choose from 14 restaurants and lounges, two health clubs, tennis, island tours, casino gaming lessons and promotional chips, watersports, and a seemingly endless white sand beach. You never have to leave the premises—you can have your hair done, have room service, or go shopping for a new outfit to wear to the multi-million dollar Las Vegas-style dinner show. In other words, you can play all day, and through the evening in what is now the biggest gaming facility anywhere.

And for those who come to play golf, be prepared for a pleasant surprise. Designed by Dick Wilson, one of the most sought-after designers of the fifties and sixties, this course takes advantage of the natural shoreline, pristine beaches, and lush tropical foliage of the island. The Atlantic borders three sides, with water coming into play on 13 holes, and tricky tradewinds playing havoc with your drives. The fourteenth hole, looking out across the beach and ocean, is a stickler. Premium is on the tee shot to a heavily bunkered uphill green. Fortunately, the Nineteenth Hole Pub awaits you with a cold beer and a comfortable seat from which to survey this paradise.

Address: Paradise Island,
Phone: 800-321-3000
No. rooms: 1200
Rates: $$, Credit Cards: AmEx, Visa
Services: Health Club, Sauna, Beauty Salon, Shopping Arcades
Restaurant: 13 Restaurants
Bar: 10 lounges
Business Fac.: FAX 809-363-3000 ext4830
Sports Fac.: Tennis, Swimming, Water Sports
Attractions: Casino, Yacht Charters, Nassau, Island Tours

Distance: 6562, Par: 72, No. of holes: 18
Guest policy: Dress code
Phone Club-House: 809-326-3925
Pro's name: Fred C. Higgs
Reservations: Call for starting times
Guest carry club: No

Atlantik Beach Resort

Address: P.O. Box F-531, Lucaya, Grand Bahama Island, Freeport

Phone: 809-373-1444 800-622-6770

No. rooms: 175

Rates: $

Services: Jacuzzi, Casino, Pool, Shopping arcades

Restaurant: 3 Restaurants

Bar: Yellow Elder Bar

Business Fac.: FAX 809-373-7481

Sports Fac.: Swimming, Driving range, Parasailing

Attractions: Goombay Park, Natural Trails Tour

Course: Lucaya Golf Country Club

Distance: 6824, Par: 72

No. of holes: 18

This Swiss-owned and managed 175 room high rise occupies a prominent stretch of white sandy beachfront at Freeport/Lucaya, a popular destination for sun, diving, casinos and night life. The pluses include three restaurants, a bar, and water sports literally right out the front door. Para-sail, snooze in the sun or swim in the pool at the Beach Club, try jet skis, or a hobicat, or go snorkeling. The International Bazaar, a 10 acre shopping village is a short drive from the hotel, and provides the ideal spot to run up the credit cards with merchandise from Swiss watches to T-shirts.

The Lucayan Golf and Country Club, owned and operated by the hotel, is about a mile inland, and accessible by "Golf Express," a complimentary service to whisk you to the tees. This Dick Wilson course was cut from dense tropical foliage, and emphasizes an intriguing and undulating terrain. There's one water hole, and that comes into play on the tee shot of seventeen, but don't think you're going to birdie every hole—there's plenty of near-jungle just beyond the rough on each hole here. You can take lessons, practice at the driving range and putting green, or sip a tall cool one at the snack bar.

Jack Tar Village Beach Resort

These are the people who bring you the "all-inclusive" packages of everything from meals to tips and drinks and sports. With 400 rooms, Jack Tar Village Beach Resort is a sprawling club-like resort with a gargantuan swimming pool, deep-water marina, 16 day/night tennis courts, sailing, water skiing and a white sandy beach. A Bahamian band entertains in the afternoons and you can twist and shout in the disco or enjoy the scheduled entertainment. Don't look for a casino here.

There are three nines here at the Grand Bahamas Hotel & Country Club, and depending on which ones you combine, the course will play from 6,389 yards to 6,666 yards. Fairways are wide on the flat layout, and water comes into play on 14 of the 27 holes. Green fees are included for Jack Tar guests, but carts and club rental are on you.

Address: West End, 1314 Wood St. Dallas TX 75202, Grand Bahama Island

Phone: 214-670-9888 800-999-9182

Innkeeper: John Hamati

No. rooms: 424

Rates: $$, Credit Cards: AmEx, Visa, MC, Other CC

Restaurant: Out Island

Bar: The Witch's Light

Sports Fac.: 16 Tennis Courts, Pool, Sailing, Bikes.

Location: Beachfront

Attractions: Lucaya, Garden of the Groves

Course: West End

Distance: 6666, Par: 72

Rating: 72, No. of holes: 27

Phone Club-House: 809-346-6211

Pro's name: Jim Delancey

Bahamas Princess Resort and Casino

Address: P.O. Box F2623, West Sunrise Highway, Freeport, Grand Bahama Island

Phone: 809-352-9661 809-352-6721

Innkeeper: T. Thurston, D. Archer

No. rooms: 965

Rates: $$, Credit Cards: AmEx, Visa, MC, Other CC

Services: Gift Shop, Full Spa

Restaurant: Crown Room, Morgan's Bluff

Bar: La Trattoria

Business Fac.: Sec.Svc., Translators

Sports Fac.: Swimming, Tennis, Sailing, Water Sports

Location: Freeport, Beach

Attractions: International Bazaar, Casino, Game Fishing

Course: Ruby & Emerald Courses

Distance: 6750, Par: 72

Rating: 72.4, No. of holes: 36

Guest policy: Dress code

Phone Club-House: 809-352-6721

Pro's name: Ben Stewart

Reservations: Recommended

This is the spot for good sports facilities, golf, grand public areas, a glittery casino showroom, and nearly a thousand rooms—all within strolling distance of the beach and the gargantuan International Bazaar. This major resort center, a short flight from Miami, enjoys a balmy average temperature in the low seventies during the winter, while the mercury climbs into the eighties during the summer.

Set on 2,500 acres, the resort has just about everything—from a newly remodeled casino and opulent restaurants to tennis courts, pool, giant hot tub and full spa and miles of unspoiled white sand beaches. Dine on lobster Bahamian style, try your luck at blackjack, then shed your veil in Sultan's Tent, a steamy disco with live island rhythms.

What to do outside the resort? These waters are wonderful for sport fishing. In addition, there's good water skiing, windsurfing, and truly beautiful beaches to stroll. All kinds of boats are available for charter, and the snorkeling and scuba diving offers incredible views of marine life. If you're a shopper, bring the credit cards and an extra suitcase, as this area has two major malls that can't survive without you. Look for everything from emeralds and Scandinavian crystal to handsome coral jewelry and perfume. Not duty-free, but often a bargain.

These two courses are very popular, so be sure to make advance reservations for starting times. They're flat, good driving courses. Designed by Joe Lee who is responsible for many outstanding resort layouts in the Caribbean, Ruby Course is a par 72, 6385 yard combination of sand, water and Bahamian flora rough. Emerald Course, site of the 1970 Bahamas National Open, a U.S. tour event won by Doug Sanders is a little longer with louder birds.

Sandy Lane Hotel & Golf Club

Barbados was probably named by Portuguese sailors referring to a type of bearded fig tree. Settled by the British, with full independence proclaimed in 1966, the island enjoys one of the highest standards of living in the Caribbean today.

Open in the 1960's, the Sandy Lane has maintained an air of formality and tradition, much like a private estate. Rest assured that from the moment the Rolls stops at the white coral Palladian entrance you'll be rubbing elbows with the beautiful people. One hundred twelve rooms and 30 suites, all with balconies and postcard-perfect views of the ocean or gardens await the visitor on this 380-acre garden paradise on the west coast of the island. Dining is part of the experience here, and guests who enjoy an evening meal under crystal chandeliers or al fresco perusing one of the best wine lists on this 166 square mile island, are bound to be content. Lively night entertainment and action in the main bar or Terrace will spruce up your evenings, as will a sunset beach stroll. There are duty-free shops, a gorgeous swimming pool and wind surfing, sunfish and hobicat sailing literally right out your door. Sunday's buffet lunch is a crowd-pleaser with a fantastic steel band providing the sights and sounds.

Barbados is worth exploring, and since much of the terrain is sugar cane, if your taxi driver knows a short-cut, you'll be in for a thrill as you whoosh through the fields. Places to visit might include the flora at Welchman Hall Gully, Harrison Caves, Barbados Wildlife Reserve, and tours of Drax Hall, an old plantation house. Cricket, the national pastime, is played just about everywhere. During winter months, there are polo matches near the resort.

Great golf is here. The first nine was completed in 1961, and the Molyneux nine was added in 1973. The layout is dotted with colorful trees in bloom and has plenty of challenging sand and water hazards. Lovely butterflies and offshore breezes are included, golf carts and caddies are extra.

Address: St. James, Barbados

Phone: 809-432-1311 800-223-6800

Innkeeper: Pierre Vacher

No. rooms: 112

Rates: $$$$, Credit Cards: AmEx, Visa, MC, Other CC

Services: Beauty & Barber Shops, Duty Free Shopping, Airport Pickup, Daily Newspaper, Welcome Tray on Arrival

Restaurant: Sandy Bay Restaurant

Bar: Terrace, Main, Oasus

Business Fac.: Sec. Svc., Translators

Sports Fac.: Tennis, Snorkelling, Sailing, Windsurf

Location: Sandy Lane Estate

Attractions: Welchman Hall Gully, Harrison Caves, Wildlife

Course: Sandy Lane Golf Club

Distance: 6576, Par: 72

Rating: 69.1, No. of holes: 18

Phone Club-House: 09-432-1145

Pro's name: Lean Geddes

Southhampton Princess

Address: P.O. Box HM 1379, Hamilton

Phone: 809-238-8000 800-223-1818

Innkeeper: Eric Brooks

No. rooms: 600

Rates: $$$$, Credit Cards: AmEx, Visa, MC, Other CC

Services: Laundry & Valet Parking, Ferry, Safety Deposit Box, High Chair Fashion Show, Bingo, Arts and Crafts Displays

Restaurant: Windows on the Sound, Newport

Bar: Neptune Lounge

Business Fac.: FAX 809-238-8245

Sports Fac.: Tennis, Swimming, Beach Club, Moped rentals

Attractions: Water Sports, Crafts Market, Duty Free Shopping

Course: Southhampton Princess
Distance: 2684, Par: 54, No. of holes: 18
Phone Club-House: 809-238-8000

Hamilton is small by capital-city standards (population about 1,700), but everything here in this picturesque self-governing dependency seems manageable, tidy and extremely friendly. This resort is large by Bermudian standards, with nearly 600 air-conditioned rooms on a grassy hilltop above the sea.

Virtually everything is here—including a new wing housing the Newport Club with extra amenities. Decor is more traditional than tropical, with Victorian touches, pastels and a lot of light wood. Views sweep across the Great Sound or the wide rolling Atlantic. There's a restaurant for every mood, appetite and age group, ranging from the mahogany, bronze, and Wedgewood formality of Windows on the Sound, to hamburgers and cools drinks on the water's edge.

This is the spot for night time action during high season, but you'll not see gambling or cutoffs here, as Bermudians refer to their style as "one of British reserve and dignified informality." Almost all hotels require jacket and tie in the evening, and daytime dress is what Americans call "casual country club." The island has a pleasant moderate year-round climate with daytime summer temperatures in the eighties, and winter days reaching into the sixties and low seventies. The resort has 11 tennis courts, two swimming pools, and a beach club with shuttle service up the hill! Arrangements can be made for all kinds of water sports.

Tourism is Bermuda's strong suit. You'll see why generations of families return year after year. Among our suggested diversions: rent a moped (tourists can't drive cars here), pick up a picnic, head for one of the beaches, visit the crafts market, shop for duty-free Liberty prints, take a buggy ride around Hamilton, hop on one of the efficient busses to Grotto Bay, pedal to the ferry that criss crosses the Great Sound, sway to calypso and sip rum aboard a Sea Gardens cruise, or pray for oceanic bonito or blackfin tuna at the end of your line.

Golf is on an 18 hole par 3 course with ample water hazards, elevated tees and 60 strategically placed bunkers. Just two and a half hours playing time. You'll need skillful iron work here, and when the wind blows off the Atlantic, the 2,684-yard course re-introduces you to every club in your bag.

Marriott's Castle Harbour Resort

Opened in 1931 by the Furness-Withy Steamship Line as a hotel for passengers travelling between United States and Britain, the elegant hotel on Harrington Sound gained a reputation as THE place for discerning travellers. After a renovation of more than $60 million, the doors reopened in 1986 with Marriott's logo, and a full complement of amenities. With more than four hundred rooms, guests can ramble around airy public rooms, choose from a myriad of restaurants, and lounges, and wonder how many bodies it takes to fill up 9,000 square feet of banquet space. It has tennis courts, three swimming pools, private marina, two beaches, a fully equipped health club, and acres of Bermuda's beauty. These waters are magnets for sailors, who know them as good sailing grounds, and here, too, in the protected waters of Harrington Sound is where you'll find good water skiing.

Shoppers can find substantial bargains in the doll-like shops where imported British goods are a fraction of their European price. Shetland sweaters, Waterford crystal, and that Royal Stewart kilt and sporran you always wanted are waiting.

This is a dramatic course, revitalized by Robert Trent Jones, with wildly undulating fairways, and majestic water views from elevated tees. A long-established island layout, it's hilly from start to finish. Let's hope you admire the pale pink sand bunkers from afar, and not when you're trying to dig out a fried egg.

Address: P.O. Box HM 841, Tucker's Town, Hamilton

Phone: 809-293-2040

Innkeeper: Stacey Evans-Coles

No. rooms: 405

Credit Cards: AmEx, Visa, MC,

Services: Child Care, Beauty Salon, Concierge, Health Club, Spa

Restaurant: Windsor Dining Room

Bar: Blossoms Lounge

Business Fac.: Fully equipped conference rooms

Sports Fac.: Tennis, Swimming

Attractions: Fishing Charters, Tour 17th-Century buildings

Course: Castle Harbour Golf

Distance: 6440, Par: 71

Rating: 69.2, No. of holes: 18

Pro's name: Bruce Fraser

Hotel do Frade

Address: Rodovia Rio-Santos Highway, Km 123, Angra dos Reis, Rio de Janeiro

Phone: 055 0243-65-1212

No. rooms: 117

Rates: $$, Credit Cards: AmEx, MC, Other CC

Services: Gift Shop, Spa

Restaurant: Escuna Restaurant

Bar: 2 bars, Disco

Sports Fac.: Swimming, Tennis, Riding, Sailing

Attractions: Island Tours, Snorkel, Windsurfing

Course: Frade Golf

Distance: 6420, Par: 72

Rating: 70.5, No. of holes: 18

Phone Club-House: 267-7375

Pro's name: Mario Gonzalez

Brush up on your Portuguese, order some cruzados from the bank, and plan to enjoy golf in a tropical forest complete with thundering waterfalls, saucy tropical birds and caddie fees to write home about. From Rio, its about two and a half hours, and for an unbeatable experience, you can arrange a leisurely schooner trip, which cruises among the hundreds of small islands. The idyllic resort is just outside Angra Dos Reis, and consists of 117 rooms and 17 suites, all with minibars, telephones, air conditioning and televisions. The hotel is right on the beach under the watchful eye of the magnificent "Pico do Frade" mountain which rises out of the center of the bay, with lounges and restaurants offering sweeping vistas of a tropical waters.

The restaurant here serves a marvelous sampling of all kinds of dishes, and you'll no doubt want to sample some of the traditional local fare. Since Brazil cannot be compared to the rest of South America, in climate, history, people or food, the cooking is a mixture of Portuguese, Indian and West African influences. Fish is plentiful and often accented with pungent spices and served with arroz Brasileiro and manioc, a root crop known to many as sweet cassava.

Swim in the pool or snorkel in crystaline waters, or have the hotel arrange windsurfing, sailing, speed boats, bicycling, an early morning gallop on the beach, or an excursion to nearby islands. There are tennis courts, a full health spa, and those Latin favorites, soccer and volleyball.

The course, completed in 1980, was designed with much of the natural foliage left intact, and herein lies its appeal. Expect to be distracted and dazzled by exotic butterflies, a turbulent river plunging down from towering peaks, and some mind-boggling Atlantic views from behind the double green at Numbers 5 and 12. An abandoned tequila still sits alongside the green on the par-three eighth hole, and just when you're concentrating on carrying a dense stand of bamboo, a local brahma bull's roar can blow it. The course was designed by Belgian, French and Dutch Open winner

Sheraton Mirage, Port Douglas, Australia

Bahamas Princes, The Bahamas

Banff Springs Hotel

Nestled amidst the rugged beauty and towering peaks of the Rockies is Banff Springs, a majestic castle-like hotel legendary to this unique wilderness area. Since Banff Springs first opened its doors in 1888, the hotel has been one of the wonders of the travel world—a grand and gracious, Scottish Baronial Castle where "rarified extravagance" is at its best.

Encounter old world elegance and regal hospitality under glittering chandeliers, high vaulted ceilings and gothic arches. Balustraded balconies encircle the palatial lobby, and throughout the hotel, a fascinating array of antiques are a treat for the eyes.

Nine dining rooms, offering everything from casual to elegant, will accommodate every mood. Start your day with a leisurely breakfast buffet style or table d'hote in the Alberta. Lunch lavishly in the summer sunshine of the great outdoors on the Bow Valley Terrace.

Swing your racquet on one of five outdoor tennis courts, or swing yourself up into the saddle and take off to the mountains on horseback. For the real adventurer, there are daily whitewater rafting expeditions with all the thrills, chills and spills you could want. Sightseers have a myriad of tours and museums to choose from, including a chance to view rare plant and animal life. But whether its sports or sightseeing, you'll treasure the chance to end a perfect day with a long soak in therapeutic mineral hot springs.

High on just about everybody's list of unmarred natural splendor offering first-rate golf is the Stanley Thompson-designed Banff Springs Golf Club. Since professional tournaments cannot be held in Canada's National Parks, and the Park is a game reserve, your gallery is likely to be a deer with her fawn, or a couple of playful bear cubs scampering after an errant ball. A masterpiece of ingenuity, the renowned 7th hole is literally carved out of Mount Rundle's granite face. As the last seven holes meander past the glistening Bow River, golfers are mesmerized by the hole called Devil's Cauldron, the par-3 175 yard 16th. A natural glacial lake has to be carried, but that's minor compared to the winds that can howl through the natural amphitheater set under the steep rock. Your game here in tranquil alpine splendor promises to be a test of club selection, as distances can be deceptive against lofty mountains which give the appearance of shortened distance.

Address: P.O. Box 960, Banff, Canada, T0L 0C0
Phone: 493-762-2211   800-828-7447
Innkeeper: Ivor Petrak
No. rooms: 841
Rates: $, Credit Cards: AmEx, Visa, MC, Other CC
Services: Valet, Library, Beauty shop, Garage and parking, Car hire, Intl. currency exchange, Babysitting, Card or other game area, Room service
Restrictions: Pets ltd.
Restaurant: Rob Roy Dining Room
Bar: The Works Night
Business Fac.: Secretarial, Telex, Conf. rm. cap.: 800
Sports Fac.: Pool, Tennis, Trail Rides
Location: Banff National Park
Attractions: Centre for the Arts, White Water Rafting, Hiking

Course: Banff Springs Hotel
Distance: 6,729, Par: 71
Rating: 71.0, No. of holes: 27
Guest Policy: Book in advance, Dress code
Phone Club-House: 403-762-2211
Pro's name: Stan Bishop
Reservations: 3 to 4 months in advance
Season: May 1st to mid-Oct.
Guest Carry Club: Yes

Jasper Park Lodge

Address: P.O. Box 40, Jasper,
Canada, T0E 1E0
Phone: 403-852-3301   800-268-9143
Innkeeper: Jacques H. Favre
No. rooms: 397
Rates: $247.00, Credit Cards: AmEx,
Visa, MC, Other CC
Services: Valet, Barber Shop, Beauty
Shop, Garage and Parking, Car hire,
International currency exchange,
Complimentary shoe-shine, Nurse,
Babysitting, Room service
Restrictions: Pets ltd.
Restaurant: Beauvert Dining Room
Bar: La Terrasse
Business Fac.: Message center,
Conf. rm. cap.: 1,000
Sports Fac.: Pool, Tennis, Croquet,
Skiing, Riding
Location: Jasper National Park
Attractions: Maligne Canyon, Jasper
Tramway, Icefields all near

Course: Jasper Park Lodge
Distance: 6,598, Par: 71
Rating: 70.5, No. of holes: 18
Guest Policy: Call for availability,
Dress code
Phone Club-House: 403-852-3301
Pro's name: Ron MacLeoud
Reservations: ASAP—very busy
Season: April–Oct.
Guest Carry Club: Yes

For those who seek treasure when they travel,
there's a jewel of a resort set high in 900 wilderness acres of the Canadian Rockies—Jasper Park
Lodge. It's an exclusive village curving along the
shores of jade-green Lac Beauvert beneath magnificent mountains. The first unit of the main
building was erected in the winter of 1922-23.
At 250 feet long and 200 feet wide, it was reputed to be the largest single story log structure
in the world. Today, the original log cabins are
accompanied by modern cedar chalets that complete the resort.

Dining comes in a variety you'll appreciate. The
Beauvert Dining Room features lakeview dining
on continental cuisine. Under the direction of
Chef Gnemmi, specialties like salmon mousse,
buffalo steaks, and fine French pastries are prepared for your enjoyment. At the Henry House,
the cozy steakhouse atmosphere sets the mood
for a hearty meal. And The Copper Kettle features an evening Italian menu.

A full selection of recreational activities are always available to guests of Jasper Park Lodge.
For the tennis player, there are four hard-surfaced tennis courts and even a resident professional for those who might want a little guidance. The heated outdoor swimming pool is the
focal point of the recreation area. Steambaths, a
weight room, as well as Shuffleboard and Billiards are all located here.

The Jasper Park course is a par-71 beauty with
snow-capped Pyramid Mountain peaks shading
many of the holes. Built in the early 20's by one
of the fathers of modern design, Stanley Thompson, construction was impeded due to thick timber and huge boulders. Thompson's reputation
spread quickly after acclaim he received for
courses at Banff Springs and Jasper Park. The
course isn't long at 6,598 yards, but its variety
will impress you—all well trapped and rolling.

Probably the course's best-known aspect isn't
even a part of the physical layout—its the wild-life for whom the area is home, a playground,
and a meal ticket. Employees and guests attest
to the congregation of friendly tame black bears
who delight in playing around the bunkers, and
help the greenskeepers haul sprinklers from fairway to fairway. This doesn't mean the others—
elk, deer, geese, coyotes and wolves aren't in
evidence; they're just upstaged.

Keltic Lodge

The wild mountainous terrain of eastern Nova Scotia's Cape Breton Island, remote and sparsely settled, is the setting for the breathtaking Keltic Lodge. This is a palatial grande dame overlooking the rocky coast, run by the government of Nova Scotia. Accommodations are in the baronial main lodge, two and four bedroom cottages, and the adjacent White Birch Inn. Dinner is somewhat formal, with coats and ties for gentlemen, and seafood to rave about.

After you've savored the dramatic mountain backdrop against the sea, you can explore the amenities at hand. For swimming, there's a large freshwater lake, a pool, or a mile-long ocean beach. We ambled up and down trails on a guided nature hike, and then headed for the nearby national park for a late afternoon sail. If you're driving the Cabot Trail, take time to explore Cheticamp, the center of Acadian life, and pop into some of the small coastal villages where lobstering is a way of life.

Our golf game at the adjacent Highland Links was truly memorable. Although the clubhouse is modest, the course is spectacular in its natural beauty. Early holes afford magnificent views of North Bay Ingonish, then the course turns toward the mountains. The undulating fairways challenge you with an unending variety of lies, and because of the considerable distance between several holes, all but ardent trekkers should consider a cart. This is a Stanley Thompson gem, but due to its remoteness, it isn't as well known as his other triumphs, Banff Springs and Jasper Park.

Address: Ingoshish Beach, Cape Breton Island, Nova Scotia NS B0C 1L0
Phone: 902-285-2880 902-285-2691
Business Fac.: FAX 902-285-2859

Course: Highlands Links
Distance: 6588, Par: 71
Rating: 73.0, No. of holes: 18
Phone Club-House: 902-285-2600
Pro's name: Joe Robinson

Manoir Richelieu

Address: 181 rue Richelieu, Pointe-au-Pic, Quebec G0T 1M0

Phone: 418-665-3703

Restaurant: Main Dining Room

Bar: Piano Bar

Business Fac.: FAX 418-665-3093

Sports Fac.: Swimming, Tennis, Riding, Ski

Attractions: Whales on St. Lawrence River, Summer Theater

Course: Manoir Richelieu Golf

Distance: 6110, Par: 73, No. of holes: 18

Pro's name: Robert Ledoux

Poised regally above the St. Lawrence, and overlooking rugged hills and pine forests, this stately 19th century castle evokes the spirit of a French manor. The area, midway between Montreal and the breathtaking unspoiled scenery of the Gaspe Peninsula, is decidedly rural French. This resort, totally renovated with taste and style, is the place to stay if eastern Quebec, whose name comes from the Algonquin word meaning "narrowing of the waters", is your destination, and castles appeal to you. Rooms and suites aren't fussy, they're tailored and grand, and public areas are spacious, with attention to detail.

Try the indoor pool, tennis courts, lawn bowling, badminton, horseback riding, volleyball, bicycling, or hopalong at hopscotch!

You can watch or play petanque, or check out the evening entertainment following an aperitif and dinner on the patio. The lawns go on forever, an outdoor sea water swimming pool seems to float above the river.

William Howard Taft, twenty-seventh president of the U.S. drove the first ball on this 18 hole course in 1925. The course is spread out on a ledge of mountainside, with a meandering stream showing up on several holes, and you'll get some incredible views out over the river. Non-walkers will rejoice at the 80 new Yamaha carts, and golfers who know this hilly course from years past will welcome the many changes, including the fully automated watering system. The catch here is reading the greens. The French refer to them as slippery, we think they're fast and rolling. If you can, come here in the fall, it's particularly colorful and the crowds have left. The neighboring hills are ablaze with fiery reds and yellows, and there's a nice nip in the air.

Gray Rocks Inn

The Laurentian villages east of Montreal, tucked in between lake-sprinkled hills and valleys, provide an ideal playground all year round. Skiers flock here, honeymooners and families with kids can't resist the call of the wild, and it's a perfect place for a conference or meeting. As you practice your French with names such as Ste. Agathe des Monts and St. Jovite, be prepared for little pockets of rusticity, roadside shacks touting "patates frites" and panoramic views of Mont Tremblant, the Laurentians highest peak. Gray Rocks is a dowager—a huge old rambling fortress perched on Lac Quimet that has facilities to suit every need and checkbook. Stay in the main inn, condominiums, or a cozy lodge called Le Chateau. Name your sport and mood, and it's probably here. There's a spa, tennis, riding stables, a children's playground with attendants, sailing, croquet, and some of the best packages we've seen. You can be as involved as you choose—try hay rides, local tours, nightly live entertainment, an outdoor pool, fitness trails, or lazing through the days on the sandy beach. Arrive by car (an easy 90-minute drive from Montreal), arrive by seaplane, or land on a 3,600-foot landing field.

The 18 hole, par 72 championship course is on the south side of the skiing mountain, basking in the sun all day. A clubhouse with bar and small dining room, and a fashionable golf shop eagerly await your credit cards or Canadian dollars. You'll cross the Devil's River Valley, maybe lose a ball in one of the deep gullies, and marvel at the Bugaboo, the fourteenth hole. The tee and green are the only lovely areas of play here, so your tee shot had better be accurate. By the way, the green is minuscule by some accounts. You can hit the basket of balls or lag some putts on the practice green. The Golf Week Package includes a private lesson, and there are 3-day golf clinics throughout the season.

Address: C.P. 1000, Mont-Tremblant, St. Jovite, Quebec JOT 2H0

Phone: 819-425-2771 514-430-4441

No. rooms: 92

Rates: $, Credit Cards: AmEx, Visa, MC, Other CC

Services: Special Children's Program

Business Fac.: Audio-Visual, FAX

Sports Fac.: Tennis, Riding, Swimming, Fitness Ctr.

Attractions: Hay Rides, Tours

Course: Gray Rocks Golf Course

Distance: 6320, Par: 72

Rating: 70.4, No. of holes: 18

Chung Shan Hot Spring Golf Club Hotel

Address: Sanxiang Commune, Zhongshan, Guangdong

Phone: 011-852-5-210377

Innkeeper: Aylwin Tai

No. rooms: 48

Credit Cards: AmEx, Visa

Services: Conference Facilities, Gift Shop, Hot Springs

Restaurant: Clubhouse Restaurant

Bar: 19th Hole

Business Fac.: FAX 011-852-5-8684642

Sports Fac.: Swimming Pools, Tennis

Attractions: Chinese Farms & Commune, Traditional Village

Course: Chung Shan Hot Spring

Distance: 5906m, Par: 71

Rating: 72.0, No. of holes: 18

Phone Club-House: 24019

Pro's name: Peter Tang

From Hong Kong's magnificent harbor, Chung Shan Hot Spring is a comfortable 50-minute Jetfoil trip across the South China Sea to the Portuguese colony of Macau, followed by a half hour drive across the border into the heart of the Zhujiang River Delta.

The attractive garden-style resort, consisting of rooms, suites and villas, sits in a peaceful rural fertile valley where oxen work the fields, and the natural hot springs have soothed the soul for centuries. Many rooms are furnished in traditional Chinese style, within a private courtyard, complete with water gardens, fish-filled ponds and spring waters bubbling from the taps.

Guests will find 4 tennis courts, 2 swimming pools, two putting greens and a separate disco. The elegant clubhouse, with its veranda overlooking rice paddies, houses a restaurant renowned for local specialties such as Portuguese vegetable soup, curried crab, and garlic steamed prawns. Don't miss the Great Wall white wine, an unpretentious conversation piece.

There are pleasant walks through the countryside to old farms and a commune, where visitors can enjoy traditional village atmosphere with friendly locals, or relax in the spa. Zhongshan is a scenic 45-minute drive, a bustling metropolis full of age-old riverboats plying teeming waterways, new buildings, and an exotic night market.

The golf course, designed by the Arnold Palmer Design Group, was built over rice paddies and rolling hills by locals using mostly oxen and hand tools. It winds around the foothills of a lush valley under a backdrop of blue-green mountains, and a river flows through the course, in addition to seven ponds that come into play. Players find undulating, well-defined fairways, and plenty of tricky dog-legs on this beautifully maintained course.

Hotel Cariari and Country Club

About three miles from San Jose, bustling capital of this peaceful Central American republic where coffee, bananas and sugar cane reign, and there's been no army in forty years, lies this modern resort. With 186 rooms, a bar, two restaurants, a casino and the El Chapuzon Wet Bar poolside, guests don't have to leave the premises. Convention and banquet facilities can handle large groups, and other amenities such as babysitting, travel agency, a gift shop and hair salon are available. El Cariari hosts dignitaries from all over the world, and busboys and photos attest to the graciousness of Henry Kissinger, Joe Dimaggio, Jose Feliciano and others.

The adjacent Country Club is where you'll find 10 championship tennis courts, an Olympic size swimming pool, gymnasium, and three children's pools.

George and Tom Fazio created the rolling 18 holes here in 1973. Trees, tropical vegetation and tight fairways characterize the lush layout, and we found the group instruction with a PGA pro to be just what the golf doctor ordered. Green fees run about $15 (US), and our caddie, was one of the best we've encountered.

Address: P.O. Box 737 Centro Colon, San Jose

Phone: 506-39-0022 800-325-1337-221

No. rooms: 186

Rates: $$

Services: Shuttle Bus, Tours, Laundry & Valet, Medical, Safety Deposit Boxes

Restaurant: La Flamme, La Terraza Tropical

Bar: El Chapuzon

Business Fac.: Audio-Visual, Telex, FAX

Sports Fac.: Health Club, Swimming, Tennis

Attractions: Tropical River Safari, Casino, San Jose Volcano

Course: Cariari Country Club
Distance: 6590, Par: 72
Rating: 70.0, No. of holes: 18

Casa de Campo

Address: P.O. Box 140, La Romana

Phone: 809-523-3333 800-223-6620

Innkeeper: Haani Ayoub

No. rooms: 850

Rates: $$$, Credit Cards: AmEx, Visa, MC, Other CC

Services: Health Spa, Gift shop

Restaurant: Casa Del Rio

Bar: Various

Business Fac.: FAX 809-541-1419

Sports Fac.: Swimming, Tennis, Riding, Sailing, Polo

Location: La Romana

Attractions: Museum, Art Galleries, Handcraft Boutiques

Course: Cajuiles I, Cajuiles II

No. of holes: 54

"La romana" refers to the sugar scales used before shipping from the local mill in this town on the southeast coast. Today, the ultra-chic resort, Casa de Campo, seems to be the main attraction for tourists who yearn for luxury service and style on 7,000 acres.

This is a sprawling resort dedicated to the pursuit of sports, with lodging in spacious rooms (850 in all) and 6 suites in casitas. In addition, there are golf and tennis villas, with Oscar de la Renta's touches in evidence. You can head for one of many swimming pools, go horseback riding, practice for your polo match, spend time trap and skeet shooting, sweat it out in the spa, browse in the gift shop, or flag down the van headed for the beach, ten minutes away. Tennis buffs will love the 13 court hillside tennis village with its own restaurant, pro shop, swimming pool and lights for night play.

Take your pick of dining spots, there are eight choices, offering varying types of cuisine in a multitude of atmospheres. Our favorite was Casa del Rio, at Altos de Chavon, a definite "must" for hotel guests. Perched on a hillside, its today's version of a 16th century Spanish style village, complete with museum, church, art galleries, handcraft boutiques, and a shop brimming with de la Renta creations.

Two magnificent championship courses await you here. Cajuiles I, "Teeth of the Dog" is a Pete Dye masterpiece featuring seven holes rimming the rocky ocean beach. The seventh, a spectacular seaside hole requires the player to carry over churning water to a small green guarded by sand, tall scratchy grass and bunkers. The other, Cajuiles II, a links style course, also sits on a base of coral, where Dye coaxed vegetation by spreading a magic mixture to create a fine inland 18 holes. You can request a caddie, and rest assured, they are worth every peso.

Jack Tar Village

Puerto Plata (port of Silver) is 130 miles northwest of the capital, Santo Domingo, and thanks to a new international airport, tourists can arrive on this side of the island and head right for great golf, tennis and nearly deserted beaches. Bargain-hunters will love the week-long "all-inclusive" packages offered at this moderately priced resort in the land of aspiring baseball big leaguers, instant divorces and the bones of Christopher Columbus. Clusters of one and two-story white stucco villas surround thatched roof buildings that are the heart of the resort, and a well-manicured golf course encircles the village. Rooms show off Dominican art, made by locals, and its worth a serious look.

Its a short stroll from your room to the beach, where you can arrange for all sorts of water sports, or relax at the bar and grill. Guests can opt for buffet or table service in the Village dining room, plus there are afternoon and late night snacks offered. Activities include tennis courts and instruction, a huge swimming pool, and a daily schedule of events such as Merengue lessons or Spanish classes. Visit the amber mine, dawdle in the craft market, take the cable car to the top of Mt. Isabel de Torres, or hop on a bike and see the other resorts. After a leisurely dinner, check out the entertainment, and by all means, catch a glimpse of the 4,000 pound crystal chandelier in the casino.

Green fees at the Robert Trent Jones course are included for resort guests. With exotic trees and flowers, a backdrop of lush green mountains, stately palms, ocean breezes and lanky eager caddies, you'll have a splendid round. The scenic 6,730 yard layout meanders around the resort, along the sugar-white beaches, and then inland through tropical foliage and past quiet ponds.

Address: P.O. Box 368, Puerto Plata
Phone: 809-586-3557 800-999-9182
Innkeeper: William Vastbinder
No. rooms: 285
Rates: $$, Credit Cards: AmEx, Visa, MC, Other CC
Restaurant: Village Dining, Elaine's
Bar: Meeting Place Bar
Business Fac.: FAX 809-586-4161
Sports Fac.: Swim, Tennis, Water Skiing, Riding, Sail
Attractions: Casino, Amber Mine Tour, Fort San Felipe

Course: Puerto Plata Golf Course
Distance: 6730, Par: 72
Rating: 72.0, No. of holes: 18
Guest policy: Green fee included for hotel guest
Phone Club-House: 809-586-3557
Pro's name: Joe Rivera

Welcombe Hotel and Golf Course

Address: Warwick Road, Stratford-upon-Avon, CV37 ONR

Phone: 0789-295252

Innkeeper: Brian A.K. Miller

No. rooms: 76

Rates: $$$, Credit Cards: AmEx, Visa, Other CC

Services: Gift Shop

Restaurant: The Restaurant

Bar: Trevelyan

Business Fac.: Secretarial Service, FAX

Sports Fac.: Tennis, Croquet, Putting, Game Room

Attractions: Warwick Castle, Cheltenham, Oxford

Course: Welcombe Golf Course

Distance: 6202, Par: 70

Rating: 70.0, No. of holes: 18

Phone Club-House: 0789-295252

This elegant 76 room Jacobean style country hotel was built in 1869. Set on 153 acres of parkland on the outskirts of this charming town on a bend of the gentle Avon, the hostelry offers comfortable quiet lodgings, a classic French menu and an outstanding wine cellar. Rooms and suites in the older parts of the manor contain local antiques, and many have oversized marble bathrooms.

Don't miss afternoon tea in the panelled lounge. Guests are treated to a ritual reflecting a gentility of yesteryear, complete with silver service, crisp linens, and a spread of cakes and clotted cream to delight the most devout calorie counter.

The attractions of Stratford with its picturesque swans gliding past half-timbered houses are but a few minutes drive. The concierge will arrange theater tickets, historic house tours, information about side trips to the Cotswolds and help you with special events such as The Boat Club's Regatta in June, riding, tennis, fishing, or tips on local shopping. There are conference facilities for as many as 200, a superb gift shop, tennis courts, and the Trevelyan Terrace Bar—just the place to share a pint with friends.

An 18 hole golf course was added in 1980. With a standard scratch score of 70, players of every level will find its 6,202 yards pleasantly undulating, attractive and not always predictable. The course meanders through the parklands, part of which was once owned by the Bard himself. You'll find a lake, gargantuan trees, and eighteen names of holes guaranteed to titillate the post-game lager. Did you bogey or birdie Dingle Bend, Will's View or Foxes Stitch?

The Belfry

Should you find yourself heading for the Birmingham area, you'll be glad to know this major industrial, business, and conference center, has plenty of other attractions going for it. The Belfry, minutes from the M6 Motorway, is an ivy-clad, stately country manor surrounded by 370 acres of parkland and two magnificent championship golf courses.

There are conference rooms and facilities, 220 rooms and suites, tennis courts, squash courts, a full health spa, snooker, (a type of billiards), driving range and putting green. Champions Suite, with splendid views overlooking the courses and lakes, is in the "olde" building and has a four-poster bed, beamed ceiling, color television, and that old indispensable favorite—a trouser press.

If you have time for exploring the environs, you might want to visit the impressive collections at the Museum of Science and Industry, the Palladian styled St. Philip's Cathedral, the Botanical Gardens and aviaries in Edgbaston, or Birmingham's well-known jewelry manufacturing factories. Britain's second largest city has some terrific shopping, and if this appeals to you, put The Rag Market, with over 500 stalls, on your itinerary.

Golf here is well known, as the Brabazon Course is the venue of the 1985 and 1989 Ryder Cup, team matches held every other year between U.S. professionals and those of Great Britain/Europe. You can play this 7,146 yard par-72 brute designed by TV commentator Peter Alliss and David Thomas in 1977. Beware the watery grave on the 18th which Payne Stewart, Paul Azinger and Mark Calcavecchia all found during the final match of the '89 Ryder Cup. Curtis Strange says he never wants to see it again. The Belfry, home of the British PGA, was built in 1979 and requires proof of a 28 handicap or less.

Address: Lichfield Road, Wishaw, N. Warwickshire B76 9PR

Phone: 044-0675-70301

Innkeeper: Mr. Rene C. Brunet

No. rooms: 220

Rates: $$$, Credit Cards: AmEx, Visa, Other CC

Services: Tea/Coffee Making Facilities, In-house Movies

Restaurant: The French Restaurant

Bar: The Belfry Bar

Business Fac.: Secretarial Service, FAX

Sports Fac.: Swimming, Tennis, Squash, Health Spa

Attractions: Warwick Castle, Stratford Upon Avon

Course: Brabazon & Derby

Distance: 6975, Par: 73

Rating: 73.0, No. of holes: 36

Phone Club-House: 0675-70301

Pro's name: Peter McGovern

Pacific Harbour International Hotel

Address: P.O. Box 144, Postal Agency, Pacific Harbour, Deuba

Phone: 0679-45022

No. rooms: 170

Rates: $, Credit Cards: AmEx, Visa, MC, Other CC

Services: Tea/Coffee Making Facilities, Laundry Service, Guest Laundry Room

Restaurant: Nautilus

Bar: Clubhouse Bar

Business Fac.: FAX 0679-45262

Sports Fac.: Swimming, Tennis, Riding, Billiards

Attractions: Dance Theatre of Fiji, Firewalkers, Boat Tours

Course: Pacific Harbour

Distance: 6908, Par: 72, No. of holes: 18

Pro's name: Greg Norman

There's a strange mesmerism about these islands, where the indigenous Fijians live side-by-side with Indians and a handful of Europeans, Chinese, and other Pacific Islanders. This resort is a forty minute drive from Suva, the capital, which happens to be one of the wettest cities on earth, and the drive itself is comparable to a journey though a year's supply of National Geographic. Head east towards Pacific Harbour, and you'll find blue cloudless skies and miles of virgin beach. Horses and goats saunter along the road, Fijian women wash colorful sulus in the river, and happy little faces offer watermelon and shout "bula" as you pass.

If a tropical vacation with a strong Polynesian influence appeals to you, search no more, for the hotel and villas at Pacific Harbour is an experience to be treasured. There's every type of water sport, bicycles, mopeds and horses to ride, all weather floodlit tennis courts, tours to native villages, cruises to bustling Suva for shopping, and a staff of smiling, affable people likely to burst into song at any time.

The resort is on a long stretch of golden sand, facing the island of Bega, home of the legendary firewalkers, with villas scattered along miles of waterways. Some very good food is to be found here. Visitors find a good balance between traditional cuisine at the Sakura House, and local specialties such as kokoda, a delicious appetizer of fish marinated in coconut milk, onion, lemon, and chilies. There's excellent snorkeling on the reefs here, as well as sailing and big game fishing charters, wind surfing, canoeing, water scootas, and top notch scuba diving.

Designed by Robert Trent Jones in the early sixties, this is a favorite tournament site and the only championship course in Fiji. It's a well-maintained layout, dotted with lagoons and wide verdant. We opted for a caddie (barefoot, of course). His humor and advice were well worth it, especially when he forded a river for a wayward ball, and beamed as he presented us with six balls and four river prawns. Greg Norman holds the professional course record, and Bobby Clampett claims the Amateur record of 69 on the par 72 course.

Hotel de Chantaco

A couple of kilometers south of St. Jean-de-Luz, whose horseshoe-shaped white beach makes it a favorite stopping-off place for those avoiding nearby Biarritz, lies this genteel ocher-colored hotel. Opened at the beginning of the century, the mansion, with gracious archways, antiques and Basque memorabilia, has 25 rooms, each furnished differently. Some overlook the golf course, others have views of the flower-filled patio. Take time to relax and enjoy the garden or a meal on the patio under a century-old wisteria, or simply lap up the Pays Basque. Nearby you'll find a wide range of water sports, as well as riding, river fishing, and the lure of the steeply rising Pyrenees.

A few kilometers away is the Iberian border, and you'll feel the influence in St. Jean-de-Luz, where Louis XIV married Maria Theresa of Spain. Be sure to visit the Maison de l'Infant, where the bride lived prior to the nuptials, and the Basque Eglise St.-Jean-Baptiste, no doubt the most sumptuous Basque church. Check out the local shops and choose a colorful linen tablecloth to take home as a reminder of your visit to the whaling port turned fishing village. Golfers will want to visit the Centre International d'Entrainement au Golf, the continent's most extensive golf training center in Biarritz.

The hotel faces the Chantaco golf course, a par 70 layout that winds through the forest, crosses creeks and sports small well-protected lush greens. The Lacoste family owns the course, so no doubt any alligators you encounter will be walking abreast.

The course isn't overly long, but when the Atlantic winds come up, you'll understand what the French call "technique". Be ready to pull every shot from your bag, because you'll have to deal with every conceivable lie on the twisting, rolling terrain.

Address: F 64500, Saint Jean de Luz, 64500
Phone: 033-59-26-14-76
Innkeeper: Claude Libouban
Rates: $$
Services: Beauty salon
Restaurant: Dining Room, Patio
Sports Fac.: Tennis
Location: Basque Country
Attractions: Surfing, Yachting, Diving, Deep Sea Fishing, Riding

Course: Golf de Chantaco
Distance: 5366m, Par: 70, No. of holes: 18
Phone Club-House: 59-26-14-22

Cazaudehore et la Forestiere

Address: 1 Av. Kennedy,
St. Germain-en-Laye, 78100

Phone: 033-1-39-73-36-60
212-696-1323

Innkeeper: Ph. Cazaudehore

No. rooms: 24

Rates: $, Credit Cards: Visa, MC,
Other CC

Restaurant: Cazaudehore

Business Fac.: FAX 033-3973-7388

Sports Fac.: Tennis

Attractions: Hiking, Paris,
Versailles, Castles, Monet's house

Course: St.Germain-en-Laye's Golf

Distance: 6024, Par: 72,
No. of holes: 27

Guest policy: Private Club

Phone Club-House: 34-51-75-90

We're departing a little from our standard golf resort by including this family-owned hostelry set in the heart of the forest of St. Germain, twenty minutes from Orly Airport, and three kilometers from a course implanted in the heart of bucolic countryside. Three generations of Cazaudehors have nurtured the 24 room hotel which has all the charm and comfort of a country house filled with antiques and family treasures. In warm weather tables are set on the terrace under ancient acacia trees, and you'll discover some very fine dishes such as Noisettes d'agneau Poelees au Thym and a well-balanced wine list.

There are tennis courts nearby, and some truly enchanting forest paths to explore, making it very much the place for those who prefer a leisurely pace not far from Paris. For a few extra francs, your dog (well-behaved, naturally) is welcome here amid impeccable service and beautifully kept gardens.

The course at St. Germain-en-Laye was designed in 1922 by Harry Colt, whose other courses include Knollwood Country Club in Lake Forest, Illinois and the remodel of Royal Lytham & St. Annes course, where Bobby Jones won the first of his three Opens in Britain. This is a private club, with admission by "relationship", meaning the hotel will arrange for you to play. Seve Ballesteros holds the course record here, with a 63. Be sure to make your arrangements well in advance.

Hyatt Regency Grand Cayman

This is a Caribbean island with a different personality. Sure, you'll find pure white beaches, pink stucco hideaways and probably the best scuba and snorkeling around, but it's also a tax haven for offshore banking and insurance, resulting in a flourishing economy.

About 500 miles due south of Miami, is George Town, an unassuming capital of mainly offices. This resort is on Seven Mile Beach which runs along the west shore, and is the site of most of the island's major resorts.

The average winter temperature here is a pleasant 75, with summer rainier and maybe eight or ten degrees warmer.

You can expect all the Hyatt Regency touches here. The British Colonial design is in keeping with the roots of islanders, and since no structure can be more than five stories here, high-rises and blocked out views are non-existent. Accommodations are in one, two and three bedroom villas located along the edge of the Britannia Golf Course, or rooms or suites in the hotel. Regency Club rooms and suites are in a separate wing. You'll recognize the Hyatt Regency touches by its open-air lobby, lush tropical foliage, waterfalls and two signature swimming pools. The colors of the Caribbean—aqua, coral, turquoise, pink and lilac -are carried throughout—and naturally, the furnishings are attractive contemporary. Amenities include tennis courts, two restaurants, private marina, a beach club, and a unique gazebo-style bar in the swimming pool. You can rent the hotel's 65-foot catamaran, go diving, or take advantage of Nick's Aqua Sports, the hotel's watersport center. For an experience classified not-run-of-the-mill, try an excursion in a submarine to view the marine life on a tropical reef. Two types of vessels offer the plunge (one descends 1,000 feet over a coral wall), and the price is quite reasonable considering it's a unique chance to witness life at the bottom.

Golf is in the form of a prototype course by Jack Nicklaus to utilize a "Cayman Ball" , which is supposed to fly half the distance of a normal ball. Dimpled outwardly and weighing about half that of a regular ball, you can play faster and on a smaller course. The Britannia has a Scottish flair—grassy mounds, rolling dunes, oversized bunkers and lakes—the hazards of a typical "links" layout.

Address: Seven Mile Beach, Grand Cayman Island

Phone: 809-949-1234 800-233-1234

No. rooms: 236

Rates: $$

Services: Concierge, complimentary continental breakfast, shops, Dive Shop Boutique, Car and Moped Rentals

Restaurant: Hemingway's

Bar: Loggia, Aqua's

Business Fac.: FAX 809-949-8528

Sports Fac.: Tennis, Swimming, Croquet, Water Sports

Attractions: Turtle Farm, Atlantic Submarine, George Town Shops

Course: Britannia

Distance: 6206, Par: 70

Rating: 70.7, No. of holes: 18

Guest policy: Dress code

Phone Club-House: 98020

Reservations: Reservations recommended

Discovery Bay Golf Club

Address: Valley Road, Discovery Bay, Lantau Island

Phone: 852-5-9877273

Innkeeper: Bertie To, Jr.

Rates: $$$$, Credit Cards: AmEX, Visa

Services: Boutiques, Curio Shops

Restaurant: West Kitchen

Business Fac.: FAX 852-5-9875-900

Attractions: Porcelain Factories, Po Lin Tse Buddhist Monastery

Lantau Island, west of Hong Kong Island, is twice as big as Hong Kong, but with a tiny fraction of the population. You can take the ferry from Hong Kong, a pleasant, fast ride, and stop en route at Peng Chau if porcelain factories interest you. The Discovery Bay bus takes guests up the hill to the self-contained low-slung modern resort. Accommodations are in attractively furnished rooms and suites, and all have views of the sea or the mountains. Many people come here for the day, but more options are available for resident guests. There are tennis courts, bicycles, a swimming pool, water sports, and squash and racquetball courts, plus many lovely beaches to explore.

Your palate, too, is catered to here, with menus offering Cantonese and Western dishes, and bars serving tall, cool Singapore Slings. There are boutiques, curio shops and banks for your convenience. Don't think you have to race back to crowded Hong Kong. See about an excursion to Po Lin Tse Buddhist monastery, or a tea plantation where you can sample the tea being picked, and purchase some to take with you.

The 18 hole championship course, 600 feet about sea level, offers breathtaking views of Eastern Lantau and nearby islands. With green hills as a backdrop, the course, designed by Robert Trent Jones, Jr., was laid out as a walking course, with water coming into play in the form of lakes, ponds, and streams. It's hilly, challenging, and extremely beautiful. You can opt for a caddie, trolley, electric push cart, or electric golf cart.

Course: Discovery Bay Golf Club

Distance: 6123, Par: 72

Rating: 72.7, No. of holes: 18

Phone Club-House: 5-9877273

Bali Handara Kosaido Country Club

Think of Bali and you'll recall a lovelorn Mary Martin crooning about a special island where the sky meets the sea. Today's Bali, part of an archipelago southeast of Asia along the Equator is an independent republic, rich in sugarcane, rice and timber.

The steamy lowlands lure beachgoers, but the cooler climate of the mountains and plateaus of this paradise offers a glimpse of an astoundingly rich culture. Upon arrival at Denpasar Airport, guests are whisked by air-conditioned coach through a winding panorama of tiers of rice fields, to alpine country and houses built of volcanic rock.

Here in the lush highlands over looking Lake Buyan at 3746 feet is a two story luxury hotel with an additional 22 rooms in Balinese style bungalows. The look is Indo-Javanese contemporary, with bamboo furniture, hand-blocked batiks, and local wood trim used lavishly.

Kamandalu is the main restaurant, where you can sample local specialties, often spicy, as well as international dishes. Be sure to try babi guling, Bali's delicacy of spit-roasted suckling pig, stuffed with ginger, peppercorn, tumeric, garlic, red chili, and aromatic leaves. A lobby bar and snack bar cater to international palates.

In a place where developers are forbidden to build anything higher than a palm tree, you'll find plenty of places to explore and things to do. There are tennis courts, boating and fishing trips, botanical gardens, fruit and flower markets, and tropical rain forests to see. The beautiful North Coast beaches are perfect for swimming, sailing and outrigger canoes, and diving and snorkeling in these waters is nothing short of fantastic. Save room in your suitcase for textiles, gold and silver work, and you can send the bamboo chairs home. A "must" is the very center of Balinese life, the dance performances at a temple festival.

Golf here is like the frosting on the cake. Five-time British Open champion Peter Thompson carved nine holes from an old dairy farm and another nine from a tropical rain forest to produce a championship course featuring tall trees and flowers in riotous colors separating the fairways. Reminders of an old volcanic crater pop up now and then, so try to keep your ball on the soft grass.

Address: P.O. Box 324 Denpasar, Pancasari, Bali

Phone: 062-0361-28866 062-0362-41646

Innkeeper: Widodo Slamet

No. rooms: 22

Restaurant: Kamandalu

Bar: Lobby Bar

Attractions: Botanical Gardens, Tropical Rain Forest, Shopping

Course: Bali Handara Kosaido

Distance: 7024, Par: 72

Rating: 73.3, No. of holes: 18

Dromoland Castle

Address: Newmarket-on-Fergus, County Clare

Phone: Shannon 061-71144
800-346-7007

Innkeeper: Mark Nolan

No. rooms: 75

Rates: $$$, Credit Cards: AmEx, Visa, MC, Other CC

Services: Full Health Spa, Gift Shop, Currency Exchange, Parking

Restaurant: Main Dining Room

Bar: Cocktail Bar

Business Fac.: Sec.Svc., Translators

Sports Fac.: Swimming, Tennis, Squash, Riding, Sail

Attractions: Fishing, Cliffs of Moher, Limerick City

Course: Dromoland Golf Course
Distance: 6098, Par: 71
Rating: 71.0, No. of holes: 18
Phone Club-House: 061-71144

This is the quintessential baronial Irish castle, sitting regally in a 450 acre park, and reeking of the noble style recently bestowed upon it by designer Carlton Varney. For years it was the ancestral home of the O'Briens, Barons of Inchiquin. Today it's a stately hotel 8 miles north of Shannon Airport, handsome with wood panelling, original paintings, hand loomed Irish carpets, crystal, damask, and plenty of sunlight. Guests can roam the gardens, take tea in the library, fish for salmon or ride through the woods. 73 rooms and six elegant suites, all high-ceilinged and offering views of the lake and golf course, await discerning travellers.

But all is not staid here, there's a dance floor, entertainment, gift shop, swimming pool, tennis, and sailing on the lake. The staff is extremely helpful, and can make arrangements for you to play golf at the two international courses within easy driving distance, Lahinch and Ballybunion. And should you prefer to tee off right here, there's an eighteen hole course. Its a par 71 with just enough water, woods, irregularly shaped mounds and wildlife to remind you that Mother Nature, architect of Irish courses is in charge.

Waterville Lake Hotel

This secluded 80 room structure is scenically sandwiched between the mountains and the eastern shore of Ballinskelligs Bay. If you're coming from Killarney, allow about two hours to drive through Macgillycuddy's Reeks and then along the coastline cliffs to this small unspoiled village, famous as an angling center.

The resort, on the shores of Lough Currane, is open May through October, and offers an indoor pool, thermal spa pool, sauna solarium, tennis courts, and a fine dining room featuring traditional Irish specialties. And when either fresh salmon or trout is available, it's fresh from the line from a nearby mountain lake or the lough.

If early Christian remains interest you, there are beehive huts, stone forts and ancient roadways scattered around Lough Currane, and if you can find a local to take you to Church Island, you'll marvel at the ruins of a twelfth century Romanesque church. The Ring of Kerry is a sight to behold. The trip around the peninsula takes a full day in good weather, and you'll be rewarded with tiny fishing villages, mountains rising 2,000 feet from lakeshores, luxurious forests, castle ruins, and pristine seaside resorts. Skellig Rocks is home to thousands of puffins, gannets razorbills, and kittiwakes, and is definitely worth the boat voyage.

The nearby countryside is exceptional and during summer months, the wide, sandy beaches are among the best in Europe.

Golf has been a way of life here for generations, and the Waterville Golf Links, created by Irish-American Jack Mulcahy in 1975, can be called a true course of hazards. Its one of the longest in Europe, with sufficient roll to the ground to give golf feature and to create natural amphitheaters. Tees and greens are large, and fairways somewhat level. The signature holes are the par-five 11th measuring 487 yards along a rugged valley between towering dunes; and the 17th, dubbed Mulcahy's Peak, an awesome par three with a tee that towers above the links on all sides, and the Kerry Mountains beyond.

Address: Ring of Kerry, Waterville, County Kerry

Phone: 353-0667-4133 800-346-7007

No. rooms: 72

Rates: $, Credit Cards: AmEx, Visa, Other CC

Services: Thermal Spa Pool, Sauna, Solarium, Tanning Beds

Restaurant: Waterville Lake Hotel

Bar: Skelligs Bar

Business Fac.: FAX 353-0667-4482

Sports Fac.: Swimming, Game of Pool, Tennis, Riding

Attractions: Pony Trekking, Boat Trips, Shopping

Course: Waterville Golf Links

Distance: 7184, Par: 73

Rating: 74.9, No. of holes: 18

Phone Club-House: 0667-4102

Pro's name: Liam Higgins

Ashford Castle

Address: Cong, County Mayo

Phone: 353-092-46003 800-346-7007

No. rooms: 86

Rates: $$, Credit Cards: AmEx, Visa, , Other CC

Restaurant: 2 Restaurants

Bar: Dungeon Bar

Business Fac.: FAX 353-924-6260

Sports Fac.: Tennis, Jogg, Trails, Hunting, Shooting

Attractions: Yacht tour, Fishing

Course: Ashford Castle GC

Distance: 2996, Par: 35, No. of holes: 9

Guest policy: Green fee included for hotel guest.

This part of Western Ireland, a land of white limestone plains, stone canal locks, the thick creamy head on a pint of Guinness, and restrooms labeled Fir, and Mna, is home of some of the best hunting and fishing in the republic, or anywhere. Cong is a tiny village known for the ruins of a twelfth century Augustinian abbey, and Ashford Castle, one of Europe's premier castle luxury hotels.

Truly a fairy-tale setting on the shores of Lough Corrib, with its hundreds of islands, bays and coves, today's castle reflects the idiosyncrasies of previous tenants. More than seventy rooms, all with views of the lake or formal gardens and rolling lawns await the visitor. Public rooms gleam with priceless antiques, paneled ceilings, Waterford chandeliers, and suits of armor to remind us that yesteryear's knights weren't line-backers. Two restaurants, a Dungeon Bar, jogging trails, and tennis courts dispel one's urge to joust at sunrise. Wet fly fishing for trout and salmon extends from March through summer, and expert instructors conduct a well-respected angling school. Topics covered include water reading, wading, tackle, fly tying, and landing and releasing. A day's tour aboard a 65 foot motor yacht, and the horse drawn jaunting car from "The Quiet Man" with John Wayne, are available for guest's enjoyment. No visitor should miss exploring the beautiful Connemara countryside, stopping for a pint and local smoked salmon at an Oyster Pub.

As luck of the Irish would have it, golf is exclusively for castle guests. You'll have nine holes of enjoyable play on an uncrowded (probably misty) fairly flat layout. And begorra, you can have a motorized cart!

Caesarea Golf & Country Club

Site of ancient Israelites, Romans, Byzantines, Crusaders and Turks, an aqueduct and a Roman theater still in use, this maritime metropolis boasts the country's only golf course. Conveniently located midway between Tel-Aviv and Haifa, Israel's mountainside port of parks and gardens, the Caesarea is easily accessible from all cities. The 110 air conditioned rooms of this well appointed modern hostelry face a large swimming pool, fairways or the rolling green hills of this city named in honor of Herod's Roman patron, Augustus Caesar.

Rain generally falls during the winter only, but it's usually sunny with temperatures rarely dipping below the mid-sixties Fahrenheit. Summers can be quite hot, but the cooling breezes from the Mediterranean make this area practically ideal.

A complete resort, guests can opt for horseback riding, bicycling, a health club, tennis, a sauna, and a good restaurant, coffee shop, bar and cafeteria-style restaurant. Evening entertainment ranges from live shows, movies and specialty nights to starlight dancing. There's meeting, party and conference space for up to 250 people, or one can host up to a thousand in the gardens. Windsurfing is minutes away, and there's fantastic skindiving and acres of countryside for jogging or searching for small archeological treasures.

Plan to spend some time exploring the area. Depending on your time and interests, you might want to visit Netanya to the south, a major diamond cutting area where you can tour factories and perhaps leave with a small bauble. Not far is the town of Hadera, where cotton and oranges are shipped to a shivering Europe. And don't miss the country's most acclaimed theater, where concert-goers enjoy a splendid sea view as they savor the sounds of opera or rock. Most of the seats are modern, but one can imagine an audience two thousand years ago admiring or booing toga-clad actors. The golf scorecard itself is a treasure—choose from Hebrew or English to learn local rules, our favorite stating "All relics of the Roman Period are integral parts of the course", thus no free drop. The picturesque course is built on sandy soil, so you'll find very little run on the ball, summer or winter, and very few water hazards.

Address: P.O. Box 1010, Caesarea, 30660

Phone: 972-06-361172-3-4
800-2237773-4

No. rooms: 110

Rates: $$, Credit Cards: AmEx, Visa, MC, Other CC

Services: Health Club, Sauna, Laundry & Dry Cleaning, Free Parking, Dannyl Children's Program

Restaurant: Caesarea Dining Room

Bar: Lobby Lounge & Bar

Business Fac.: FAX 972-636-2392

Sports Fac.: Swimming, Tennis, Volleyball, Basketball

Attractions: Ancient site of Roman city, Windsurfing,

Course: Caesarea Golf Club
Distance: 6245m, Par: 73
Rating: 70.7, No. of holes: 18

La Meridiana

Address: Via ai Castelli, 17033 Garlenda (SV),

Phone: 039-0182-580271/2/3

No. rooms: 31

Rates: $$$

Services: Daily Newspaper, Sauna, Massages

Restrictions: Small dogs permitted

Restaurant: Il Rosmarino

Business Fac.: FAX 039-580150

Sports Fac.: Swimming, Riding, Tennis

Attractions: 13th Century Cathedral and Baptistery

Course: Golf Club Garlenda

Distance: 5851m, Par: 71

Rating: 70.0, No. of holes: 18

Phone Club-House: 0182/580012

Think Liguria and you'll visualize terraced hillsides dotted with grapes and pungent olives, fields of gladioli, and the sleek set sipping chilled Vermentino at seaside cafes in Portofino and Rapallo. And if you're thinking golf in conjunction with a mild winter, gentle spring and temperate summer, this rustically elegant red tile roofed sanctuary, with 15 spacious rooms and 16 suites might well be for you. Each room affords views of lush greenery, brilliant flower gardens, and the silvery olive trees that dot the golf course. Furnishings are a delightful combination of regional antiques and expanses of glass which create an indoor-outdoor effect. You'll receive a warm welcome, attentive service and a cuisine with a strong regional bent highlighted by some fine local wines. The restaurant, "Il Rosmarino", is a favorite among locals as well as those who seek the talents of Fabio Dagrada, the young chef.

You can have a sauna and massage, saddle up at the nearby stable, or revel in the throes of the 13th century cathedral and baptistery in Albenga, a few kilometers away. If you like stalactites and stalagmites, don't miss the Basura grottoes, a stone's throw from Albenga. Liguria is famous for its olive oil, and the amiable propietario of the hotel, Edmondo Segre, will gladly point you to a local producer where visitors are welcome.

Golf is popular here on the Italian Riviera, and especially at this demanding 18 hole course, where the first few holes can lull you into relaxation (especially after a lunch of home made pasta). Then comes the twelfth hole, a long and treacherous par four, followed by a long par 3 that crosses the Torrente Lerrone, surely a something to avoid. There's a putting green, driving range, attractive clubhouse, and a serene valley that beckons golfers. A glance at the course's calendar reveals such stellar events as the Trofeo Guy Laroche, the Coppa Nike, and the Coppa Relais & Chateau. Electric carts are available, in addition to the pull carts. Be sure to check out the special discount for La Meridiana's guests.

Villa d'Este

If the lifestyle of a lakeside villa amid elegant public rooms, wide marble staircases and gleaming chandeliers appeals to you, you should head for this grand old dowager to experience gracious old-world country living. Once the home of the ruthless Dukes of Ferrara, and later inhabited by King George 1V's wife, the property later fell into the hands of Milanese businessmen who transformed the estate into a luxury hotel. It's the breathtaking backdrop—standing near a beautiful park under jagged snow-capped peaks facing an azure lake—that makes it worth the visit. You will be received here with exemplary courtesy, and attentive, efficient service, as you marvel at the modern sports facilities clad in its Renaissance facade. Floating right on the lake is a heated swimming pool, a favorite haunt of wealthy Italians who flock here in their Lamborghinis and Maseratis. Indoors, you'll find a squash court, gymnasium, and sauna, turkish bath and massage room. With its own sandy beach, bronzed bodies can contemplate a myriad of watersports. Tennis courts are tucked away unobtrusively above the cypress-lined eighteenth century garden near the renowned mosaic. Sip an aperitif on the terrace overlooking the lake as the sun sets—everything conspires to make you fall in love with the drama of a land where Roman ruins blend with German and French architecture. One of Italy's four casinos is nearby, and an excellent restaurant serving classic Lombardian dishes will render you utterly content. .

The best way to explore the lake is by boat, you can eat on board and savor unparalleled scenery. The Lombardy Lake area is rich in diversions, whether you prefer sightseeing, shopping, or hiking in the rolling hills, forests and mountains. Many resorts and restaurants close in winter, so best time to visit is in late spring, before the crowds converge.

Address: Via Regina 40, 22010 Cernobbio
Lake Como, 031-200200
Phone: 031-511471 800-223-6800
No. rooms: 182
Rates: $$$, Credit Cards: AmEx, Other CC
Services: Sauna, Turkish Bath, Massage Room

Restaurant: Restaurant
Bar: Poolside Bar
Business Fac.: Conference facilities
Sports Fac.: Swimming, Squash, Gymnasium, Tennis
Attractions: Casino, Shopping, Hiking, Sightseeing, Wineries

Distance: 5585, Par: 69
No. of holes: 18

Is Molas Golf Hotel

Address: 09010 S. Margherita di Pula, Cagliari, Sardinia

Phone: 070-9209422
070-9209447-457-466

Innkeeper: Eligio Orru

No. rooms: 81

Rates: $$$, Credit Cards: AmEx, Visa, Other CC

Services: Children's Playground, Beauty Salon, Private Parking

Restaurant: Al Prato Verde

Bar: Piano Bar

Business Fac.: Sec.Svc., Translators

Sports Fac.: Swimming, Tennis, Riding, Sailing

Location: Is Molas

Attractions: Nuraghi di Barumini, Rovine de Nora Antica

Course: Is Molas Golf Club

Distance: 6383m, Par: 72, No. of holes: 18

Phone Club-House: 070-920906

Pro's name: A. Paolillo

If you fly or take the ferry into Cagliari, the Sardinian capital founded by the Phoenicians, you'll have a 35 kilometer drive to this 81 room hotel which faces the sea. Or, better yet, request the services of the hotel's private limousine. This resort, opened in 1984, has a swimming pool, tennis courts, and facilities for riding and riding and sailing. There are conference rooms for as many as 90 people, as well as secretarial service for busy travellers, and translators. Al Prato Verde is the main restaurant, and guests can choose from local specialties, including pastas and freshly caught seafood. The piano bar and dance floor are lively spots for checking out the night life. And don't pass up a sip of the fiery Filu di Ferru.

This championship course is laid out with numerous natural hazards intact. Open since 1975, golfers rave about the long holes, the steep ditch in the fifth, the quirky pond on the 9th, and the clever use of strategic mounds and depressions. Luxuriant wooded hills are the backdrop for this Henry Cotton layout that skirts the sea front as well as inland terrain.

Costa Smeralda Hotels

This sophisticated, expensive resort development caters to those seeking la dolce vita in a sleek, well-planned consorzio in Sardinia's sun-drenched northeastern corner. The heart of it all is Porto Cervo, where gorgeous yachts, cafes and social events play host to jet setters. Accommodations range from Moorish-style clusters of whitewashed towers housing grandiose suites and rooms in the Hotel Cala di Volpe, to 6 room villas on private beaches. The four hotels offer amenities such as water skiing school, a jetty for small yachts, fantastic cuisine, a lively nightlife, and even children's special events. The inlets and bays are perfect for snorkeling, all sorts of sports are offered, and after thirty years in operation, the result has been a harmonious combination of buildings blending in with and enhancing the landscape. Not only can you come here and enjoy eighty sheltered beaches, a glass of sparkling white Vermentino di Gallura, and the pleasures of hedonism, you can arrange a conference here, or even purchase your own villa!

Robert Trent Jones carved a smashing 18 hole course from a rocky promontory between two bays. Fairways and greens twist through the hills dotted with wind-sculpted rocks, lupin, lavender, Mediterranean marquis, lakes and ponds, and patches of granite outcroppings. Tees are exceptionally long, views of the bays exhilarating, and there's no shortage of rough. You can rent an electric cart, or a hand trolley, to carry your clubs around this par 72 course, rated numero uno by Italian golf media. Green fees vary with the season, but during the summer, your best bet is to book a tee time far in advance.

Address: 07020 Puerto Cervo, Costa Smeralda, Sardinia

Phone: 039-0789-94000 800-223-6800

No. rooms: 731

Rates: $$$$

Services: Bridge Room

Restrictions: No Pets

Restaurant: Cervo Grill

Bar: Lord Nelson Pub

Business Fac.: Audio-Visual, Translators

Sports Fac.: Swimming, Tennis, Squash, Boat Tours

Attractions: Shopping, Marina, Carnevale (during Lent)

Course: Pevero Golf Course

Distance: 6175m, Par: 72, No. of holes: 18

Phone Club-House: 0789-96210

Reservations: Tee times recommended

Tryall Golf, Tennis & Beach Club

Address: Sandy Bay Post Office, Hanover

Phone: 809-952-5110-3 800-237-3237

Innkeeper: Josef Berger

No. rooms: 52

Rates: $$$$, Credit Cards: AmEx, Visa, MC, Other CC

Services: Gift Shop, Card Room, Concierge, Babysitting, Beauty Salon, Laundry/Valet

Restaurant: Tryall Great House Restaurant

Bar: Great House Bar

Business Fac.: Sec. Serv., Conf. Fac.

Sports Fac.: Tennis, Riding, Water Sports, Swimming

Location: Sandy Bay, Hanover

Attractions: Ocho Rios & Dunn's River Falls, Carinosa Gardens

Course: Tryall Golf Course
Distance: 6680, Par: 71
No. of holes: 18
Phone Club-House: 809-952-5110
Pro's name: Nelson Long

Tryall, clinging to a hilltop overlooking the Caribbean, is one of those fashionable resorts of the twentieth century—well tended, tastefully furnished and oozing tranquility and tradition. It isn't overwhelming, with 52 rooms and 42 villas with 2, 3, or 4 bedrooms. The hub of this 2200 acre former sugar plantation is the 153-year old Great House, which has not only maintained its past charm, but has kept current with every conceivable amenity. Rooms are newly decorated, and are filled daily with fresh flowers. some have private patios and all overlook the sea or open to mountain views. Most villas have private pools, and come with staff eager to help you unwind. Evenings are dress-up events and for eight or more, the chef will prepare a special Jamaican dinner.

This is an ideal place to stay if activity, pampering and the perfect terrace for sunset watching are high on your list. The pool is complete with swim-up bar and waterfall, and the tennis courts, boutique, beauty salon, gift shop, beach bar and evening entertainment all assure guests of a grand hotel lifestyle. An amenable concierge will help you arrange babysitting, shopping and exploring the environs, an appointment with a masseuse, dry cleaning and laundry service, horseback riding, scuba diving and deep-sea fishing, or point you to the veranda where tea, finger sandwiches and cakes are served each afternoon.

Watersports offered at the beach include snorkeling, Sunfish sailing, windsurfing, pedal boats and a glass-bottom boat for reef viewing. The golf course's 18 holes begin by the sea on low, flat land. Seven holes stretch along the water, where wind and sand are major hazards. The rest wind inland onto sloping foothills leading to a high plateau with such features as tree-lined tees and several dogleg holes. The 6th tee is the one to write home about—a gigantic water wheel 200 years old and still turning. Caddying at Tryall is a prestigious position, and the sight of golf bags balanced astride a head is a time-honored tradition older caddies are proud to keep alive. In the 1981 annual caddies tournament, four of them broke 80 when they "hit de ball, mon!"

Half Moon Golf, Tennis & Beach Club

This is a refreshing departure from the typical Caribbean beach resort. You'll not see rooms swathed in bamboo and pastels, instead, visitors find an air of elegant informality in the form of Queen-Anne-style reproductions, colorful local art, and architectural details such as white-washed columns, arches and brick-paved floors. The resort sits on a long stretch of beach, and is comprised of villas, rooms, apartments, and cottages with private pools.

Not in the mood to cook? Request the services of one for your apartment, and plan to fall in love with local specialties such as Duckanoo (sweet potato dessert), pepper pot soup, and Matrimony. Nothing's crowded here, you have 400 acres of colorful gardens, lawns, tennis courts, and a jitney in case all this vacationing renders you immobile. A plantation-style pavilion used for barbecues, crab races, dinner shows with calypso and a hundred other events is the hub for villa renters.

A full range of water sports can be yours for the asking, plus horseback riding, squash courts, saunas and massage facilities. General Manager Heinz Simonitsch, past president of the Caribbean Hotel Association, recently masterminded a $3 million renovation here. Touring companies offer trips to all sorts of places including a pineapple and coffee plantation, old Jamaica with stately homes, craft markets, bamboo rafting through a tropical forest, and a rollicking open bar train into the country's interior to a rum distillery.

If you're here in August, you can catch the Reggae Sunsplash—right where it all started, and where its pulsating rhythms are part of everyday life.

Golf is complimentary for hotel guests on a Robert Trent Jones layout that is fairly flat with a devilish little irrigation ditch that crisscrosses several fairways. Scenic little ponds dapple the course, and when the afternoon breezes come in from the sea, you'll be glad you have all those clubs.

Address: P.O. Box 80, Montego Bay

Phone: 809-953-2211 800-237-3237

Innkeeper: Heinz Simonitsch

No. rooms: 107

Rates: $$, Credit Cards: AmEx, Visa, MC, Other CC

Services: Shopping Arcade, Sauna, Massages, Champagne on Arrival

Restaurant: Seagrape Terrace - Sugar Mill

Bar: Cedar Bar

Business Fac.: Secretarial Service, FAX

Sports Fac.: Swimming, Tennis, Squash, Riding, Sailing

Location: Rose Hall

Attractions: Tours Historic Great Houses, Public Market, Crafts Markets

Course: Half Moon

Distance: 7160, Par: 72, No. of holes: 18

Guest policy: Green fee included for hotel guest,

Phone Club-House: 809-958-2560

Pro's name: Bryon Bernard

Wyndham Rose Hall Beach Hotel

Address: P.O. Box 999, Montego Bay

Phone: 809-953-2650 800-822-4200

No. rooms: 500

Rates: $

Services: Full Health Club

Restaurant: Cat Cay Brasserie

Bar: 4 Lounges

Business Fac.: FAX 809-953-2617

Sports Fac.: Tennis, Swimming, Water Sports

Attractions: International Shopping Mall, Horseback Tours

Course: Wyndham Rose Hall Beach

Distance: 6598, Par: 72, No. of holes: 18

Guest policy: Green fee included for hotel guest,

With meeting and convention facilities capable of handling up to 1,200 serious people, this 500 room high rise hotel overflows with amenities. Sitting on 30 acres of private beach about 15 minutes east of the airport, this well-maintained property offers a well-trained staff and all the latest luxuries. For dining and snacks, you can choose from various eateries, and for a more formal lunch or dinner, don't miss the Country Club. The Great House Veranda, for continental cuisine, is in an elegant island setting, and you can unwind to reggae or jazz in any or all of the four lounges.

Head for the beach for a wide variety of watersports, or check out the tennis, which is big here. A Wimbledon and Davis Cup tennis director runs special daytime clinics, and you can play in the evening, should you choose. An international shopping mall, with imports from the Orient, Mexico, and various far-flung outposts will tempt your credit cards. No need to disturb your solitude in one of the three interconnecting pools, float on over to the swim-up bar and order a cool one.

Think about exploring Jamaica's inland wonders —woods, waterfalls, plantations—on horseback. There are various equestrian centers, and some offer trail rides with picnics, evening rides, etc. Ask at the hotel. You might want to rent a moped, go spearfishing, hike to the top of Dunn's River Falls, watch a cricket match, or, if you're lucky enough to be here for Jonkanoo (a celebration similar to Carnival) you'll see plenty of action.

What a course this is! You'll have some blind holes, surely some wind, a cemetery, and a lovely waterfall. Named "Chinaman's Reef," the par 4 eighth is only 322 yards from the rear tees. It's a dogleg left with the Caribbean lurking along the left side of the fairway, and a stream to the right of the green. The 18th century Rose Hall Great House overlooks the course, which was built in the seventies by Henry C. Smedley.

Runaway Bay H.E.A.R.T.
Country Club

This twenty room resort, nestled in the lush tropical hills of Cardiff Hall is a training and service program for young aspiring students of the hospitality industry. The country club overlooks the Runaway Bay Golf Course, and is but a short stroll from the beach. Amenities at the resort include tennis, a swimming pool, and an eager young staff dedicated to catering to vacationer's pleasures.

Cardiff Hall, the restaurant on the premises, serves local and international fare. Wednesdays you'll want to sample the Jamaican buffet with an array of jerk dishes, and Friday is barbecue night, Jamaican style. Transportation may be arranged to all restaurants in the Ocho Rios area.

If greathouses intrigue you, don't miss Good Hope, the eighteenth century home of a very rich planter. There are excellent craft markets, daily trains Kingston and Montego Bay, trips to Dunn's River Falls, bicycle rentals, and the Governor's Coach Tour, for a glimpse of the mountainous interior. This is the place to shop for unusual wood carvings and art by contemporary artists and textiles. Check the weekly tourist newspaper or ask Mr. Wint, the manager of this charming resort for details on the best places to shop. Jamaican coffee is a swell gift for the guys you left behind.

The 18 hole course here is a product of Commander John Harris, who attained his rank with the Royal Navy during World War II. Among his masterpieces are Lahinch (Castle Course) in Ireland, and the Royal Hong Kong Eden Course. Hotel guest have unlimited green fees on this par 72 layout whose course rating is 72 from the white tees. Golfers get vistas of the azure Caribbean as well as wide fairways, generous bunkers, and some demanding par threes.

Address: P.O. Box 98, Runaway Bay, St. Ann

Phone: 809-973-2671-4
1-800-526-2422

Innkeeper: Hugh Wint

No. rooms: 20

Rates: $$$$, Credit Cards: AmEx, Visa, MC,

Restaurant: Cardiff Hall Restaurant

Bar: Bar

Location: Cardiff Hall

Attractions: Daily Island Tours, Dine Around Program

Course: Runaway Bay Golf Course
Distance: 6884, Par: 72
Rating: 73.5, No. of holes: 18
Phone Club-House: 809-973-2561
Pro's name: Seymour Rose

Kawana Hotel

Address: 1459 Kawana
Ito City, Shizouka Prefecture 414
Phone: 081-0557-45-1111
213-388-1151
Innkeeper: Yoshiharu Yoneyama
No. rooms: 140
Rates: $$$, Credit Cards: AmEx,
Visa, Other CC
Services: Billard Room, Card Room,
Gift Shop
Restaurant: Dining Room
Bar: Bar
Business Fac.: Sec.Svc., Translators
Sports Fac.: Swimming, Tennis
Location: Fuji Hakane Izu Park
Attractions: MOA Museum of Art,
Izu-Hakone Nat'l Park.

Course: Oshima & Fuji Golf
Distance: 6187, Par: 72,
No. of holes: 36
Pro's name: K. Sugimoto

The hotel, Japan's first golf resort for foreigners,is located in the suburbs of Ito City, on the Izu peninsula, which comes from the old Japanese words meaning "hot water gushing". Baron Okur, businessman and pioneer of tourism, intended to develop a country estate similar to one he had seen in England. Upon visiting the site a year later, he discovered the man in charge had started a golf course. In 1928 the Kawana Hotel opened a course with a small western style hotel, which now has 140 air conditioned rooms, an Imperial Suite, and banquet halls, all overlooking sweeping green lawns, Mt. Fuji's majestic outline, and the Izu National Park.

Other amenities include all-weather tennis courts, three outdoor swimming pools, a gift shop and a game room for table tennis, Mah Jong, and quoits. Dining here is an exhilarating experience. The menu in the main dining room caters to European palates, while the visitor can expect a sampling of tasty Japanese fare in a separate 350 year old farm house transported from the mountains. For drinks, there's a spacious main bar, a grill bar and a golfer's bar aptly called the "37th Hole".

Autumn is best here, there's a crispness in the clear blue sky, and trees are spectacular. Between January and May, Sakura or cherry blossoms are everywhere, and during summer months many vacation spots tend to be crowded. It's easy to take the train here from Tokyo or Atami, and you'll see some lovely scenery en route.

The area has parks, gardens, amusement centers, hot springs, museums, and restaurants galore. Sports facilities are everywhere, but the area is well-known for hiking, ocean fishing, and bicycling. And you can't ignore Mount Fuji in all its splendor. It's there to ponder, climb, sketch or photograph.

You can tee off in sight of the magnificent mountain on the Fuji Course. Designed by British golf architect C. H. Alison, this course is typical of the layouts in the mountainous regions, where agricultural crops have priority over golfers. Green fees in a land where players don $100 golf shirts are thirty thousand yen on weekends! On a clear day you can see Oshima Island with its live volcano from Oshima Course.

Genting Highlands Resort

Peninsular Malaysia, with one of Asia's highest standards of living, is a prosperous blend of Portuguese, Dutch and British influence, and Malay, Chinese, Thai and Indian exotica and charm.

As you leave the administrative capital of Kuala Lumpur, and wind through rubber forests and tin mining operations towards the hills, you'll see Chinese temples, Muslim mosques, Sikhs in turbans, tourists carted about in rickshaws, and road signs in Bahasa.

Here in the Genting Highlands, 32 miles out of K.L., and away from the tropical heat of the lowlands is a modern resort consisting of three hotels, a dazzling casino, an indoor stadium, tennis, swimming pools, a gymnasium, restaurants, disco, convention hall and facilities for family fun such as boating, a narrow-gauge train, amusement arcade, and a cable car. The resort is well promoted, with excursions to nearby sights, entertainment and always the soothing invigorating mountain breeze that sweeps across the sculpted terraces and emerald hills of Genting.

Nature lovers will want to visit Kinabalu National Park, and everybody should see The National Museum in Kuala Lumpur, with its gold, silver and samples of aboriginal life. Don't leave without a few colorful batiks, a couple of wood carvings, and certainly some woven place mats are in order. Your Malaysian dollars, called ringgits, will buy marvelous food here—you can sample everything from a Madras curry to spicy saytay, beef or chicken on a skewer. You'll play at the Awana Golf and Country Club, a well-maintained eighteen holes offering both caddies and carts. Between the sixth and seventh holes lurks a largish pond, no doubt lined with wayward Titleists, and in case you think you've seen enough water, the par 5 eighth will re-introduce you. Your game will be enhanced by jungle foliage, animal statues, small huts and some tricky sand traps.

Address: 8th Mile, Kuala Lumpur, Selangor/Pahang 69000

Phone: 03-211-3015 800-448-8355

Innkeeper: Col Martin Loo

No. rooms: 680

Rates: $, Credit Cards: AmEx, MC,

Services: Gift Shop, Jaccuzi, Full Health Spa

Restaurant: Rejawali Restaurant

Business Fac.: Secretarial Service, FAX

Sports Fac.: Swimming, Tennis, Squash, Riding, Polo

Attractions: Casino, Narrow-guage Train, Kinabalu National Park

Course: Awana Golf Course

Distance: 5474m, Par: 72, No. of holes: 18

Phone Club-House: 03-211-3015

Pro's name: Mr. Selarus

Pierre Marques

Address: P.O. Box 474, Acapulco, GRO

Phone: 748-4-20-00 800-223-1818

No. rooms: 332

Restaurant: La Pergola, La Terraza

Bar: Pierre Bar

Business Fac.: FAX 52-748-43395

Sports Fac.: Swimming, Tennis

Attractions: Acapulco, Parasailing, Deep Sea Fishing

No. of holes: 36

Acapulco, where the green Sierra Madre meet the sea, and rich Mexicans retreat to opulent hillside villas, has always spelled

F-U-N. Add wall-to-wall bikinis, a pretty sophisticated nightlife, bargain shopping, good body-surfing and watersports, a picture-postcard bay, and a quite respectable convention/performing arts center, and just about any sybarite can find his niche. This resort shares the Revolcadero Beach with its sister, the Acapulco Princess, and is about a ten minute drive from the airport.

Atmosphere is casual and relaxed, yet this isn't for the cutoff jeans-and-tee-shirt set. Rooms and suites are in low rambling wings overlooking pools, gardens and the ocean. Casitas dot the landscaped gardens, and an uncrowded stretch of beach lures sunbathers, surfers and aspiring castle-builders. Swimmers can head for any of the three pools, and five tennis courts, all lit for night play, or a mirrored exercise room. The hotel maintains a water purification system, laundry and valet services, and there are convention facilities for as many as 500. Arrangements can be made for sailing, water skiing, snorkeling, horseback riding, nightclub trekking, and the spectacle of bullfighting. Acapulco is a deep-sea fishing paradise, with the Pacific yielding pompano, yellowtail, bonito, and everybody's favorite shark! Guests can hop on the shuttle or stroll along the beach to the Princess, whose facilities you can share.

The 1982 World Cup was held on this course, and the pros managed only 17 individual rounds under par. Lagoons, palm trees, hibiscus and deep bunkers characterize a course that keeps regulars coming back. But don't count on walking away with the money—there are some tricky carries here, especially when the wind comes up, and many a wayward ball has gone into the drink.

Southampton Princess, Hamilton, Bermuda

Chang Shan Hot Springs Golf Club, China

Puerto Azul Beach Hotel

You'll know you are in the Philippines when your hop aboard a brilliantly festooned jeepney to be taken to your suite here. As it lurches up the jungle pathway, affording a bird'seye view of Manila Bay with Corregidor Island and the Bataan Peninsula, you hope you didn't forget the insect repellent. This is a sprawling tropical resort, on virgin hills and forests, with 17-room clusters of three and four floors. Interiors have a local flair, with lots of wood and brass, and rates are moderate. Everything is here, including a spa, pool, indoor games, tennis, squash, badminton, bowling, conference and shopping areas, entertainment, bars and restaurants.

Paniman Beach is a ten-minute jeepney ride away, where you can find a wide range of water sports. Excursions in the area afford guests a glimpse of Filipino country life while visiting a fishing village, public market, old churches and the Taal volcano, the world's smallest. How about shooting the rapids at the giant Pagsanjan Falls, or exploring the hidden islands surrounding Cavite and stopping for a San Miguel beer on the way back?

You'll play golf at the Puerto Azul Beach and Country Club, a Gary Player course that opened in 1978. You can request a caddie, and there are carts to rent. From the middle tees, its 6.061 yards on this championship par 72 layout whose front nine twists through the forest and whose back nine has plenty of water to carry. The seventeenth, skirting Caysubic Bay is a nerve-wracking test of skill where many a hooker has found a watery grave.

Address: Ternate, Cavite 4111
Phone: 574731 212-397-2449
Innkeeper: Rigo Hartmann
No. rooms: 340
Rates: $, Credit Cards: , Visa, MC, Other CC
Services: Complimentary Coffee and Tea Sachets
Restaurant: La Parilla
Bar: Mardicas Bar
Business Fac.: Secretarial Service, FAX
Sports Fac.: Swimming, Tennis, Squash, Pony Rides
Attractions: Cavite Village, Corregidor Is. Tours, Banca rides.

Course: Puerto Azul Beach & CC
Distance: 6082, Par: 72
Rating: 75.0, No. of holes: 18
Phone Club-House: 57-47-31
Pro's name: Joe Mari Alid

Quinta do Lago

Address: 8100 Loule, Almancil, Algarve

Phone: 089-96666 800-445-5322

No. rooms: 141

Rates: $$

Services: Billards, Health Club, Massage

Restaurant: Ca d'Oro, Navegadores

Business Fac.: Audio-Visual

Sports Fac.: Swimming, Tennis, Riding, Water Skiing

Attractions: Windsurfing, Clay Shooting, Deep Sea Fishing

Course: Quinta do Lago

Distance: 6400m, Par: 72

Rating: No. of holes: 27

Phone Club-House: 809-94529

Sleek and uncluttered, this whitewashed, red-tile-roofed contemporary resort cascades down the hill facing the estuary and sea. Half an hour from Faro airport in Portugal's sun-blessed Algarve, guests find sporting facilities, 141 luxury rooms and 9 suites, and conference facilities for up to 200. Nothing is lacking here—the estate has stables with experienced instructors, and horsepower in abundance for a fast gallop through the undulating sun-parched hills. Windsurfers can skim a small lake, there are tennis courts, swimming pools, billiards room, a spa, and the services of a friendly Portuguese staff. Devotees rave about the food here. The Ca d'Oro serves Italian fare, and the Navegadores Restaurant concentrates on traditional Portuguese dishes as well as other specialties. Don't pass up freshly caught sardines, or the tangy cheese, Serpa. We were partial to the light, dry Vinhos Verdes from the Minho region in the north, perfect with fresh seafood. Beach aficionados have only to stroll across a foot-bridge spanning an estuary to enjoy azure water and golden sands.

There are twenty-seven holes here, with another nine under construction. Designed by William Mitchell, the three nines are among the top ten in Europe, and any two can be combined for a par 72 round. Hilly it isn't, nor are there a lot of bunkers, but you'll have to figure out which iron to use to get out of the umbrella trees. As creatures of habit, we were amused by the local rule stating that it isn't necessary to replace divots (due to the type of grass).

Hotel Dona Filipa

The Algarve, a ribbon of fine sandy beaches backed by huge sandstone cliffs along Portugal's entire southern coast, was al-Gharb, the "west", to early Arab settlers. Frequented by Europeans in search of warm secluded beaches, picturesque fishing villages, and small market towns tucked in the hills, the area has some of the best golf courses on the continent. This hotel is surrounded by the Vale do Lobo estate, a large development of whitewashed villas, beautifully landscaped grounds, and miles of golden sandy beaches.

The hotel is comfortably modern, and decor is tasteful, with Portuguese ceramics, carved furniture, and flowers everywhere. Rooms are large with balconies facing the sea or golf course, and you'll find a pool, tennis courts, and for aspiring champions, the Roger Taylor Tennis School, a few minutes away. A high spot here is the restaurant with its hand-carved ceiling, and a lively bar, as well as nightly entertainment. You'll need to book well in advance here, as the hotel, with first-rate service, is a mecca during the spring, summer and fall.

You'll find lots to do near here. Pottery, embroidery, and 18 karat gold jewelry are all good buys. If you have a car, you can head for Faro, with its stunning Gothic cathedral, and the Algarve Ethnographic Museum, and Loule, a small town known for copper and leather. You can rent boats, go horseback riding, visit a winery, visit a 12th century castle, check out the bikinis, or visit the Prince Henry Navigational School, now a hostel.

The Clube de Golfe at Vale do Lobo consists of three nines, with some holes running along the Atlantic interrupted by deep gorges of sandstone cliffs. You'll play through almond trees, cross a river, and with any luck, avoid the patios bordering the fairway.

Address: Vale do Lobo, 8106 Loule, Almansil, Algarve

Phone: 351-089-94141

Innkeeper: Manuel V. Rocha

No. rooms: 129

Rates: $$

Services: Card Room

Restaurant: Dining Room, Terrace Grill

Bar: Gothic Bar

Business Fac.: FAX 357-89-94288

Sports Fac.: Tennis, Swimming, Table Tennis

Attractions: Algarve Ethnographic Museum, Maritime Museum

Course: Clube de Golfe

Distance: 6541m, Par: 72, No. of holes: 27

Penina Golf Hotel

Address: P.O. Box 146, Penina,
Portimao Codex, Algarve 8502

Phone: 351-82-22051-58

Innkeeper: Luis de Camoes

No. rooms: 200

Rates: $$

Services: Sauna, Massage,
Hairdresser, Boutiques

Restaurant: Club Bar & Restaurant

Bar: Cocktail Bar

Business Fac.: Audio-Visual, FAX

Sports Fac.: Swimming, Tennis,
Bowling Green

Attractions: Casino, 12th Century
Fortress, Shopping

Course: Penina Championship GC

Distance: 6394, Par: 73

Rating: No. of holes: 36

Guest policy: Green fees included
for hotel guests,

The Algarve's oldest and probably most revered golf hotel, situated on 360 well-maintained acres, is attractive and impressive without being pretentious. It has spacious, elegant public rooms with attractive appointments set amid contemporary Algarve architecture, an especially attractive dining room with a vaulted ceiling and beautiful tapestries. Many guest rooms and suites have balconies, and all are air conditioned. Rooms in the back have delightful views of the violet blue Monchiqye peaks. Swimmers and sun worshippers will find an Olympic-size pool in the garden, a sauna, tennis courts, bowling green, and a pool bar and restaurant serving lunch. During the summer, guests can hop aboard the special beach-bound bus, for a five minute ride, where the hotel maintains beach beds, and soft drinks are available. If you're looking for some action in the evening, stroll over to the plush Alvor Casino (with your passport in hand). The restaurant is quite good, and there's a floor show.

For diversion, you might check out the fishing port of Portimao, the center of the canning industry, and if you are in the mood to explore, drive up to Lagoa, a market village famous for its wine. Then, turn north to Silves, and take a look at the 12th century fortress, restored over a hundred years ago.

If you came for golf, you won't be disappointed. There's an 18 hole championship course, plus two nine hole courses. Built on a former rice paddy, and lined with thousands of trees, Henry Cotton let his imagination serve him well. Although the area is essentially flat, old drainage canals now define fairways, provide hazards, and give depth and character to the green sites. The elevated greens are a major feature of this layout which has hosted the 1976 World Amateur Team Championship, and the Portuguese Open five times in a ten year period. Handicap certificate is required to play the Championship course only, and you'll find a driving range, practice holes and putting greens to get you in shape.

Dom Pedro Golf Hotel

Slightly west of the Algarve's center, and a little north of the region's main thoroughfare, is Vilamoura, one of the most highly developed resort centers in Portugal's premier playground. Virtually every conceivable summer recreational facility abounds, and visitors will find a wide variety of hotels, bungalows and apartments in the area. The nine story Dom Pedro, not far from the beach, isn't the newest or the most expensive, but it is convenient to the many golf courses in the area. There's a nice pool and garden, a large Gazebo Bar, tennis, a buffet, gift shop, ping pong, volleyball, hair salon, and a grill.

The real drawing card, of course, are the two great courses at the Vilamoura Golf Club, which tends to attract more serious golfers than Sunday hackers. The original course, designed by Frank Pennink follows the concept of the rugged moorland courses in England. Greens are relatively flat, and fairways are tight on the course that has hosted the Portuguese Open twice. Beware of the tricky par three holes, many of which are in the shadow of the Monchique Mountains. The newer course, called Vilamoura II is a fairly flat course with smashing ocean views. The first few holes are wide open, and the last nine, enhanced by Robert Trent Jones' deft hand, weave through heavily scented umbrella pines. These courses are in top condition, and you'll find a practice area, polite caddies, and lessons available year round.

Address: 8125 Vilamoura, Quarteira, Algarve
Phone: 351-089-35450-60-70
No. rooms: 260
Rates: $$
Services: Beauty Salon
Restaurant: Buffet
Bar: Bazebo Bar
Business Fac.: Sec. Svc., Audio-Visual
Sports Fac.: Tennis, Swimming, Ping Pong, Volleyball

Course: Vilamoura I & II
Rating: No. of holes: 36

Turnberry Hotel

Address: Ayrshire, Strathclyde, KA26 9LT

Phone: 44-0655-31000 800-223-6800

No. rooms: 130

Rates: $$$, Credit Cards: AmEx, Visa, Other CC

Services: Sauna, Billiards Room, Library, Barber and Beauty Shops, Full Health Spa, Ten Concierges

Restaurant: Dining Room

Sports Fac.: Swimming, Tennis, Croquet

Attractions: Culzean Castle, Gallorway Forest Park

Course: Alisa & Arran Courses

Distance: 6653, Par: 70, No. of holes: 36

Our cover property, the venerable Turnberry Hotel, was built at the turn of the century by the railroad company primarily for golfers. Totally refurbished recently, this Edwardian symbol of British golf at its best is perched on the curving shoreline, with ever-changing views across the links and the Firth of Clyde. The 130 room landmark has changed with the times. Requisitioned as an officer's mess during the first World War, and used as a hospital during the second, Turnberry has managed to strike a happy balance between tradition and today's amenities such as enormous warmed towels and Jacuzzis. Bedrooms and suites are individually furnished, and bathrooms are enormous by hotel standards. And surprise! the restaurant has received well-deserved acclaim for its imaginative fare—a Scottish French cuisine that makes full use of local delicacies. The food is excellent, and the wine list an especially good one.

There is an indoor swimming pool, a sauna, billiards room, tennis courts, library, barber and beauty shop, croquet, and full health spa for your pleasure. And if this isn't enough, an airport limousine and ten concierges are on hand to be of service.

The Ayrshire coast, marked by extraordinary weather effects, rocky promontories, endless rolling green fields ablaze with poppies and daisies and a delightful absence of billboards and roadside enterprises, provide interesting territory for exploration. Visit Culzean castle (open during summer), Galloway Forest Park, or Ayr, where Robert Burns sowed his oats. A motor boat will take you to Ailsa Craig, a major bird sanctuary, or you can visit Brodick Castle with its woodland gardens.

According to Sandy Lyle, the Alisa course is the most spectacular, most dramatic, and the most compellingly beautiful. Home of many great golfing events, including the 1986 British Open, The scenery, particularly on the first nine, is awesome. Running closely along the rocky shoreline, it begins with a series of par fours. The craggy ninth tee is high among the rocks, and if you don't suffer from vertigo, you should play from it. You'll need a carry of 200 yards to the fairway across an inlet often whipped by gale-force winds. Arran course, immediately adjacent, isn't as long, but is almost as tough.

Gleneagles Hotel

The Tayside of Scotland is a region rich in legends. Site of the oldest Scottish capital at Scone, Glamis Castle, scene of Princess Margaret's birth, where Macbeth was hailed as Thane, and Gleneagles, the Scottish "palace in the glens", where the Guinness Group has recently poured in over eleven million pounds to restore and upgrade the luxury flagship perched on 750 acres.

The 249 high-ceilinged rooms and suites are spacious, with Edwardian reproductions of fine quality, and views over the gardens toward the Ochil Hills. Grounds and gardens are lovingly tended, with extensive facilities for serious sportsmen and occasional pleasure-seekers. Guests can peruse the list of daily activities and choose from full Scottish afternoon teas in the Drawing Room, dining in the Conservatory, croquet, lawn bowling, squash, a multitude of tennis courts, a fully equipped spa, salmon and trout fishing, table tennis, a children's room, putting greens, and miles of Highland trails for jogging or cycling. The new Mark Phillips Equestrian Centre, a private club, with membership available to hotel guests, covers every aspect of horsemanship for individuals and groups—whether it be for dressage and carriage driving or polo or Riding for the Disabled. Be sure to contact management should you choose to board your horse for schooling.

The Library, sedate, very British and stocked with books and periodicals is a peaceful haven perfect for a quiet drink away from the buzz of the hotel's bars.

Golf is on 4 world class 18 hole courses. King's course is carved out of rising hills splashed with purple heather and golden gorse, with ample sculptured bunkers. One of the most memorable is Braid's BNrawest, referring to James Braid's 13th fairway that rolls narrowly away from the tee, requiring a long straight drive to carry a ridge plagued by two deep bunkers. We rather like the understatement from a fellow who characterized Gleneagles as a "hill course that a mountain goat would or did find home before it was cut into a glen."

Address: Auchterarder, Tayside-Perthshire, PH3 INF

Phone: 44-0764-62231 44-0764-62134

Innkeeper: Vivien Sirotkin

No. rooms: 249

Rates: $$$, Credit Cards: AmEx, Visa, MC, Other CC

Services: Gift Shop, Library

Restaurant: The Strathearn Restaurant

Bar: 4 Bars

Business Fac.: Sec.Svc., Translators

Sports Fac.: Tennis, Squash, Croquet, Riding

Location: Waverly: 50 miles

Attractions: Antique Shops, Scone Palace, Glenturret Distillery

Course: Kings, Queens, Princes

Distance: 6471, Par: 70

Rating: 71.0, No. of holes: 72

Phone Club-House: 0764-63543

Pro's name: Ian Marchbank

Greywalls Hotel

Address: Muirfield, Gullane, East Lothian EH 3 2EG

Phone: 44-0620-842144 800-544-9856

Innkeeper: Jim Lennox

No. rooms: 23

Rates: $$$, Credit Cards: AmEx, Other CC

Restaurant: Dining Room

Business Fac.: FAX

Sports Fac.: Tennis, Croquet, Riding

Attractions: Lasmmermuir Hills, Shooting, Fishing, Edinburgh

Course: Muirfield Golf Course

Distance: 6806, Par: 71, No. of holes: 18

This is the most exclusive place to stay in Gullane, a pleasant 25 mile drive east of Edinburgh. An Edwardian country house designed by renowned architect Sir Edwin Lutyens, Greywalls was frequented by King Edward VII, who admired the views across the Firth and south to the Lammermuir Hills, immortalized by Scott.

Most of the 23 bedrooms are furnished with period pieces, and the paneled library and dining rooms offers guests views of the 9th and 18th greens of Muirfield, home of the Honorable Company of Edinburgh Golfers, generally recognized as the world's oldest club. Within the grounds are a hard tennis court and a croquet lawn, and there's fine fishing nearby.

The jewel in the crown here is the walled country garden created by the master of English gardens, Gertrude Jekyll. A Lutyens house with a Jekyll garden was an outward symbol of good taste and financial success among the aristocracy.   Sightseers can head for Edinburgh, ancient castles such as Tantallon, and the famous bird sanctuary on Bass Rock. Don't miss the Heritage of Golf Museum in Gullane, and history buffs should plan to visit Lufness Castle near Aberlady, a 16th century edifice with a 13th century keep, moat and gardens.

Muirfield Golf Course is one of the few strictly private clubs in Scotland, but guests at Greywalls are offered a limited number of starting times, providing you can demonstrate a handicap of 18 or lower if you're male, and at least a 24 for females.

Its a beautifully simple and testing links, with continuous records since 1744. There are only three successive holes played in the same direction, an asset for a layout played nearly always in wind.

Greens aren't enormous, there are no trees, no water and the player can see his approach to the green, making it a great test of driving. The final hole has few peers in the annals of golf, for the wicked island bunker guarding the green is not forgiving.

Old Course Golf and Country Club

Adjacent to the world-famous Road Hole (17th) of the Old Course, this hotel, which opened in 1968, is the logical place to stay if you plan to explore and play the official "Home of Golf." The atmosphere is relaxed, and everything is here to promote congeniality among golfers and their families. Over half the guest rooms overlook the Old Course, and the rest look out to the Eden Course and the estuary of the River Eden. The hotel was recently purchased by a consortium, and every effort is being made to spruce up the facility before the British Open is held here in 1990. The hotel's four bars and two restaurants have magnificent views across four golf courses to the jagged coastline which borders them. The old station master's cottage has been converted into a pub, and the Member's Bar exudes a rich club atmosphere. Put on your leisure suit and head for the Leisure Centre, where you'll find a large pool, gymnasium, sauna, and Turkish bath.

Take time to explore beyond St. Andrews. The magnificent (and often windy) and safe beaches, the harbor, the lovely parks and gardens are all worth visiting. To the north of the town, you'll find unspoiled pastoral scenery sprinkled with ancient villages, and you can always spend time in Dundee, which is an eighteen minute drive across the Tay Road Bridge.

Many changes are taking place, and millions of dollars are being spent on the town's greatest drawing card—the golf courses. All four courses are open to the public, with a fifth opening in 1989. New clubhouses are on the drawing boards, but for now, visitors can play the Old Course, considered to be the greatest links course in the world, the New Course, and the shorter Jubilee, nearest the sea and bordered by sand dunes. The Eden Course is best suited for average players.

Address: Old Station Road, Saint Andrews, Fife KY 16 95P

Phone: 44-0334-7-4371

Innkeeper: Russ Furlong

No. rooms: 125

Rates: $$$$, Credit Cards: AmEx, Visa, Other CC

Services: Sauna, Turkish Baths, Masseuse, Beautician, Hair Stylist

Restaurant: Eden, Road Hole

Bar: Jigger Inn, 17th

Business Fac.: Audio-Visual FAX

Sports Fac.: Pool, Health Spa, Indoor Golf School.

Attractions: Many Historical Sites in St. Andrews, Beaches,

Course: Old, New, Eden, Jubilee

Distance: 6700, Par: 72

Rating: 72.0, No. of holes: 72

Guest policy: Carts not allowed on Old Course

Pro's name: John Philp

Sun City Hotels, Casino & Country Club

Address: Bophuthatswana,
P.O. Box 2, Johannesburg

Phone: 01465-1-21000 800-448-8355

Innkeeper: Edgar van Ommen

No. rooms: 687

Rates: $, Credit Cards: AmEx, Visa, MC, Other CC

Services: Babysitting, Hairdresser, Safe Deposit Boxes, Laundry/Dry Cleaning, Shopping, Valet Service

Restaurant: Grotto, Raffles, Palm Terrace

Bar: Vistas, Pool Bars

Business Fac.: Sec., FAX, Audio-Visual

Sports Fac.: Swimming, Bowling Green, Tennis, Squash

Attractions: Casino, Pilanesberg National Game Park

Course: Gary Player Country Club
Distance: 7033m, Par: 72,
No. of holes: 18

This is a gargantuan sports resort complex rising out of the Bophuthatswana bush like an oasis, a half hour flight from Johannesburg. Consider Cascaes Hotel, a 15-story tropical engineering marvel, Sun City Hotel with casino, theater and non-stop entertainment, and Cabanas, situated on the lakeside offering deluxe and standard accommodations catering to families. Add conference facilities, bars and restaurants, swimming pools and the romance of the wild outdoors in the Pilanesberg National Park, 10 minutes away. You also have the opportunity to stay and play in a development that calls itself "Fun City."

Sporting and recreational facilities include a bowling green, horse riding school center with resident trainer, squash courts, tennis ranch, ten pin bowling, and Waterworld, a man-made lake in the center of the African bush, where you can water ski, wind surf, jet ski, or go parasailing. You'll have access to the Gary Player Country Club, with a pro shop, mini golf, tennis shop, and health spa.

If you've come for golf, you're at the right place. The course burst into the limelight in 1981 when it hosted the game's first million-dollar tournament, won by Johnny Miller in a sudden death-playoff with The Spaniard, Seve Ballesteros. The 18 holes border a game preserve, so finding a wide-eyed baboon eyeing your Titleist isn't unheard of. Our favorite is the par 3 sixteenth, a pretty little hole that doesn't seem to bother the better players. The smaller pot bunkers are a legacy of Gary Player's numerous treks to Scotland. Notice the "fingered" greens and try to avoid the bunkers, finger-perfect monsters.

Hotel Byblos Andaluz

This is possibly the place for you if the idea of a complete health spa in a sparkling new luxury hotel appeals to you. You'll find everything for a pampered vacation here, starting with fabulous swimming pools with poolside bars and buffets, tennis courts, a gift shop, and access to horseback riding. The Andalusian-style hotel and villas is set in a huge garden of babbling fountains, palms, and mature cypresses. Renowned for its health program, guests can soak up the cure in steam baths, underwater showers with filtered and warm sea water, saunas, a gymnasium, and even a teahouse. Special diets are addressed by a professional staff, or you can splurge and opt for French cuisine at Le Nailhac. How does fried anchovies with lemon, followed by sherbet, roast lamb, gratineed tomatoes and spinach, cheese and wild strawberries sound? Disco-lovers won't be disappointed, for there's a lively one here, as well as a more sedate piano bar. You might go for the Presidential Suite—it's huge and overlooks the golf course, with a marble bathroom large enough to accommodate forty friends. Decor is a most attractive mixture of antiques and expensive contemporary. Not far is the picturesque 2,500-year-old village of Mijas, where you can see the bullring and shop for quality gifts.

You'll have two courses at hand: Los Lagos, and Los Olivos, both Robert Trent Jones par 72's. Laid out in 1976 on fairly rolling terrain, there's a feeling of spaciousness, with generous fairways and some large irregularly-shaped bunkers. Jones didn't overlook water hazards. Take a moment to savor the clubhouse, an old Andalusian hacienda between the two courses.

Address: Mijas Golf, Apt. 138, Fuengirola, 29640

Phone: 34-952-473050 800-323-7500

Innkeeper: Pierre Aron

No. rooms: 144

Rates: $$$$, Credit Cards: AmEx, Visa, MC, Other CC

Services: Gift Shop, Spa

Restaurant: Le Nailhac

Bar: Saint Troper

Business Fac.: Sec., Translators, FAX

Sports Fac.: Swimming, Tennis, Riding

Attractions: Bull Fighting, Ancient town of Ronda

Course: Los Olivos, Los Lagos

Distance: 5955m, Par: 72

Rating: 72.0, No. of holes: 36

Phone Club-House: 52-47-6843

Pro's name: Juan Rosa

Son Vida Sheraton

Address: Castillo Son Vida, Palma de Mallorca, 07013

Phone: 34-971-790-000

Innkeeper: Peter P. Tschirky

No. rooms: 165

Rates: $$, Credit Cards: AmEx, Visa, Other CC

Services: Gift Shop

Restaurant: Panoramico & El Jardin

Bar: Bar Armas

Business Fac.: Sec.Svc., Translators

Sports Fac.: Swimming, Tennis, Squash, Fitness Ctr.

Attractions: 13th Century Cathedral, Almudaina Palace,

Course: Son Vida

Distance: 5642m, Par: 72

Rating: 70.0, No. of holes: 18

Guest policy: Special Green Fee for hotel client

Phone Club-House: 34-71791210

Pro's name: Florecio

Mallorca, long favored by throngs of Europeans in search of sparkling clear days, dazzling seascapes, moderate prices, bullfights and exquisite leather, is roughly 100 miles southeast of Barcelona, and is easily accessible by air or car ferry. The Balearic Islands are jammed during the summer, and with one of the highest concentrations of hotel rooms per capita, it's wonderful to know of a respite that caters to individuals. The Son Vida Sheraton is a converted 13th century palace, with antiques and original paintings enhancing its character, and amenities for all. Perched serenely on a hillside with breathtaking views out over the bay, city, and mountains, this completely air conditioned towered and turret hostelry offers comfortable rooms and suites, sumptuous public rooms, and a gorgeous expanse of poolside terrace, perfect for daytime sunning and evening dinner. There's also an indoor swimming pool, four tennis courts, and a fitness club, all in a quiet park-like atmosphere. Children can burn off their energy in a play area, while parents peruse the gardens, check out the game rooms and ballrooms, sip hierbas in one of the assorted bars, or arrange for a lesson at a nearby riding academy. Bustling Palma is a 5 kilometer shuttle bus ride away, with boutiques, some beautiful 18th century townhouses, and the wide promenade (or rambla) that is the heart of the city.

The course, right outside your doorstep, opened in 1964, boasts narrow fairways with some tricky doglegs, and a sixteenth hole guarded by a small lake. The trees are quite pretty, especially the fragrant flowering almonds and the carob. With a Standard Scratch Score of 70, you'll use most of your clubs. Don't concentrate so hard on your game that you miss seeing some of the island's more grandiose casas. Everything's here—a well-stocked golf shop, driving range, and special green fees for hotel guests.

Hotel Los Monteros

Here it is—a smart luxury resort complex spread over the grounds of a former estate, in a picturesque little town on the Costa del Sol. The major attraction here, where Moorish arches mingle with Swedish, German and Arabic accents, is the stretch of beach resorts along this high-rise heaven for the well-heeled. Los Monteros, with 169 rooms boasts tennis courts, swimming pools, a gymnasium, riding, a gift shop, and the tranquility of an elegant hostelry.

Rooms have views of gardens, the pools or the sea, and are furnished tastefully with attention to details. Art isn't mass-produced, bedspreads and draperies are custom-made, and personal service is stressed. The sybarite has only to look for amenities such as billiards, a bridge lounge, an open air buffet, bars, a night club, a beach club complete with thatched roof cabanas and bars, and room safes for one's baubles. You can request the services of the Hotel Nanny, should you choose to leave the little darlings while you play golf or sightsee.

Ideal time to visit Costa del Sol is during the spring months, when the temperature is in the sixties, days are sunny, and evenings are cool. Summertime is jammed here, and the mercury hits the low nineties, while September and October are usually lovely. Surrounding towns such as Torremolinos and Malaga have lively night spots and good shopping. Visit the marina at Nueva Andalucia, Picasso's birthplace or the archaeological museum in Malaga, or Fuengirola's 10th century Moorish castle. You can catch the ferry to Tangiers in Malaga, or tour the bullfight arena.

Green fees are included in the room rate, but a hand cart will set you back about 350 pesetas for the eighteen holes at "Golf Rio Real." The late Javier Arana, renowned golfer and a leading contemporary course architect, is responsible for the design of the layout here. The par 72 course is situated in a beautiful valley between sea and mountains, crossed at various points by the Real River, with an abundance of trees. Look for Arana's trademark—an isolated tree on a fairway.

Address: Carretera de Cadiz, Km. 187, Marbella, Malaga E-29600

Phone: 34-52-77-17-00

Innkeeper: Gonzalo Lasso

No. rooms: 169

Rates: $$$, Credit Cards: AmEx, Visa, MC, Other CC

Services: Gift Shop, Sauna, Massage

Restaurant: Main Restaurant

Bar: Blue & Flamingo

Business Fac.: Sec.Svc., Translators

Sports Fac.: Swimming, Tenis, Squash, Riding, Gym

Attractions: Costa del Sol, Shopping, Moorish Castle

Course: Golf Rio Real

Distance: 6130m, Par: 72

Rating: 72.0, No. of holes: 18

Guest policy: Green fees included for hotel guests,

Hotel du Golf

Address: Crans-Montana 3963

Phone: 41-027-414242

Innkeeper: J. Bonvin

No. rooms: 80

Rates: $$, Credit Cards: AmEx, Visa, MC, Other CC

Restaurant: Dining Room

Business Fac.: Translators

Sports Fac.: Swimming, Tennis, Skiing, Riding, Sail

Location: Haut Plateau Valaisa

Attractions: Hiking, Plaine Morte Glacier, Histroical Landmarks

Course: Crans-sur-Sierre

Distance: 6811, Par: 72, No. of holes: 27

Crans-Montana, twin resort boomtowns perched high in the canton of the Valais, are "the" fashionable spots for skiing, golf, hiking, fishing and simply taking in the splendors of the 10,000 foot Point Plaine-Mort. The plateau overlooks the upper Rhone valley and more than 100 miles of the Alps' snowy summits. Montana, hugging the shores of a pristine lake, has been a resort for a century, with Crans, site of the Hotel du Golf, and the Swiss Open, coming on the scene later. This most pleasant five-star hotel, dating from 1914, sits in a 6-acre park adjoining the golf course, with a most intimate and charming air. Public areas are inviting, with tasteful antique reproductions, warm colors, fresh flowers and unsurpassed vistas of Alpine majesty. There are eighty rooms, and 8 suites of varying age and decor, depending on the particular wing. We were partial to the junior suite whose parlor overlooked the golf course and the Alps. Mobility comes in the form of a gondola here at nearly 5,000 feet, and you can head for the Cry d'Err and its dining room, or take your meals at the hotel. A swimming pool, sauna, tennis courts, riding, sailing, and certainly shopping and bar hopping are all at your fingertips. You'll recognize the bags, they're all here—YSL, Chanel, Piaget, Cartier, Nina Ricci, and Rolex, to name a few.

But the real attraction is 6,811 yards of gently undulating terrain of the Crans-sur-Sierre Golf Course, which has been the venue for seven Swiss Opens. 1905 was the year and Plan-Bramois was the genius who masterminded the course. The sixth, a 328-yard par-four is surrounded by tall pines and demands a carefully judged approach shot to a long, elevated green that seems out of place among large bunkers. We loved the fairly level greens, minimal rough, and the way the ball soared in the altitude. Jack Nicklaus designed a fine nine hole course nearby—same snowy mountain peaks, same melezes (pines), different strokes for different folks.

Brenner's Park, Baden Baden, Germany

Hotel Quellenhof, Bad Ragaz, Germany

Quellenhof Golf Hotel

This is "Heidi" country—isolated villages where you'll hear a wide range of dialects, (Romansh is still spoken here) spruce-covered mountains, distant white church towers, and the romance of the Rhine. This is THE most elegant hotel Switzerland's best-known spa, and it commands a genteel following, year round. Set in a private park and surrounded by seemingly enchanted gardens, returning guests will find extensive redecorations, additions and improvements, thanks to a hefty influx of Swiss francs.

Generations have taken the mineral waters here, where standards are high and one's daily regimen is given top priority, and you can make full use of the sauna, solarium, and fitness room. With 126 rooms and junior suites, guests are offered scores of amenities such as a choice of restaurants and grills, a cavernous lounge resplendent in its aura of the last century, the America Bar with musical entertainment at aperitif time, a sun terrace, bridge corner, boutique, hair salon, tennis courts and banquet facilities. Bring your weary body here for the renowned cure. You'll have direct access from your room to the thermal pool and the sports swimming pool. The Medical Center offers a wide range of treatments and remedies for cardio-vascular rehabilitation, and just about everything else-except a high handicap. And as long as you're thinking fitness, a quick consultation with a dietician will ensure a daily low calorie menu.

A pleasant five minute stroll puts you in the village center, a delightful melange of shops and diversions. Ask the concierge about horseback riding and fishing in the area. Now that you're committed to fitness, consider some side trips such as an excursion to Lichtenstein's museums and galleries, shopping in Chur, an ancient town with medieval houses, taking the cableway to Pardiel-Pizol, popping in for a sip at some local wineries, or looking for Lady Di in St. Moritz.

The golf course dates from 1895, when Englishmen, stopping over for a few days en route to the Engadine would take to the links. At the turn of the century a new nine hole course was built, and after World War II, the second nine was completed. Greens and fairways are immaculate, and in keeping with the Swiss mandate for quality, maintenance and service are tops.

Address: Bad Ragaz, 7310

Phone: 085-9-01-11 800-223-6800

Innkeeper: Pierre Barrelet

No. rooms: 126

Rates: $$$, Credit Cards: AmEx, Visa, MC, Other CC

Services: Spa, Medical Center, Concierge, Hairdresser, Boutique, Parking

Restaurant: Dining Room, Grill Room

Bar: American Bar

Business Fac.: Sec.Svc., Translators

Sports Fac.: Swimming, Tennis, Skiing, Riding

Attractions: Hiking, Cross Country Skiing, Lichtenstein,

Course: Bad Ragaz
Distance: 5766m, Par: 70
Rating: 71.0, No. of holes: 18
Phone Club-House: 85/9-15-56

Burgenstock Hotels

Address: CH 6366, Burgenstock

Phone: 041-632525 800-223-6800

Innkeeper: Dirk J. Post

Rates: $$$

Services: Valet, Dry Cleaning, Laundry, Fitness Center, Beauty Salon, Shops

Restaurant: Grand Hotel, Golf Club House

Bar: Peter Paul Rubens

Business Fac.: FAX 41-61-76-88

Sports Fac.: Swimming, Tennis, Jogging

Attractions: Lake Lucerne, Hiking, Disco, Chapel

Course: Burgenstock Hotels Golf

Distance: 1935m, Par: 34, No. of holes: 9

We're not exaggerating when we say the setting here, atop a mountain peninsula 1500 feet above Lake Lucerne is stupendous. In the world of international hostelries, this complex of three luxurious hotels with its panorama of lakes, snow-clad mountains, forests and meadows invite you to partake of the highest possible standards. The most romantic way to arrive is via paddle steamer from Lucerne, followed by an unforgettable trip on the hotel's funicular. You'll find all the amenities here—restaurants, bars and lounges, a heated indoor pool, and an outdoor pool, tennis courts, a horticultural center, shops, and an ultra-contemporary fitness center consisting of sauna, steam baths, solarium and exercise room. Take a trip through history and savor the paintings, tapestries and antiques adorning public rooms here. Not to be missed are the gothic sculptures dating from the 15th and 16th centuries in the chapel.

As you stroll the grounds, always with a stunning view of Lucerne across the lake, you'll find an infinite variety of fine spots for relaxing, sipping a drink or dining. And don't forget hiking shoes if that's your idea of seeing it all, for here on the largest privately owned estate in Switzerland the vistas can be all yours.

This is true alpine golf, on nine holes of open fairways bordered by pines and mountain shrubbery. During high season, (July and August) you can request a caddie, or you can take cart— either way, you'll be so entranced with the scenery, you won't worry about your score.

Les Chevreuils

This is a country house over a century old in a tranquil garden setting just nine kilometers from the French-Swiss city of Lausanne. With 31 rooms, this unassuming hotel is comfortable and cozy, with many of the rooms looking out to the terrace, the Alps, or Lac Leman below. In addition to riding and excellent hiking, you'll find bicycle touring, a fitness course, and a conference room for 10-30 people. The menu is primarily French, and the cooking light and delicate, using regional produce, and there are good French wines. Not to be missed is the chef's foie gras. In warmer months, dinner is served in Le Jardin Gourmand, the lovely panoramic terrace, or you can opt for the less formal cafe.

Don't miss the medieval streets in the old part of the city. Climb the tower at one of the most spectacular monuments in Switzerland, the Gothic Cathedrale, famed for its rose window. And don't miss the Musee Olympique for an historic journey through the Olympic Games past.

You can tee off at Golf Club de Lausanne—a pleasant 18 hole par 72 course dating from 1921. Its right across the road. With a Standard Scratch Score of 72, the visiting player will find it difficult to concentrate on his game when surrounded by towering Alps, wildflowers and the hilly terrain.

Address: Vers-Chez-les-Blanc, Lausanne, 1000Lausanne 26
Phone: 41-021-784-2021
Innkeeper: Alexandre Tannaz
No. rooms: 31
Rates: $, Credit Cards: AmEx, Visa, Other CC
Services: Gift Shop
Restaurant: Le Jardin Gourmand
Bar: Bar
Business Fac.: FAX 41-021-784-15-45
Sports Fac.: Skiing, Riding
Location: Vers-Chez-les-Blanc
Attractions: Hiking, Bicycle Touring, Fitness Course

Course: Golf Club de Lausanne
Distance: 6295m, Par: 72
Rating: 74.0, No. of holes: 18
Phone Club-House: 021-784-1316
Pro's name: O. de Baeuvois

Dolder Grand Hotel

Address: Kurhausstrasse 65, Zurich, CH-8032

Phone: 41-01-251-6231 800-223-6800

Innkeeper: Henry J. Hunold

No. rooms: 200

Rates: $$$

Restaurant: La Rotonde

Business Fac.: FAX 41-251-88-29

Sports Fac.: Tennis, Swimming, Jogging, Ice Skating

Attractions: Shop the Bahnhofstrasse, Swiss National Museum,

Par: 30, No. of holes: 9

Guest policy: No green fee for hotel guests

Zurich—swathed in opulence, prosperity and the mystique of the "gnomes" of the international money scene sits on the northern tip of the Zurich See. This famous luxury hotel in the Zurichberg forest with its fairy tale castle appearance can be reached by car or the Dolder funicular which runs every ten minutes from the city below. Accommodations exceed 200 rooms, both older and furnished with antiques, and newer ones in a modern wing. If you book well in advance, ask for a room or suite with a view of either the lake, forest, or those majestic snow-capped Alps.

La Rotonde, one of the continent's top restaurants, offers Swiss and Continental fare in its renowned panoramic dining room. Taste regional specialties such as smoked brook trout or classics such as Kalbssteak "Prinz Orloff" with chanterelles in cream sauce from the clever fixed-price menu. A good choice of Swiss wines awaits you in addition to a judicious selection of notable French vintages.

Stroll, jog, or contemplate the park paths surrounding the hotel with its three pointed towers peeking through the trees. Ride the tram into town and shop the Bahnhofstrasse, "the most beautiful shopping street in the world", graced in summer with flower pots and the scent of linden trees. Play tennis or make waves in the pool with huge artificial waves. Don't miss touring the lake by boat, or the Swiss National Museum, and an absolute must is Beyer's Watch and Clock Museum, with rare watches dating from the fifteenth century.

Didn't bring your clubs? Not to worry, the Swiss think of everything, and as a hotel guest, there's no green fee to play here. Its an executive course with three par 4 holes and six par threes scattered on a hilly layout. The third, eighth and ninth holes are bedded in steep hills, so bring your hill-climbing muscles. This is one of the few courses in Europe located within a city limit. If you want to walk off that ice cream souffle with Grand Marnier cookies, you can pull a hand cart. We'll opt for a caddie.

Central Plaza Hotel

If Bangkok is on your itinerary for business, shopping or an urge to explore upcountry temples or the beautiful beaches of Phuket, this large modern hotel, only 15 minutes from the airport, could be the answer. Part of the Central Plaza Complex, the imposing 26 story structure features 3 tennis courts, a wide selection of restaurants and bars, a fitness center, jogging track, shopping arcade, and the lively Hollywood Discotheque. Most of the rooms overlook Chatuchuk Park and the skyline of the "City of Angels," and the Dynasty Club, with its exclusive accommodations and special concierge, can be reached by elevator passkeys.

Golf has attracted a lot of attention in Thailand, and the visitor will find a broad choice of good courses. Low labor costs mean that courses can afford the luxury of large staffs to maintain the grounds in top shape. Many of the leading courses are located within greater Bangkok, including the splendid Krungthep Kritha, Unico and the celebrated Navatanee, about 40 minutes from the city center.

Here, golf is a ten-minute walk across the road to the Railway Golf Course, not actually situated on hotel property. The layout is flat, with a few ponds for water hazards. There are no golf carts here, but caddies are more than happy to carry your bag the 18 holes. Days are generally hot, especially between February and June, when the mercury hovers in the nineties, but play is possible at almost any time of the year. Even the rainy season, with its heavy but short lived downpours, rarely stops a game. New Year celebrations, special Thai dances, and colorful ceremonies at the temples are a sight to behold, should you be here at the end of December. Your satang and baht will come in handy during your round of golf, and the girl caddies are quite knowledgeable about the game, and eager to keep track of the bets.

Address: 1695 Phaholyothin Road, Bangkhen, Bangkok 10900

Phone: 66-2-5411234 800-448-8535

Innkeeper: Kamthorn Chaturachinda

No. rooms: 607

Rates: $$, Credit Cards: AmEx, Visa, MC, Other CC

Services: Gift Shop

Restaurant: Dynasty

Bar: Lobby Lounge

Business Fac.: Sec.Svc., Translators

Sports Fac.: Swimming, Tennis

Location: Lardprao

Attractions: Railway Golf Course, Weekend Market, Temples

Course: Navatanee Golf Course

Distance: 6241, Par: 72, No. of holes: 18

Mount Irvine Bay Hotel

Address: P.O. Box 222, Scarborough

Phone: 809-639-8871-2-3
800-448-8355

Innkeeper: Carlos Dillon

No. rooms: 108

Rates: $$, Credit Cards: AmEx, Visa, Other CC

Services: Beauty Parlor, Arts & Crafts Shop, Boutique, Babysitters

Restaurant: Sugar Mill

Bar: Cocrico

Business Fac.: Sec.Svc., Translators

Sports Fac.: Swimming, Tennis, Sailing

Location: Mount Irvine

Attractions: Water Skiing/Windsurfing, Tour to Buccoo Reef

Course: Mount Irvine Golf Course

Distance: 6793, Par: 72

Rating: 71.9, No. of holes: 18

Phone Club-House: 639-9971/73

Pro's name: Carlton Fawtin

Lying eight miles off the northeast coast of Venezuela in the Caribbean Sea, the sister Islands of Trinidad and Tobago have been one independent country since 1962. Tobago has been the sleepier of the two, but plans are underway to accommodate cruise ships and increase the number of hotel rooms. Not to worry though, there'll always be a frosty Old Oak rum punch and a mouth watering Robinson Crusoe roll on the clubhouse porch overlooking the dazzling golf course and the sea. Rooms are scattered about in cottages, each with 2 rooms, patio and views, or in the main building. The patio and gardens around the old sugar mill serve as the hub for daily activity and local steel bands in the evening.

If romantic dinners under tropical stars are on your wish list, this could be the place. The menu is imaginative while taking advantage of local fresh ingredients. We tried lobster and shrimp cocktail, followed by Tobago Pigeon Pea Soup and a tasty beef Wellington. There are lobby shops, two flood-lit tennis courts, a grand swimming pool, separate conference wing, and water sports. Expect to share the idyllic beaches and coves with Trinidadians and Europeans, who flock here in droves for the laid-back lifestyle, golf course, and scuba diving. Head for Fort King George, 400 feet above the town of Scarborough, Tobago's capital, where you'll hear the sing-song Creole patois in the marketplace each morning. Even if you're not a confirmed ornithologist, you shouldn't miss the bird sanctuary on Little Tobago, a teeny island off the coast near Speyside where you are bound to catch a glimpse of one missing from your list. Some of the most beautiful stamps come from here, too, so you can shop for your philatelic friends.

Golf is taken seriously here, and it should be , for this course is a classic of Commander John Harris. Carved in gently rising country along the sea, there are Caribbean vistas from all holes. The par three holes are especially challenging, with only two under 200 yards. The 7th is spectacular. At 215 yards, you'll need a shot to a long, narrow green with bunkers on both sides, and a small lake guarding the left front. With a course rating of 71.9, fine water features and plenty of massive palms, this course warrants checking out.

Grand Hotel

This rambling structure of weathered cypress, known as "The Queen of Southern Resorts," covers about 550 acres of aged magnolias, and moss-draped live oaks on Mobile Bay, a short drive southeast of Mobile. The first hotel appeared in 1847, and history logs reveal it has witnessed Confederate soldiers needing hospitalization, fires, replaced structures, hurricanes, and a US Marine Training School. Hospitality and a sense of tradition are maintained in the recently renovated resort, which Marriott bought in 1981, right down to daily tea, fresh mint juleps and dressing for dinner. Three separate buildings and 16 cottages house more than 300 guest rooms, which offer views of the marina, lagoon, or the bay.

The chef will prepare your catch for a sumptuous repast in the Magnolia Room. Others will want to try the Bon Secour oysters, bay shrimp and seafood gumbo, all fresh daily. The Grand's orchestra plays for dancing each evening in the Grand Dining Room, and guests will find The Bird Cage Lounge a lively spot.

You can board the resort's 53-foot Hatteras yacht for a local cruise, drop a line or crabtrap off the wharf, sail, water ski, jog, bike, stroll or ride horseback. The extensive facilities also include card rooms, a swimming beach, lawn bowling, croquet, ten tennis courts, and a 750,000 gallon swimming pool constructed from an old ship's hull.

The 40-slip marina can accommodate your dinghy, or you can rent their paddleboats, powerboats, windsurfers or skiffs. If its water-sports oriented, its here. The Grand also offers a supervised children's program during summer. If you like antiques, the area's full of irresistible shops laden with historic treasures.

Golf here is unhurried on two fine 18 hole layouts at Lakewood Golf Club which zigzag through white pines and sleepy lagoons. (Watch out for alligators!) Built in 1945, the original 27 holes played host to notables such as Julius Boros, Sam Snead and Byron Nelson, and is now home of the Women's Western Amateur Championship. What was once mosquito-ridden swampland, and later a Confederate cemetery is today 36 holes of championship pleasure with majestic tree-lined fairways. And to think you can have one of Bucky's famous mint juleps (he picks the mint from his private patch) after you've double-bogeyed Dogwood!

Address: Scenic Highway 98, Point Clear, 36564
Phone: 205-928-9201 800-228-9290
Innkeeper: John Irvin
No. rooms: 308
Rates: Credit Cards: AmEx, Visa, MC, Other CC
Services: Valet, Library, Beauty shop, Garage and parking, Babysitting, Card or other game area, Laundry, Room service
Restrictions: No pets
Restaurant: Grand Dining Room
Bar: Birdcage Lounge
Business Fac.: Kelly Svc., Audio-vis, Conf. rm. cap.: 900
Sports Fac.: Swimming, Tennis, Croquet, Riding, Sail
Location: Gulf Coast
Attractions: Antebellum homes, Bellingrath Gardens, Antique shop

Course: Dogwood
Distance: 6,331, Par: 71
Rating: 70.5, No. of holes: 18
Guest Policy: Open to Marriott's guests & club members
Phone Club-House: 205-928-9201
Pro's name: Joe Glasser
Reservations: May be made one week in advance
Season: Year round
Guest Carry Club: No

Boulders Resort

Address: 34631 N. Tom Darlington, Carefree, 85377
Phone: 602-488-9009   800-223-7636
Innkeeper: Richard A. Holtzman
No. rooms: 123
Rates: $$$$, Credit Cards: AmEx, Visa, MC, Other CC
Services: Valet, Parking, Car hire, Babysitting, Card or game area, Laundry, Room service
Restrictions: Pets ltd.
Restaurant: Latilla, Palo Verde
Bar: Discovery Lounge
Business Fac.: Copiers, Telex, Conf. rm. cap.: 175
Sports Fac.: Tennis, Pool, Croquet, Fitness Center
Location: Maricopa
Attractions: Day trips/flights Grand Canyon; desert jeep tours

Course: The Boulders/Lake
Distance: 7,105, Par: 36
Rating: 74.4, No. of holes: 27
Guest Policy: Members and hotel guests only, Dress code
Phone Club-House: 602-488-9028
Pro's name: Bob Irving
Reservations: With hotel res., or any time avail.
Season: Sept. 14–June 15
Guest Carry Club: No

You have to like a place called Carefree, where asterisks on your scorecard denote saguaros, huge boulders harbor cottontails, and your cocktail comes with blue corn tortillas. The adobe buildings of the Main lodge and 120 casitas blend in so seamlessly with the Sonoran desert north of Scottsdale, it could be a mirage. From austere desert topography, Rockresorts has carved an opulent oasis, where nature has been left untouched. The Boulders is truly an experience; contemporary in feeling, yet a place to unwind amid Indian handicrafts, and regional art. Even the main door is made of natural woods.

Dining here is definitely au courant, whether its in the formal, subtly colored Latilla Room, or the more casual Palo Verde Room. The menus reflect a style of cuisine focusing on innovative dishes using natural ingredients, plenty of fresh fish and regional specialties.

The wine list here is impressive—not only will you recognize the traditional renowned vintages, but some of Napa Valley's finest premium wines are to be found here, such as the intense Duckhorn Merlot.

You can be as active or as lazy as your spirit moves you. The free-form turquoise pool evokes the feeling of a natural desert water-hole, or maybe you'd prefer cruising over the clear desert air in a balloon, airplane or on horseback. Six all-weather tennis courts, and a fitness center round out sporting facilities.

If you'd like to visit another desert habitat, venture out to nearby Taliesin West, Frank Lloyd Wright's studio and home, or head for Paolo Soleri's prototype in urban architecture, Arcosanti. Feeling energetic? You could play golf in the morning, helicopter through the Grand Canyon in the afternoon, and sip a margarita in front of a fiery sunset at the Boulders.

Three tough golf courses await you, with tees, fairways and greens framed by and often virtually a part of the dramatic, time-carved scenery. The courses roll gently with undulating greens, grass bunkers and beautiful desert specimens which often make it difficult to concentrate on one's game. Boulders #9 is a post-card scenic par 5, 583 yard gem which requires over a 200 yard carry to the fairway from the back tees. Your second shot has to favor the left, and the approach shot, if played from the left will keep you out of the lake. This is assuming you didn't slice into the 300 year old saguaro near the tee and lose your ball.

The Wigwam

Built in 1919 as an organization house for executives visiting the Goodyear Tire & Rubber Company's cotton plantations, The Wigwam has become a favorite winter vacation resort. Its low-rise casas are architecturally faithful to the original building which still stands as part of the lobby. Stately palms, ornamental orange trees, and annually replanted flower gardens complete the Southwestern atmosphere of the beautiful 75-acre oasis.

Explore the native desert on a breakfast horseback ride. Or, arrange to have a desert steak broil at Sunset Point, where you'll witness the spectacular beauty of an Arizona sunset. A horse-drawn hay wagon, complete with banjo players and cold drinks, will transport you to Sunset Point. There, you'll find The Wigwam chefs at work over an old-fashioned barbecue grilling steaks to perfection, a buffet laden with hearty Western-style dishes and a full bar.

In addition to golf, other sports activities are naturally suited to the desert surroundings, including tennis, trap and skeet shooting, bicycling, shuffleboard, lawn sports and, of course, swimming.

You'll enjoy shopping or simply visiting the 14,000-acre ranch surrounding the resort and village with crops of cotton, alfalfa, grains, citrus, vegetables, melons and other fruits.

There are three championship courses here. The most challenging is Robert Trent Jones', matured to perfection and offering a wide variety of play with the many tee and pin placements that are possible. For instance, the 10th tee can be stretched out to play 610 yards (from the normal tees it is a mere 556 yards). Even the exceptional golfer will find that this long course requires a high degree of skill and accuracy. This is a par 72, with 7,220 yards of wicked traps, undulating greens and long lakes.

Jones also was responsible for the Blue Course thirty-three years later, a par 70 with many water holes, tree-lined fairways and the famous Trent Jones tricky greens. The West Course, by Robert "Red" Lawrence, designed around a meandering stream and five lakes is a par 72 extremely fine test of golfing skill.

Address: , Litchfield Park, 85340
Phone: 602-935-3811   800-327-0396
Innkeeper: Marj Mahoney
No. rooms: 245
Rates: $$$$, Credit Cards: AmEx, Visa, MC, Other CC
Services: Library, Barber shop, Beauty shop, Garage and Parking, Car hire, International currency exchange, House doctor, Babysitting, Laundry, Room service
Restrictions: Pets ltd.
Restaurant: Terrace Dining Room
Bar: The Owl Lounge
Business Fac.: Copiers, Telex, Conf. rm. cap.: 490
Sports Fac.: Pool, Tennis, Croquet, Riding, Spa
Location: Phoenix/Scottsdale
Attractions: Shopping Fifth Avenue, Borgata, Spanish Village

Course: Gold Course
Distance: 7,074, Par: 72
Rating: 74.9, No. of holes: 54
Guest Policy: Resort guests have priority, Dress code
Phone Club-House: 602-935-3811
Pro's name: Doug Allen
Reservations: One Week in advance, 2 on package
Season: Open all year
Guest Carry Club: No

Arizona Biltmore

Address: 24th St. & Missouri, Phoenix, 85016
Phone: 800-228-3000   800-528-3696
Innkeeper: Cecil Ravenswood
No. rooms: 551
Rates: $$, Credit Cards: AmEx, Visa, MC, Other CC
Services: Valet, Beauty shop, Garage and parking, Card or game area, Laundry, Room service
Restrictions: No pets
Restaurant: Gold Room
Bar: Aztec Lounge
Business Fac.: Audio-visual, telex, Conf. rm. cap.: 1,250
Sports Fac.: Pool, Tennis, Croquet, Exercise Salon
Location: Phoenix
Attractions: Shuttle to Biltmore Fashion Park

Course: Arizona Biltmore, Links
Distance: 6,400, Par: 71
Rating: 72.2, No. of holes: 36
Guest Policy: Call for tee times, Dress code
Phone Club-House: 602-955-6600
Pro's name: Randy Beaupre
Reservations: May be made 7 days in advance
Season: Year round
Guest Carry Club: No

Inspired by the patterns, geometric shapes and textures of Frank Lloyd Wright, this "Jewel of the Desert", on 39 lushly landscaped acres offers today's guests a tradition of service and grandeur from a classic era. The resort has never looked better—thanks to a recent improvement and expansion program under the direction of the Taliesin Associated Architects. The original system of hand-cast, patterned concrete blocks has been retained in the additions, stained glass windows dazzle, new roofs are gleaming Arizona copper, the famous Dixon/Hamlin murals are enhanced by contemporary new lighting, all harmonizing with the Wright conception of a dream resort destination. Many rooms have private patios or balconies with views of gardens, Squaw Peak, Camelback Mountain or the pool area. Mrs. Frank Lloyd Wright selected the color schemes; and colorful and vibrant they are—striking combinations of greens, blues, purples and oranges. A sunken living room dramatized by ruby and forest green upholstered pieces characterizes the Bougainvillea Suite, complemented by a walnut wet bar, fireplace, and large patio overlooking the pool.

The elegant Gold Room, for fine dining and dancing under the gold-leaf vaulted ceiling, is a local landmark. Cocktails and live entertainment are featured in the historic octagonal Aztec Lounge, while southwestern specialties and American favorites are found in the more casual Cafe Sonora. Orangerie, for lunch and dinner, is an intimate garden spot offering Continental favorites and nightly piano music.

Resort activities include bicycling, an exercise salon, three heated pools, tennis courts, badminton, croquet, horseshoes, a putting green, and lawn chess. A complimentary shuttle will whisk you to Biltmore Fashion Park, truly a shopper's paradise, while the Concierge can direct you to just about any diversion in the area, ranging from Grand Canyon Tours to the A's and Giant's Spring Training.

Golfers will want to play one or both of the PGA-rated championship courses. Try flat Adobe, built in 1930, where Clark Gable lost his wedding ring, with 6900 yards of tree-lined fairways, streams and lakes. Or play the long, narrow Links, with its unusual rolling terrain, five lakes and scenic views of the resort. #15, a par 3, is straight downhill with a clear shot of Phoenix.

Hyatt Regency Scottsdale

Are you ready for swaying palms surrounding a glitzy air conditioned Taj Mahal in the dry desert air of the Valley of the Sun? Throughout this spectacular 493 room Hyatt Regency, winds one of Water Wizard Howard Fields more elaborate freshwater creations.

This hotel has all the luxuries and comforts for which Hyatt is famous. Rooms have a southwestern feeling with bleached oak furniture and brass and marble accents. Balconies and decks have views of mountains, fairways and that unforgettable pool of pools with its swim-up bar, four water slides and a subterranean grotto whirlpool. You'll find seven casitas, a Regency Club, fourteen club suites, parlor suites, VIP suites and one Regency Suite. Two restaurants and a high-energy lobby bar provide refreshing outlets for meeting and relaxing. Conference planners will find a full range of meeting rooms and facilities for just about any type of gathering.

A full health spa, 8 Laykold tennis courts, lawn tennis, croquet, and bicycle, jogging and walking paths will help keep you in shape. If you're bringing the kids, you can enroll them in Kamp Kachina, the children's program for ages 5-12.

Excellent shopping adjacent to the resort awaits the non-golfer as well as numerous other area adventures.

There are three separate individually designed nine hole courses that make up a 27 hole championship course. Benz and Poellet designed this 6818 yard masterpiece of rolling desert terrain. Dunes, first of the three, is characterized by sand dunes amidst rolling greens. Golfers will find five lakes cropping up on the next nine, oddly enough called Lakes. The most difficult of the three is Arroyo, with a winding dry river bed and two lakes. Beware—its three finishing holes were designed to be particularly challenging, for that's where the game is frequently decided.

Address: P.O. Box 6211, Scottsdale, 85261
Phone: 602-991-3388   800-228-9000
Innkeeper: James K. Petrus
No. rooms: 493
Rates: $, Credit Cards: AmEx, Visa, MC, Other CC
Services: El-safes, TV, Radio, Fully stocked mini-bar, Children's program: ages 5-12
Restrictions: No pets
Restaurant: Golden Swan, Sandolo
Bar: Andiamo, Lobby
Business Fac.: Sec. Svc., Audio-visual
Sports Fac.: Full Health Spa, Tennis, Pool, Jogging
Location: Gainey Ranch
Attractions: Jeep Tours, Hot-air Ballooning,

Course: Arroyo/Lakes Combination
Distance: 6,818, Par: 72
Rating: 70.0, No. of holes: 18
Guest Policy: Private, Hyatt guests have privileges
Phone Club-House: 602-951-0022
Pro's name: Derek Crawford
Reservations: Seasonal—allow more time on season
Season: Year round
Guest Carry Club: No

Marriott's Camelback Inn Resort

Address: 5402 E. Lincoln Dr.,
Scottsdale, 85252
Phone: 602-948-1700   800-228-9290
Innkeeper: Wynn Tyner
No. rooms: 423
Rates: $, Credit Cards: AmEx,
Visa, MC, Other CC
Services: Valet, Barber shop, Beauty
shop, Garage and parking, Car hire,
House doctor, Babysitting, Card/game
area, Laundry, Room service
Restrictions: Pets ltd.
Restaurant: Chaparrall
Bar: Oasis, Chaparral
Business Fac.: Sec. Svc., Audio-
visual, Conf. rm. cap.: 2,200
Sports Fac.: Pool, Tennis, Full
health spa
Location: Maricopa County
Attractions: 5th Ave. Shopping,
Mountain Climb, Desert Jeep Tours

Course: Indian Bend Course
Distance: 6,486, Par: 72
Rating: 70.9, No. of holes: 18
Guest Policy: Open to public on
space available basis
Phone Club-House: 602-948-0931
Pro's name: Chuck Eade
Reservations: May be made 7 days
in advance
Season: Year round
Guest Carry Club: No

Camelback Inn, situated on 125 scenic desert acres in prestigious Paradise Valley, has become a
respected landmark as generations have enjoyed
the rustic Southwestern charm created by Jack
Stewart in 1936. In the shadow of majestic Camelback mountain, the Inn radiates from a main
lodge, where, for fifty years, lettering on the
tower has declared the resort to be a place
"Where Time Stands Still." Sun-drenched days
and refreshingly cool evenings are the attraction
here, amidst untouched desert surroundings,
majestic palm trees and lush gardens.

Dining is as memorable as the unsurpassed
beauty of the desert backdrop. The elegant
Chaparral Dining Room, renowned by locals, offers its celebrated rack of lamb, topped off with
a decadent chocolate truffle cake. Less formal
meals are served in the authentic southwestern
decor of the Navajo Room, or on the North Garden Buffet terrace.

Tennis enthusiasts will thrill to discover ten all
weather courts, five of which are illuminated.
Two huge outdoor pools with adjacent whirlpool
baths beckon guests, and surrounding the property are well-maintained paths—ideal for jogging, walking or bicycling. You'll have the option
of working out in the Fitness Center, playing volleyball, table tennis or shuffleboard. A pitch-
and-putt course, as well as a nine-hole putting
green are but a short distance from your "casa"

The area abounds in diversity—such as jeep
tours through the desert, horseback adventures
into the mountains, scenic trips to the Grand
Canyon, and hot air ballooning.

Minutes away are award-winning Desert Botanical Gardens, Scottsdale's charming galleries and
the famous Borgata . . . the epitome of shopping
elegance.

Camelback Golf Club, offering 36 holes of championship golf, awaits you. The long and open Indian Bend Course was designed by Jack Snyder,
and lies within a verdant natural wash basin. Its
links-type layout provides the golfer with
stretches of gently-rolling terrain and incredible
mountain vistas. Camelback's original 18-hole
Padre course is short but tight—but don't be
lulled into thinking it's a snap—there's plenty of
challenge here. Sweeping eucalyptus and stately
palms line the well-manicured fairways, and for
most of the year, you'll be invigorated by the
desert air.

Scottsdale Princess Resort

This is the first resort in this country for Princess Hotels International, and it's made a big splash. Part Mexican Colonial, part ultra-chic, and pure Southwestern in style, the 525 rooms and suites blend unobtrusively into the 450 acres. The largest ballroom in Arizona, a constellation of outstanding restaurants, a major spa, and close proximity to Horseworld, with its 480 stables and polo field, are big attractions. Guest rooms and suites feature the earthy subtle patterns of desert country, phones in oversized bathrooms, and many have fireplaces, wet bars and defined living and work areas.

Restaurants run the gamut from casual to elegant La Hacienda with its garden atrium and golf course view. Recreational amenities are nothing short of spectacular. Among the ten tennis courts is a 10,000 seat stadium court, site of the annual WCT Scottsdale Open. Other diversions include swimming, water volleyball, racquetball and squash and aerobics.

The lure of Scottsdale's shopping tempts most visitors, and you'll want to visit the Borgata and Biltmore shops. How about seeing the Grand Canyon from the air?

As a guest here, you're guaranteed a starting time on one of the two 18 hole, Tournament Players Courses. Designed by Tom Weiskopf and Jay Moorish to facilitate more than seventy thousand spectators, you'll have a chance to go for par on the fifteenth—the one with the island green. This is the home of the Phoenix Open, remembered by many as the spot where Scottish-born Sandy Lyle walked away with the winner's check in gorgeous shirtsleeve weather while most of the country shivered.

Address: 7575 E. Princess Dr., Scottsdale, 85255
Phone: 602-585-4848   800-255-0080
Innkeeper: Gratien Kruczek
No. rooms: 525
Rates: Credit Cards: AmEx, Visa, MC, Other CC
Restrictions: No pets
Restaurant: La Hacienda
Bar: Cazadores
Business Fac.: Sec. Svc., Audio-visual
Sports Fac.: Tennis, Pool, Full Health Spa
Location: Scottsdale
Attractions: Arabian Horse Farms, Grand Canyon, Heard Museum

Course: Tournament Players Course
Distance: 6,992, Par: 71
Rating: 73.9, No. of holes: 18
Guest Policy: Resort guests guaranteed tee times, open
Phone Club-House: 602-585-4848
Reservations: Suggest 10 days in advance
Season: Year round
Guest Carry Club: No

Loews Ventana Canyon Resort

Address: 7000 E. Ventana
Canyon Dr., Tucson, 85715
Phone: 602-299-2020   800-243-5117
Innkeeper: John Thacker
No. rooms: 400
Rates: $$, Credit Cards: AmEx,
Visa, MC, Other CC
Services: Valet, Beauty shop,
Parking, Babysitting, Laundry,
Room service
Restrictions: No pets
Restaurant: Canyon Cafe
Bar: Cascade
Business Fac.: Msg. Ctr., Secretarial
Sports Fac.: Pool, Tennis Aerobics,
Weight room
Location: Northeast area town
Attractions: Shuttel to Sabino Canyon and two malls

Course: Resort Course, Lowes
Distance: 6,818, Par: 72
Rating: 74.0, No. of holes: 18
Guest Policy: Call for availability,
Dress code
Phone Club-House: 602-577-1400
Pro's name: Mike Abbott
Reservations: May be made 5 days in
advance
Season: Year round
Guest Carry Club: No

High on a plateau, virtually hugging the Santa Catalina Mountain foothills, sits a unique merger of man and nature. With Tucson sprawled below, rugged canyons above, and magnificent expanses of desert terrain in every direction, this sleek, low-rise resort is true integration into the rocky landscape. The lobby is a cool, beautifully appointed symphony in mauve, sage, and bleached-wood whites, with some of the area's best artwork displayed. A glistening lake is fed from a cascading waterfall, and graceful blue paloverde shade paths and terraces offering a quiet respite.

The 400 guest rooms and suites each have a bar, stocked refrigerator and private terrace, three telephones, and an immense spa-like tub.

Included in the attractions here are a sophisticated tennis training center featuring 100 lighted courts including an exhibition court, two heated swimming pools with adjacent hot tubs, aerobics room, massage therapy, weight room, lap pool, spa, par course jogging track, picnic areas, and horseback riding nearby. When it snows on Mount Lemmon, an hour away, you can take a few runs in the morning, and come back for a round of golf. Meeting and conference planners love this resort, with 26 separate function rooms with 37,000 square feet of space for exhibits, banquets and meetings.

Among the points of interest in the area are Sabino Canyon, Saguaro National Monument, old Tucson, several good museums, concerts and theater. Clevelanders can watch their Indians in the winter, and Greyhound racing fans have a chance to bet the hounds. Shuttle services are provided to the Golf and Racquet Club, and shopping malls.

Guests at the resort have playing privileges at the Ventana Canyon Golf and Racquet Club—two spectacular Tom Fazio creations for players of every level. Chosen for the 1987 and 1988 Merrill Lynch Shoot-Out Championship, the PGA Resort Course leads pros and novices through rocky canyons, stony washes and crevasses of the foothills. Like his masterpiece at Wild Dunes, outside Charleston, the eighteenth hole is a smashing finish. This par 5 is a real challenge, with water to the right and behind the big green. Beware the Ventana Wash guarding the green in front—it must be carried for par.

Sheraton Tucson El Conquistador

As you turn onto El Conquistador Way the mesquite-tree-lined drive leads you to the resort's porte cochere. Step into the lobby and your eyes are immediately drawn to the high copper-encased dome. And behind the front desk, two 12′x20′ murals painted on; pure copper sheets by Dutch-born Tucson artist Anke Van Dun blend perfectly with the hotel's Spanish and Indian inspired decor.

Dining at El Conquistador brings alive that Southwestern flair. Dos Locos Cantina features Mexican cuisine in a casual setting, while The Last Territory serves up mesquite-grilled steaks, ribs, chicken and fish with a live Country-Western band. For a special evening of fine dining, The White Dove provides the intimate and elegant atmosphere you're looking for. Savor the creations of Chef Molly McCall's swordfish, veal and beef dishes covered with her famed gourmet sauces.

From your spacious room, decorated in either turquoise or rose color schemes, you'll enjoy a glorious view of the grassy courtyard or the natural desert and mountain scenery that surrounds the 150-acre site, nestled beneath the dramatic 2,000-feet Pusch Ridge cliffs at the western end of the Santa Catalina Mountain range.

Plenty of sports activities will let you experience the great outdoors, including 16 lighted Laykold tennis courts, horseback riding, and swimming.

45 holes await the golfer staying at El Conquistador. Nine holes are at the resort itself, with another 36 at Oro Valley's Canada Hills Country Club. These are desert courses, with a spectacular backdrop of jagged mountain peaks and seemingly cloudless azure skies, gullies, dry washes, and a variety of cacti. Six miles away, at Canada Hills, the fairways are tight with rolling hills, large, undulating double-tiered greens, clustered sand traps, and plenty of mesquite and palo verdes to avoid. #6 is a stickler—a difficult par three of 167 yards. You'll need a straight tee shot, because only the front third of the green is visible from the tee, and hooks and slices will be penalized. The green has 100 feet of putting surface behind the left front bunker that can't be seen. Events hosted here have been the 1985 Southwest Section PGA Match Play Championship, the 1987 Oldsmobile Scramble, and numerous mini-tour events.

Address: 10000 North Oracle Rd., Tucson, 85737
Phone: 602-742-7000   800-325-3535
Innkeeper: Yogi Hutsen
No. rooms: 440
Rates: $, Credit Cards: AmEx, Visa, MC, Other CC
Services: Valet, Barber shop, Beauty shop, Car hire, Doctor on call, Baby-sitting, Card/game area, Laundry, Dry cleaning, Room service
Restrictions: Pets ltd.
Restaurant: Sundance Cafe, White Dove
Bar: 6 bars
Business Fac.: Copiers, Telex
Sports Fac.: Pool, Racquetball, Riding, Health spa
Location: Catalina Mt.Foothill
Attractions: Tucson Movie Set, Arizona Sonora Desert Museum

Course: Sheraton El Conquistador
Distance: 7,073, Par: 72
Rating: 73.6, No. of holes: 18
Guest Policy: For private members & guests of Sheraton, Dress code
Phone Club-House: 602-742-7000
Pro's name: Jeff Bass
Reservations: Tee times made 7 days in advance
Season: Year round
Guest Carry Club: No

Tucson National Resort & Spa

Address: 2727 West Club Dr.,
Tucson, 85741
Phone: 602-297-2271   800-528-4856
No. rooms: 170
Rates: $$, Credit Cards: AmEx,
Visa, MC
Services: Unisex beauty salon, Skin
care salon
Restaurant: 2 Restaurants
Bar: 3 bars, Conf. rm. cap.: 350
Sports Fac.: Full Health Spa,
Tennis, Pool

Course: Green & Gold Courses
Distance: 3,361, Par: 36
Rating: 71.2, No. of holes: 9
Guest Policy: Must be guest at resort,
Dress code
Phone Club-House: 602-297-2271
Pro's name: Don Powes
Reservations: Tee times given one
week in advance
Season: Year round
Guest Carry Club: No

You'll think you've gone to heaven after a few days in the sunny dry foothills at one of the country's leading spas, which also happens to be a fantastic golf facility. The resort is a low, rambling, and comfortable newish-looking group of buildings accented by a pleasing combination of arches, colonnades and fountains that appear to be jet-propelled. Gardens, weeping willows and lounging areas are everywhere, and you get the idea that you're here to be pampered.

167 villa suites constitute lodgings, and you'll have your own patio, refrigerator/wet bar and stunning view. Many have fireplaces, kitchens and other extras. You won't have to leave the premises for fine dining—two good restaurants and three cocktail lounges cater to guests' appetites.

Two separate, divisible ballrooms, and nine meeting rooms offer 15,000 square feet of meeting space, and outdoor areas can expand meeting capabilities to more than 30,000 square feet.

Few European spas can surpass the variety of services and amenities available here. You can opt for a spa plan, or pick and choose what appeals to you, sort of a salad bar approach. Not to be missed are the Scotch water massage, Orthian equipment massages, loofah rubdown, and the renowned salt glow scrub. The Russian bath in the men's spa is guaranteed to loosen you up, and the Finnish sauna for women is one you'll want to repeat.

Tennis lovers will have four hard-surfaced courts, with two lighted, and that wonderful sound of the ball popping off the racket in the quiet desert air. Naturally, there's a gorgeous swimming pool to complete the picture. Tucson is not a desert wasteland when it comes to the arts. It's one of only 14 U.S. cities claiming its own symphony, theatre, ballet, and opera company. Not too shabby for a golf town that maintains a cool, dry average yearly temperature around 70.

Golf is taken seriously here. Consisting of three nines, it's hosted the NBC Tucson Open for 15 years, and the Arizona Amateur. This is a von Hagge/Devlin redesign on gently rolling terrain sprinkled with the occasional saguaro—pocked with gashes and holes from nesting birds and errant shots. As a permanent site for the *Golf Digest* Schools, anyone wanting putting pointers or intensive instruction will be in good hands.

Burgenstock, Germany

Hotel du Golf et Sport, Crans Montana, Switzerland

Ashford Castle, Cong, County Mayo, Ireland

Westin La Paloma

Reverence for the desert's natural gifts was the primary concern of landscape architects Rogers, Gladwin and Harmony in designing this resort complex which earned them an Award of Merit from the American Society of Landscape Architects. Over 7,000 Saguaros were transplanted and saved, and environmental zones were planted with drought-resistant brittlebush, desert marigold, Arizona poppies and Chochise lovegrass to create the unspoiled setting for this 487 room resort in the foothills of the Santa Catalina Mountains.

Jack Nicklaus' 27-hole championship layout encircles the resort which is conveniently located just 10 miles from downtown. 24 two-story complexes in a village setting give each guest a patio or balcony with private exterior entrance, and inside, shades of dusty rose, sage, cobalt, mauve and muted grey are echoed in nubby cottons, woven raffia and copper accents. Restaurants emphasize healthy fare for the active life. If the tennis, (on competition-calibre lighted courts), hiking, volleyball, croquet and bicycling have tired you out, why not try Room Service with its motorized carts, specially outfitted with heating and refrigeration units to bring you fresh selections 24 hours a day?

Other amenities include an aerobics room and weight room with Lifecycle and Nautilus equipment, and a Personal Services Center for skin and hair pampering, and massages. Shoppers and browsers have the option of exploring the ten on-premises stores or heading for nearby Old Tucson.

Not only are the three challenging 9 hole courses in excellent condition, the putting greens and driving ranges are worthy of note. Each course is a par 36, but each has a different rating. Built in 1984, the combined yardage is 9776 yards, with 4-5 tees for varying expertise on each green. Nicklaus has designed a desert course with large bunkers, no water, but plenty of grassy hollows, swales and mounds, with the mountains forming a magnificent backdrop to the lush greens and desert fairways. Hill Course's #5, a 465-yard, par 4 is a beauty. From the back tee it takes two big shots to "get home." The approach to this green—which is guarded on the left by a grassy swale and to the right by a sand trap—is through a long valley that opens up behind the green with views of the entire city of Tucson several miles away.

Address: 3800 E. Sunrise Dr., Tucson, 85718
Phone: 602-742-6000 / 800-742-6000
Innkeeper: Andrew MacLellan
No. rooms: 487
Rates: $$, Credit Cards: AmEx, Visa, MC, Other CC
Services: Valet, Beauty shop, Garage and Parking, Car hire, Babysitting, Card/game area, Laundry, Room service
Restrictions: Pets ltd.
Restaurant: La Villa
Bar: Desert Garden
Business Fac.: Msg. Ctr, Secretarial, Conf. rm. cap.: 2,100
Sports Fac.: Pool, Tennis, Racquetball, Croquet
Location: Catalina Foothills
Attractions: Old Tucson (movie location), Shopping

Course: Ridge Course
Distance: 3,554, Par: 36
Rating: 71.8, No. of holes: 27
Guest Policy: Open to guest only, Dress code
Phone Club-House: 602-299-1500
Pro's name: Don Pooley
Reservations: Reserve time with shop
Season: Year round
Guest Carry Club: No, Caddies: Yes

Rancho de los Caballeros

Address: Box 1148, Wickenberg, 85358
Phone: 602-684-5484
Innkeeper: Dallas C. Gant, Jr.
No. rooms: 74
Rates: $$$, Credit Cards:
Services: Valet, Library, Car hire, Babysitting, Card/game area, Laundry, Children's counselor
Restrictions: No pets
Restaurant: 4 dining rooms
Bar: Service bar
Business Fac.: Message, Secretarial, Conf. rm. cap.: 100
Sports Fac.: Pool, Tennis, Riding, Skeet & Trap
Location: Maricopa County
Attractions: Gold Rush Days 1st weekend Feb. Square dancing

Course: Rancho de los Caballeros
Distance: 6,577, Par: 72
Rating: 72.5, No. of holes: 18
Guest Policy: You must be guest at resort, Dress code
Phone Club-House: 602-684-2704
Pro's name: Gordy Berg
Reservations: No problem getting tee times
Season: Year round
Guest Carry Club: Yes

Rediscover a less complicated era when time was measured, not by the tyranny of clocks but, by soft shadows darkening against majestic mountainsides. Stroll amid flowering gardens and emerald green lawns and watch keen-eyed hawks soar above rugged Vulture Peak. Escape into the rapidly vanishing past and encounter the sheer pleasures of 20,000 acres of the unspoiled southwest when you stay at Rancho de los Caballeros.

Bring your family, your sense of adventure, and most of all, bring along your healthiest appetite. The outdoor activities and the clean desert air will make you hungry for fabulous "home cookin" prepared over glowing mesquite. Sample Rancho's breakfast of griddle cakes, a leisurely buffet luncheon on the poolside patio, or an intimate and elegant dinner of thoughtfully prepared cuisine.

Besides golf, there's also tennis on four acrylic courts, trap and skeet shooting, swimming at the teardrop-shaped pool, and of course, riding over miles of open countryside, an old favorite here. Their 60 horse stable is one of the finest collections in Arizona.

Spend a day exploring The Vulture Mine, the source of $30 million in gold bullion during Wickenburg's heyday. Visit Heard Museum, a notable hacienda housing the finest collection of Indian arts and artifacts in the Southwest. Then simply relax and enjoy a quiet moment with other guests in the ranch living room.

Golf is at a private club for members, their guests, and guests at Rancho de los Caballeros. There are three sets of tees, a driving range, putting green and a clubhouse featuring men's and ladies' locker rooms, pro shop, and kitchen with bar and grill room. The course was completed in 1981, and was designed so that there are no crossing fairways. Undulating greens of "tif" are elevated and the lush bermudagrass fairways are overseeded with perennial rye to insure a deep green playing area all year. Three lakes and a variety of cacti (preferably to admire) will test your skill and concentration on this demanding course.

La Costa Hotel & Spa

One of the world's leading resorts, La Costa Hotel & Spa features extensive spa facilities that attract prominent figures from the worlds of entertainment, sports, and arts. The men's and women's Spas at La Costa serve as twin centerpieces for this 1,000-acre private world of resort pleasures. Here the natural scenic splendor of Southern California's Costa Brava combine with world-class golf and countless other amenities that make La Costa living an experience of timeless elegance.

Enjoy tennis on your choice of the Racquet Club's 23 courts—including two grass, four clay and 17 hardcourt surfaces—and swim in heated pools featuring a lovely aquatic center overlooking the golf course. But, don't miss the Spa that will keep you coming back. Relax in a sauna, rock steam bath, Swiss shower, Roman pool, whirlpool or a solarium. And for that extra boost, schedule yourself for a facial, massage, herbal wrap or loofah scrub. It's a world dedicated solely to the deep satisfaction and sensual pleasures of vibrant health and radiant good looks.

The pros who play in the annual MONY Tournament of Champions have dubbed the last four holes of the South Course "the longest mile in golf". What they find so tough isn't their length as much as it is the head winds which come off the ocean, according to Jack Millard, head professional who also serves as assistant director of the nationally televised PGA tournament. You'll no doubt want to tackle both of these highly-acclaimed eighteen-hole courses, which are surrounded on three sides by towering hills.

A tee shot on the North Course's picturesque 16th, 181-yard par three, involves a lake that edges into play from the left and leads to a large, undulating green—well protected by bunkers and backed by a beautiful waterfall.

Greens are well-elevated, rolling to flat fairways which are an ample 35 to 40 yards wide, and players find a generous supply of sand traps—calling for careful follow-through on recovery shots. The South Course features the famed par-5, 546 yard 17th hole, a true test of driving skill and shot-making at every stroke, while the North Course consists of classic holes with a variety of intriguing water hazards.

Address: Costa Del Mar Rd., Carlsbad, 92009
Phone: 619-438-9111   800-544-7483
Innkeeper: Gerald T. Gleason
No. rooms: 487
Rates: $$, Credit Cards: AmEx, Visa, MC, Other CC
Services: Valet, Beauty shop, Car hire, House doctor, Babysitting, Laundry, Card/game area, Room service
Restrictions: No pets, no children in spa
Restaurant: Brasserie, Spa Dining Room
Business Fac.: Msg. Crt., Secretarial, Conf. rm. cap.: 1,000
Sports Fac.: 2 pools, Tennis, Health spa
Attractions: Sea World, San Diego Zoo, Wild Animal Park

Course: South Course
Distance: 6,896, Par: 72
Rating: 73.7, No. of holes: 36
Guest Policy: 18 holes open daily to guests, Dress code
Phone Club-House: 619-438-9111
Pro's name: Jack Millard
Reservations: May be made 1 week in advance
Season: All year
Guest Carry Club: No, Caddies: Yes

Carmel Valley Ranch Resort

Address: One Old Ranch Rd.,
Carmel, 93923
Phone: 408-625-9500   800-422-7635
Innkeeper: Cal Jepson
No. rooms: 100
Services: Valet, Babysitting, Room
service
Restrictions: No pets
Restaurant: Hotel dining room
Bar: Service bar
Business Fac.: Copiers, Audio-
visual, Conf. rm. cap.: 250
Sports Fac.: Pool, Tennis
Location: Monterey Peninsula
Attractions: 17 Mile Drive, Monterey
Bay Aquarium, Cannery Row

Course: Carmel Valley Ranch
Distance: 6,005, Par: 70
Rating: 69.6, No. of holes: 18
Guest Policy: Hotel guests and mem-
bers only, Dress code
Phone Club-House: 408-626-2510
Pro's name: Harry Turner
Reservations: May be made 7 days
in advance
Season: Year round
Guest Carry Club: No

For anyone who enjoys a sunny, warm climate, splendid golf and tennis facilities, and an exclusive resort featuring graciously appointed guest suites, the Carmel Valley Ranch Resort is the answer. Based in Carmel, Oak Tree Hotels, Inc., also operate Mission Hills Country Club Resort Condominiums, and Palm Beach Polo and Country Club, among other properties.

The 100 suites are set in clusters among old oak trees and gardens, and are individually decorated with rustic textures and soft natural colors. Against a backdrop of the Santa Lucia Mountains and clear blue skies, the cathedral ceilings, private decks, wood burning fireplaces and fairway views lend an air of country refinement. Many have private outdoor spas.

The Lodge, housing an intimate dining room specializing in fresh fish from Monterey Bay, and local produce, changes its menu every other day. The cozy lounge is a showpiece of local craftsmen whose talents are displayed in the weavings, art, and a massive stone fireplace. A pianist and freshly cut flowers add to the ambience of this informal gathering place.

Meeting and banquet rooms are designed to accommodate a group of 10, or one as large as 250, and the sweeping Oak Tree Courtyard along with the terrace area offers ample space for an outdoor conference or dining. Golf is superb here. The Club is private, and available only to resort guests and club members. There are tennis courts, an inviting freeform pool and full spas, and a choice of scenic walks in the valley.

If your goal is to play a Pete Dye creation, especially after watching the 1988 PGA Tournament at Oak Tree, and you can't make it to Ponte Verda Beach to the TPC course, here's your chance! As one of the courses in the Spalding Pro-Am featuring PGA stars such as Greg Norman, Craig Stadler and Johnny Miller, this championship design has the Carmel River bordering several holes on the north, and luxurious mountain greenery on the south. Test your prowess on some of Dye's trademarks here—a layout dappled with numerous deep sand and grass bunkers, undulating greens, and railroad ties and telephone pole bulkheading which are deemed an integral part of the course. Five of the holes climb the mountainside affording some incredible views of the valley, and the cooling fog banks that hover over the coast.

La Playa Hotel

Tucked away on a side street shaded by California live oaks, this Mediterranean-style villa is Carmel's only full-service resort.

The subtly exquisite decor accents pastel walls and upholstery with custom hand-loomed area rugs. Cope family (owners of San Francisco's venerable Huntington) California antiques and heirlooms. Many of the 75 rooms afford views of the garden or the Pacific. Bathrooms feature marble floors and inlaid decorative tiles.

The Spyglass Restaurant's terrace, where masses of bright flowers meet the eye, is the perfect spot to watch the sunset over the ocean. An extensive international wine list and a fine collection of aged Ports and Sherrys whet the appetite. We retain the delicious memory of veal and scampi in a Dijon mustard sauce accompanied by a Duckhorn Merlot, and the sinful elegance of chocolate whiskey cake.

The boutiques and galleries of Carmel are a few short blocks away, and the numerous attractions of the Monterey Peninsula are within easy access. A heated swimming pool in the garden beckons, while the beach is but a five minute stroll.

Three conference rooms, with a capacity ranging from 10–125 are available, as well as an on-premises coordinator.

There are many golf courses within a half hour's drive, and the concierge will gladly telephone for particulars. Choose from the Pebble Beach course, Spyglass, or Spanish Bay, Del Monte Golf at Hyatt Regency, or the 9 hole Peter Hay, Jr. par 3 course. Poppy Hills Golf Course, a stunning show of Robert Trent Jones, Jr's. artistry was carved out of the Del Monte Forest, and is the permanent home of the Northern California Golf Association. Not enough? Consider Rancho Canada, Carmel Valley Golf and Country Club, or Carmel Valley Ranch Resort.

Address: Camino Real & 8th, Carmel, 93921
Phone: 408-624-6476
Innkeeper: Tom Glitten
No. rooms: 75
Rates: Credit Cards: AmEx, Visa, MC
Services: Laundry, Garage and parking, House doctor, Babysitting, Cable TV, Radio, Shampoo, 2 soaps, shower caps, bath gel, Room service
Restrictions: No pets, handicap: 3 rms.
Restaurant: Spyglass
Bar: Spyglass Lounge
Business Fac.: Audio-visual, Copiers, Conf. rm. cap.: 125
Sports Fac.: Pool
Location: Carmel
Attractions: 11 nearby golf courses

Quail Lodge

Address: 8000 Valley Greens Dr., Carmel, 93923
Phone: 408-624-1581
Rates: Credit Cards: AmEx, Visa, MC, Other CC
Restaurant: On The Park Bar & Grill
Attractions: Le Petit Cordon Bleu Gourmet Cooking School

Course: Quail Lodge Golf Club
Distance: 6,141, Par: 71
Rating: 70.8, No. of holes: 18
Guest Policy: Open to members & resort guests
Phone Club-House: 408-624-1581
Pro's name: C. Lynch, PGA
Reservations: May take tee time 3 mo. in advance
Season: All year
Guest Carry Club: Yes

This is the Quail Lodge's 25th anniversary, and to celebrate it, they've redone several areas. To top it off, visitors will note the new flag poles proudly bearing the American flag, the Quail Lodge "walking quail," and the Mobile Five-Star Flag. Some of the events held here have included the Monterey Wine Festival luncheon, the Monterey Film Festival Grand Finale Party and the International Bugatti Rally. The lodge's low profile, cedar-siding and heavy shake roofs exude rustic charm on ten manicured acres surrounding a picturesque lake. The three-story lobby features timbered redwood and cedar, Spanish tile and oak flooring. Large ficus trees and a gurgling fountain dominate the central area with cozy adjoining sitting room and fireplace.

Rooms are spacious and have fireplaces, and balconies with views of the golf course, lakes and mountains of the Carmel Valley. Executive suites, Oriental in feel, feature stocked bars, private gardens, stereo, VCR and hot tubs.

The Covey Restaurant, overlooking a lake with panoramic views of a lighted fountain and arched bridge, serves dinner fare such as quenelles mousselines, abalone Morro Bay, and for dessert, vacherin au chocolat.

Perhaps the Inn's most memorable feature is The Meadows. An ardent conservationalist, Lodge President Ed Haber takes pride in maintaining this 600-acre stretch of meadows and wooded groves as a nature reserve. You may spot goats, wild boar, deer, quail, and an abundance of small game and schools of trout. The newest members are a mother and son breed of hearty cattle developed in Western Scotland. Be sure to say "hello" to them. This is peaceful California golf at its best on a well-manicured course. You probably will see lots of wildlife if you take time to look towards the pines and acacia trees and eleven lakes. Home of the Spalding Invitational Pro-Am held in January, the course also hosts the Annual Women's California Amateur. A special treat here is a lesson from Ben Doyle, whose students book way in advance for advice, using props such as mops, brooms, and old tires. Best part is, it works!

Furnace Creek Inn

If you've never visited the driest, lowest, hottest area of the United States, you're in for a real treat—for in it's foreboding isolation, between October through May, it's also starkly beautiful. To those hardy souls seeking California's riches, the Valley was a deadly obstacle to overcome, and as a study in extremes, this 3,000 square mile national monument reigns supreme. The boom towns went when the mines were no longer producing, and most of the action today centers around Furnace Creek, site of a visitor's center, a small airport and the resort. Consisting of the Inn and the Ranch, guests can choose between a luxurious 69 room inn, and a rustic ranch complete with old wagon wheels and an informal cafeteria. The rambling adobe brick Inn welcomed its first guests in 1927, and became a destination for the well-heeled who came to be pampered in the oasis of swaying palms and cool, gurgling water. The atmosphere at the Inn is relaxed, an unpretentious, intriguing because of its quiet surroundings. Desert colors, large plants, ceiling fans, wicker furniture and after-noon tea in the lobby characterize the Inn, which caters to many repeat guests.

Well-known valley landmarks worth visiting are Titus Canyon, Telescope Peak—11,409 feet high —and Badwater, directly below it, the lowest place, and of course, Devil's Golf Course, a bed of salt pinnacles, some as high as four feet, and still growing.

Maybe you'll want to explore the canyons and nearby sights on horseback, or play tennis, or you can bicycle or jog on meandering paths, and there are miles of scenic trails to hike. The golf course is fun to play and surprisingly verdant for an area whose average rainfall is 1.7 inches yearly. Tamarisk trees and stands of date palms line the fairways, but you'll probably want to use every club in your bag, as the out of bounds areas are unexpected and numerous. As you ap-proach the fifth fairway, take note that you'll be putting at 214 feet below sea level, and should you land in a bunker, you won't need your sand wedge, as all bunkers are grass. Water comes into play on several holes, fed by a mountain stream. This tough course with its outstanding layout was designed by William Bell, who is also credited with such winners as Bel Air, Ojai Val-ley, Riviera, and Stanford.

Address: Furnace Creek Box 1, Death Valley, 92328
Phone: 619-786-2345
Innkeeper: Alpheus C. Bruton II
No. rooms: 70
Rates: $$$, Credit Cards: , Visa, MC, Other CC
Services: Library, Barber shop, Beauty shop, Card or game area, Laundry, Room service
Restrictions: No pets
Restaurant: Main dining room
Bar: Oasis
Business Fac.: Copiers, Audio-visual, Conf. rm. cap.: 150
Sports Fac.: Pool, Tennis, Croquet, Riding, Bicycle
Location: Inland Empire Desert
Attractions: Scotty's Castle, Nt'nal Park, Amargosa Opera House

Course: Furnace Creek
Distance: 5,750, Par: 70
Rating: 66.3, No. of holes: 18
Guest Policy: Call for availability, Dress code
Phone Club-House: 619-786-2301
Pro's name: Brad Taylor
Reservations: Not needed week days, tee times weekend
Season: October–May
Guest Carry Club: Yes

La Quinta Hotel Golf Resort

Address: 49-499 Eisenhower Dr., La Quinta, 92253
Phone: 619-564-4111   800-854-1271
Innkeeper: Judy Vossler Woodard
No. rooms: 603
Rates: $, Credit Cards: AmEx, Visa, MC, Other CC
Services: Valet, Barber shop, Beauty shop, Babysitting, Laundry, Room service
Restrictions: Pets ltd.
Restaurant: La Mirage
Bar: La Cantina
Business Fac.: Secretarial, Copiers, Conf. rm. cap.: 575
Sports Fac.: Pool, Tennis, Balloons, Polo, Riding
Location: Palm Springs area
Attractions: Hotel tours, ballooning, Palm Springs Aerial Tram

Course: La Quinta, Dunes Course
Distance: 5,775, Par: 72
Rating: 67.8, No. of holes: 18
Guest Policy: Open to resort guests, Dress code
Phone Club-House: 619-346-2904
Pro's name: Greg Abadie
Reservations: May be made one week in advance
Season: Year round
Guest Carry Club: No

This is where the stars and the moguls of the thirties came to play. During long treks when California was Spanish and Mexican, travel between settlements and missions was arduous, and sustenance was meager. The fifth day was designated as one for good food, music and conviviality, thus the day was known as "La Quinta." Some of Hollywood's biggest names including Bette Davis, Ginger Rogers, Erroll Flynn and Frank Capra were regulars at this California desert hideaway. La Quinta is one of those small towns about 20 miles southeast of central Palm Springs, and a stone's throw from Indio. The small luxurious hotel has been expanded and revitalized without losing any of its charm or original flair. Guests stay in adobe Spanish-style casitas and have 45 acres of meticulously landscaped grounds under the imposing Santa Rosa Mountains to explore. Furnishings are expensive contemporary, with a 20's flair, and you may choose from single or double rooms, suites, or rent a private residence.

Swim in any of nine pools scattered about the property. With an average temperature a comfortable 82 degrees daytime, it's possible to relax in the pool while gazing at snow-capped mountains. A beauty salon, masseur, and gift shop are found on the premises.

Away from the resort, guests will find desert hot air ballooning, a tram to whisk you to the top of Mt. San Jacinto, the Palm Springs Desert Museum, horseback riding, polo during the winter, Oasis Water Park, a Coachella Valley Agricultural tour, hiking or sightseeing in Joshua Tree National Monument, or you can go to Indio for a date.

La Quinta is a top tennis resort, and the reasons are obvious. With a tennis stadium, sunken club court, and 40 immaculate courts, (all 3 surfaces), its an impressive setup. The resort offers 18 holes of Pete Dye's mastery at its best. Look for typical Dye touches such as railroad ties in the center of fairways, big waste bunkers, elevation changes in unexpected spots (greens), and mirror-smooth water hazards. And nothing can match the drama of the desert in bloom under the barren treeless mountains. Number seventeen is one of the toughest 18 holes in America according to pros. The acclaimed course hosted the 1985 World Cup Pro-Am, the PGA Tour Qualifying in 1985 and 1988, and the 1986 and 1987 PGA Club Professional Championship.

Silverado Country Club and Resort

All of Silverado centers around an historic mansion which was designed to incorporate adaptations of Italian and French architecture. Its surroundings suggested quiet grandeur, and today, guests gather on the terrace overlooking the creek to behold the maze of vineyards, majestic oak, and magnolia trees and manicured gardens.

Silverado Country Club is comprised of individual studios and suites which are private, low-rise clusters around gardens and swimming pools. Vintner's Court, an elegant chandeliered dining room in dusty rose and sand, is a distinctive setting for classic cuisine. The wine list is exclusively Napa Valley.

Eight swimming pools in varying shapes and sizes dot the grounds of the resort, and you'll find the largest tennis complex in the area. This is jogging country, where it's possible to see as many as twenty wineries on an hour's moderate run if you head towards Oakville.

The area is rich in diversions such as the Napa Valley Wine Library, a substantial collection on wine and gastronomy, much of it drawn from winemaker's personal libraries.

Ready for the golf course? Silverado's two courses are almost a dream come true. Maybe not that hole-in-one fantasy, but here are two challenging courses, both by Robert Trent Jones, Jr. Each bear the mark of their distinguished architect—with gigantic trees arching the fairways, and bunkers and greens placed with the touch of an artist. These are championship layouts which host the Kaiser/Anheuser-Busch Tournament, the Northern Cal Open, and many corporate tourneys.

The South Course is the newest of the two. It's a par 72 nicely contoured design with deceiving side-hill lies and over a dozen water crossings. The North Course, also a par 72, stretches to 6700 yards and is occasionally more forgiving. No matter how you play, you'll be treated to some pretty spectacular scenery on these links which have been honored by the National Groundskeepers Association, and by a staff of top professionals. There are ponds, lakes, even three sweet-water creeks, and always, the mystic of the grape.

Address: 1600 Atlas Peak Rd., Napa, 94558
Phone: 707-257-0200   800-532-0500
Innkeeper: Kirk Candland
No. rooms: 280
Rates: $, Credit Cards: AmEx, Visa, MC, Other CC
Services: Valet, Parking, Car hire, Babysitting, Laundry, Room service
Restrictions: No pets
Restaurant: Vintners Court, Royal Oak
Bar: Patio Terrace
Business Fac.: Copiers, Telex, Conf. rm. cap.: 500
Sports Fac.: Tennis, Jogging, 8 pools
Location: Napa Valley
Attractions: Winery tours, mud baths, Marine World/Africa USA

Course: North Course
Distance: 6,620, Par: 72
Rating: 73.9, No. of holes: 36
Guest Policy: Hotel guests & members
Phone Club-House: 707-257-5460
Pro's name: Jeff Goodwin
Reservations: 48-hrs. non guest, at reservation
Season: Year round
Guest Carry Club: No

Ojai Valley Inn and Country Club

Address: Country Club Dr., Ojai, 93023
Phone: 805-646-5511   800-422-6524
Innkeeper: William G. Briggs
No. rooms: 218
Rates: $, Credit Cards:
Services: Terry cloth robes, turn-down service, Valet, Laundry, play yard for children, Room service
Restaurant: Main Dining Room
Business Fac.: Audio-visual, Conf. rm. cap.: 550
Sports Fac.: Tennis, Pool, Croquet, Spa
Location: Ojai Valley

Course: Ojai Valley Inn
Distance: 5,909, Par: 70
Rating: 68.9, No. of holes: 18
Guest Policy: Members and guests have preferred times
Phone Club-House: 805-646-5511
Pro's name: Scott Flunn
Reservations: Guests up to 90 days in advance
Season: Year round
Guest Carry Club: Yes

The setting always was nothing short of incredible, and after its $35 million expansion and renovation, the exclusive retreat of rambling adobe under the towering Topa Topa Mountains continues to attract the elite. Northwest of Los Angeles and 30 minutes east of Santa Barbara, this new addition to the Hilton Group has pulled out all the stops. A new conference center, 108 new guest rooms and suites, and exquisite regional art are a few highlights. A fantastic tennis center, swimming pools, and a chef brimming with impressive credentials and innovative ideas completes the picture. Wines are carefully chosen—many from neighboring vineyards.

Ojai Country Club was one of the first great California golf courses. The course was designed by George C. Thomas, Jr. and Billy Bell, who also are credited with Riviera Country Club, and Bel-Air. Course historians tell us that throughout his career, Thompson never accepted a fee for his services as designer. The scenic natural contours have been retained in the layout's facelift by Jay Moorish, and today's golfer will find a little bit of everything. The new 18 was made more challenging by rebuilding the greens. Plans are underway to host the Southern California Amateur Championship. Try the new driving range, its one of the best.

Inn & Links at Spanish Bay

Clinging to the sloping sand dunes on a rugged sweep of coastline perched on the edge of the vast Pebble Beach Resort area is a bold new resort—The Inn and Links at Spanish Bay. Today's visitors to Pebble Beach can appreciate what visionary Samuel F. G. Morse believed; that development of the land always should enhance nature's bounty.

The Dining room is a pleasant surprise. Mediterranean specialties typical of Piedmont, Lombardy and the Pyrenees using local herbs and vegetables are found in the Inn's premier restaurant, the Bay Club.

Eight tennis courts, a complete health spa with an exercise pool and miles of forest and beach trails for hiking and exploring are available for guests.

Spanish Bay neighbors some of California's most appealing towns. The fantastic Monterey Aquarium, a blend of the historic and the modern, is around the corner, and Carmel isn't far. Quiet Pacific Grove is winter home to millions of Monarch butterflies. The course here has been called "instant tradition," meaning it's a true seaside links course modeled after the demanding layouts of Scotland and Ireland, a unique challenge of sand and soil, sea and foggy weather. An outstanding trio is responsible for the design: Tom Watson, Robert Trent Jones Jr., and Frank "Sandy" Tatum, former USGA president. Linksland golf is played close to the ground to avoid the wind—"Running like a rabbit toward the hole," as Jones puts it.

Among the highlights:

*the third hole, a fearsome 425 yard par-4 from a dramatic elevated tee;

*the 13th, which turns the player back toward the Pacific and into the dunes, a 130-yard par 3 patterned after the "Postage Stamp" at Scotland's Royal Troon; Jones calls it his "Christmas Seal because it's a gift when you get on";

*the fourth, a stunning 185-yard par 3 with the putting surfaces tucked into the side of sand dunes.

Varieties of fescue grasses are blended for the fairways, greens and roughs. Native to Scotland, they adapt well to cool, humid regions and are reputed to give golf balls more "bite." Pack your windbreaker, a few extra golf balls and prepare to spend some pleasant time in the brome.

Address: 2700 17-Mile Dr., Pebble Beach, 93953
Phone: 408-647-7500
No. rooms: 270
Rates: $$$$, Credit Cards: AmEx, Visa, MC, Other CC
Services: Valet, Car Hire, House Doctor, Robes, Barber and Beauty shops, Room service
Restrictions: No pets
Restaurant: The Dunes
Bar: Traps
Business Fac.: Audio-visual, Copier, Conf. rm. cap.: 675
Sports Fac.: Tennis, Full Spa, Riding, Jogging
Location: Monterey Peninsula
Attractions: Monterey Aquarium, Cannery Row, Fisherman's Wharf

Course: The Links at Spanish Bay
Distance: 6,195, Par: 72
Rating: 72.7, No. of holes: 18
Guest Policy: Check for availability, Dress code
Phone Club-House: 408-646-1122
Pro's name: Bob Hickam
Reservations: May be made with hotel reservation
Season: Year round
Guest Carry Club: No, Caddies: Yes

Lodge at Pebble Beach

Address: 17 Mile Drive, Pebble Beach, 93953
Phone: 408-624-3811   800-654-9300
Innkeeper: Eric Calderon
No. rooms: 161
Rates: $$$$, Credit Cards: AmEx, Visa, MC, Other CC
Services: Valet, Barber & Beauty shops, Car Hire, House Doctor, Robes, Room service
Restrictions: No pets
Restaurant: The Cypress Room, Gallery
Bar: Terrace Lounge
Business Fac.: Audio-visual, Copier, Conf. rm. cap.: 300
Sports Fac.: Tennis, Jogging, Full Spa, Massage
Location: Monterey Peninsula
Attractions: 17-Mile Drive, Monterey Bay Aquarium, Cannery Row

Course: Pebble Beach Golf Links
Distance: 6,357, Par: 72
Rating: 72.7, No. of holes: 72
Guest Policy: Changes, Dress code
Phone Club-House: 408-624-3811
Pro's name: R. J. Harper
Reservations: 30 days in advance
Season: All season
Guest Carry Club: No, Caddies: Yes

Mention Pebble Beach, and note the reactions. Visions of a rugged stretch of ocean-hugging coast. Gnarled cypress trees and fog rolling in. Samuel F. B. Morse, determined to build a golf course, motoring through windswept Del Monte Forest. Bing Crosby's annual Clambake. Celebrity players in tournament-ending dramatics. As a landmark destination on scenic 17-mile Drive, the Lodge since 1919 has been the epitome of tranquil dignity. The architecture is California traditional, c. 1919, and void of any vestiges of commercialism. Eleven rooms are available in the main building, which are unpretentiously elegant. 150 are found in 12 separate 2 and 3-story buildings, each offering stunning views of the ocean, gardens, or fairways. The Cypress Room is the main restaurant. Characterized by bouquets of oversized fresh flowers, light woods, natural fabrics in soft colors, Bauscher china and a panoramic view of the bay, the feeling is that of a grand establishment. Try Club XIX for a candlelit French meal par excellence. The Tap Room, ornamented with a fascinating collection of golf mementos, is the spot for conviviality, afternoon or evening. Guests enjoy full privileges at the Beach and Tennis Club, with fourteen plexi-paved courts (stadium court included), and two paddle tennis courts. Perched just above the surf is a heated pool, children's wading pool, viewing deck, and a spa with massage rooms, saunas and exercise studios. Equestrian trails reach every corner of the forest, sea lions bask on the rocks above pounding surf, and the 16 mile drive south of Carmel to Big Sur is a journey not to be missed.

A round of golf here is special, as these courses are among the most famous, and its unusual for tournament-class courses to be available to the public. Both the challenging Robert Trent Jones-designed Spyglass Hill, which traverses dense pine forests and sand dunes, and the Grand Daddy of them all, Pebble Beach Golf Links, are open to the public. These two beautiful courses, together with private Cypress Point, are the home of the prestigious AT&T National Pro-Am, a premier PGA tournament whose players are household names such as Willie Mays, Peter Ueberroth, and George C. Scott. Pebble Beach course starts out along the ocean, then swings back and forth along the coast for holes 4 through 10. 11 through 16 are inland, and 17 and 18 return to the rugged shoreline are second to none as a finish to this supreme course by the sea.

Ritz-Carlton

This three-story Mediterranean-styled addition to the clear, dry Coachella Valley commands a sweeping view of the Palm Springs area. The full-service resort rests on a 650 foot plateau and boasts a Wildlife Park Sanctuary for desert big-horn sheep, who roam free in the hills behind the hotel. Accommodations include 240 guest rooms with 19 executive suites and two Ritz-Carlton suites. All guest rooms feature balconies with French doors, honor bars and spacious marble bathrooms. Guest activities include use of the fitness center, tennis courts, swimming pool and spa. Summers are unbearably hot, but for nine months it's one of the most agreeable climates anywhere. Guests rave about the four hour jeep "safari" into the rugged Santa Rosa Mountains behind the resort. They're led by drivers knowledgeable in mountain wildlife and vegetation, and the lunches are prepared to order by a gourmet chef. Afternoon tea and cocktails in the lobby lounge is a favorite, and the restaurant and cafe serve meals that are acclaimed throughout the valley. There's a sundry shop, and apparel boutique in addition to a multilingual staff.

Guests have preferred tee times at the Rancho Mirage Country Club and the Mission Hills Resort Course. Pete Dye's Mission Hills is a gently rolling tough layout with some of his trademarks—large, deep bunkers, wide, rolling fairways. Greens are handsomely framed by palm trees, with large lakes on five holes. Over on Bob Hope Drive, the Rancho Mirage course offers some tremendous views from its parallel fairways. This is a very well-maintained course, with small to medium greens.

Address: 68-900 Frank Sinatra Dr., Rancho Mirage, 92270
Phone: 619-321-8282   800-341-3333
Innkeeper: Wolfgang Baere
No. rooms: 240
Rates: $$$, Credit Cards: AmEx, Visa, MC, Other CC
Services: VCR's in all suites, Color TV, Valet, Babysitting, Concierge, Auto rental, Room service
Restrictions: No pets
Restaurant: The Cafe
Bar: The Bar
Business Fac.: Complete bus. fac., Conf. rm. cap.: 1,500
Sports Fac.: Jeep safari tours, Hot air balloons
Location: Palm Springs
Attractions: Downtown Palm Springs and El Paseo, Aerial Tram.

Course: Mission Hills Resort
Distance: 5,678, Par: 70
Rating: 68.8, No. of holes: 18
Guest Policy: Guests have priority tee times
Phone Club-House: 619-324-4711
Pro's name: S. Wickliffe
Fees: $55.00, Carts: Included
Reservations: Call for availability
Season: All year
Guest Carry Club: No

Inn at Rancho Santa Fe

Address: P.O. Box 869, Rancho Santa Fe, 92067
Phone: 619-756-1131   800-654-2928
Innkeeper: David Royce
No. rooms: 75
Rates: $, Credit Cards: AmEx, Visa, MC, Other CC
Restaurant: Vintage Room, Garden Room
Business Fac.: Audio-visual, Copiers, Conf. rm. cap.: 100
Sports Fac.: Tennis, Pool, Croquet
Location: San Diego County
Attractions: San Diego Zoo, Wild Animal Park, Sea World, Mexico

Course: Rancho Santa Fe
Distance: 6,497, Par: 72
Rating: 71.3, No. of holes: 18
Guest Policy: Inn guests have limited play privileges
Phone Club-House: 619-765-3094
Pro's name: Chuck Courtney
Reservations: 5 days in advance through Inn
Season: Year round
Guest Carry Club: No

Partially hidden among towering eucalyptus and citrus groves, the low, rambling inn remains one of those spots to which a loyal clientele returns year after year to enjoy the gentle climate and hospitality of a family-owned hostelry. Accommodations are in cottages or the main building, which houses a lounge furnished with family antiques, including a collection of models of sailing ships. Cottages have secluded porches or sun decks, and many have fireplaces, kitchens or wet bars. Diners find many options in a variety of settings. Choose from The Library, book-lined and cozy, or the Vintage Room, a replica of an early California taproom which opens onto a patio for dining and dancing under the stars in summer. The Garden Room, festooned in flowers, affords a sweeping view across emerald lawns and pool. The 20 acres of landscaped grounds provide a self-contained community offering leisurely seclusion with a swimming pool, tennis courts, and croquet. For ocean swimming and sunning, the inn maintains a beach cottage with showering and dressing facilities at nearby Del Mar. Within an hour's drive are Balboa Park and San Diego's Zoo, shopping and browsing in La Jolla, Sea World, and the new waterfront complex at San Diego's Seaport Village.

Inn guests play at private Rancho Santa Fe Golf Club, a rolling, wooded, challenge designed by Max Behr, also credited with Pasadena Golf Club and Hacienda Country Club, and the first editor of *Golf Illustrated* magazine. The par 72 design claims #13 as its most noteworthy—no doubt due to a couple of small lakes to be carried.

Rancho Bernardo Inn

When the United States regained control in 1846 of what is now San Diego, they found themselves with rich agricultural valleys, a perfect climate (average annual temperature of 72 degrees), and a Mexican-Spanish cultural tie that has spawned a paradise. Rancho Bernardo Inn, thirty miles northeast of downtown San Diego, is a low-slung, red-tiled rambling beauty of low-beamed ceilings, charming small public rooms, and a beautiful view of the San Pasqual Mountains. Add decorative touches of Indian, Mexican and early California artifacts, first-class accommodations, a championship golf course, a spa, excellent conference facilities, and the bottom line is a resort worthy of its accolades.

Composed of 187 rooms including 55 suites, the Inn is enveloped by gardens, old sycamores and pines, and the meandering golf course with its lush fairways and little lakes. Just off the public foyer are smaller hideaways accented by unusual trinkets. A lute, a zither, an ancient accordion, horns, and cymbals of old brass blend in with assorted memorabilia—all part of the Inn's dedication to hospitality in attractive surroundings. Seven haciendas, of varying types, house guests. Decor is casual, yet spacious, with live plants, original artwork, and sliding doors that seem to bring the gardens to you.

Group facilities are sought after for style, attention to detail, and the expert assistance of an assigned coordinator. The 3600 square feet of the Santiago Room, with its own plaza and surrounding garden, is highlighted by a fountain from Vicenza, Italy.

North County is ideal for year round golf. Here one finds a gem of an eighteen hole par 72 course, and three executive nines. William Frances Bell designed the West Course, and the 27 holes of Oaks North was by Ted Robinson, architect of Tokatee in Oregon, and Sahalee Country Club's links in Washington, both rated as top courses. Home of the Honda Civic Classic, West's 6,388 yards weave through a long, winding valley, with streams and lakes seeming to be everywhere. On the eighteenth hole you drive from an elevated tee. It's a par 5 and the second shot must be placed between a lake on the left, and trees on the right. Your shot to the three-tiered green must clear a cascading waterscape across the center front.

Address: 17550 Bernardo Oaks Dr., San Diego, 92128
Phone: 619-487-1611   800-542-6096
Innkeeper: John M. Morton
No. rooms: 287
Rates: $$$, Credit Cards: AmEx, Visa, MC, Other CC
Services: Valet, Barber shop, Beauty shop, Garage and parking, Car hire, Babysitting, Card or other game area, Laundry, Room service
Restrictions: No pets
Restaurant: El Bizcocho
Bar: Labodega
Business Fac.: Sec. Svc., Audio-visual, Conf. rm. cap.: 450
Sports Fac.: Pool, Tennis, Full Health Spa
Location: North County
Attractions: Sea World, Zoo, Old Town, Wild Animal Park

Course: West Course
Distance: 6,388, Par: 72
Rating: 70.5, No. of holes: 45
Guest Policy: Call for reservations, Dress code
Phone Club-House: 619-487-1611
Pro's name: Tom Wilson
Reservations: May be made one week in advance
Season: Year round
Guest Carry Club: Yes

The Alisal

Address: 1054 Alisal Rd., Solvang, 93463
Phone: 805-688-6411
Innkeeper: Jack Austin
No. rooms: 66
Rates: $$, Credit Cards: Visa, MC
Services: Library, Garage and Parking, Babysitting, Card or other game area, Laundry, Rec. Room pool & ping pong, Playground, volleyball, Room service
Restrictions: No pets
Restaurant: Ranch Room
Bar: Oak Room
Business Fac.: Copies, Audio-visual, Conf. rm. cap.: 80
Sports Fac.: Pool, Tennis, Croquet, Riding, Sailing
Location: Santa Barbara County
Attractions: Solvang, Pac. Conservatory Summer Outdoor Theater

Course: Alisal Guest Ranch
Distance: 6,286, Par: 72
Rating: 70.0, No. of holes: 18
Guest Policy: Call for availability, Dress code
Phone Club-House: 805-688-6411
Pro's name: John Hardy
Reservations: Depends on availability
Season: Year round
Guest Carry Club: Yes

Secluded 40 miles north of Santa Barbara, the West Coast's country club of guest ranches dates back to an 18th century land grant to Raimundo Carrillo for his service to the newly established Mexican government. The present owners bought the property in 1943 and shortly thereafter welcomed its first guests, and the rest is history. Today, cattle and deer graze on some of the last real California hill country devoted to cattle ranching, and an air of peaceful tranquility reigns over the manicured estate-like grounds. It's like the perfect summer camp, where there was a lot to do, but you didn't have to do any of it.

At the Alisal, you dine on some of the finest food anywhere, and you never need reservations, (Modified American Plan) so you have the same table for breakfast and dinner, and the busboy (who could double as a wrangler) might become your children's best friend. Fresh fish is brought in every day from nearby Morro Bay and Santa Barbara, and pastries and desserts are temptingly rich. The Oak Room Lounge, trimmed with handsome Western appointments and a roaring log fire, is the focal point for socializing.

The Alisal, which in Spanish means "sycamore grove," has seven tennis courts, a 100 acre freshwater lake for fishing, boating, sailboats and windsurfs, plus a heated swimming pool, archery, volleyball, shuffleboard and croquet. Spacious lawns surround the guest areas, and the "down home" atmosphere is conducive to a pickup game of touch football, or Frisbee.

The Gainey Vineyard and Zaca Mesa, both within easy reach of the Alisal, are fine examples of the Santa Ynez Valley's emerging wine industry. Visitors can tour the grounds, taste selected current releases and purchase wine. Take a bottle of Firestone Vineyard's noted Johannisberg Riesling on your picnic, visit a mission or two, shop in quaint Solvang or hike up a tree-shaded canyon. If you've been dying to take square-dancing lessons, there's all the "yahhooing" you'll need to get you in the mood.

As a golf resort, the Alisal ranks high. The par 72 course, designed by Billy Bell, blends ideally into the natural surroundings of the rolling terrain, dotted by 300 year old oak, sycamore and eucalyptus trees. The course, home of the 1986 South California Seniors, meanders along a seasonal creek and affords plenty of variety.

Meadowood Resort & Country Club

What began as a country club for Napa Valley residents a quarter of a century ago, is now a dreamlike resort where you can share the good life with members and local vintners. Your initial impression as you enter along a vineyard-bordered country lane is that you are a guest at a country home with large verandas, lush lawns and wooded hillsides. You'll feel the pulse of the Napa Valley wine and food world here, sequestered on 250 acres of Oak and Madrone amid buildings patterned after a 1910 New England lodge.

Gastronomes and neophytes alike will marvel at the immersion into the world of the finest Napa Valley wines, and a chef dedicated to a cuisine reflecting simple, imaginative fresh fare. Overlooking the golf course, the casual bistro-style of the Fairway Grill will tempt you with lighter salads, fresh grilled fish, and a sampling of the neighboring vineyards offered by the glass. As shadows lengthen, you might want to savor the magic of this unhurried paradise with a wedge of Doux de Montagne and a glass of local cabernet. Warm evenings lure diners outside to the terrace for dinner under the stars.

The secluded enclave offers six tennis courts, a swimming pool, miles of walking and jogging trails, a par course and a croquet court built to comply with international standards.

The valley's fame, and thus its drawing card, rests largely with its climate—ideally suited to growing the Cabernet Sauvignon grape, with Pinot Noir not far behind. Meadowood offers unique courses in wine and food appreciation, as well as hosting the annual Napa Valley Wine Auction in June. The concierge will be happy to assist you with arrangements to local wineries, the mud and mineral baths of Calistoga, quaint nearby shops, hot air ballooning, or maybe you deserve a laid back afternoon of gliding over the panoramic valley. If you'd like to explore some of the area's more renowned eateries, the list is mind-boggling.

There's a nine-hole executive course here with four par fours and five par threes. The par 62 layout winds around California Live Oak lined fairways which are tight, but demand accuracy. Players of all levels, genders and ages await the Century Pro-Am, a scratch best-ball 18-hole event in which the combined ages of partners must be at least 100 years.

Address: 900 Meadowood Ln., St. Helena, 94574
Phone: 707-963-3646   800-458-8080
Innkeeper: Maurice Nayrolles
No. rooms: 58
Rates: $$, Credit Cards: AmEx, Visa, MC
Services: Valet, Parking, Card or other game area, Laundry, Wine School and instructor, Room service
Restrictions: No pets
Restaurant: Fairway Grill
Bar: at Starmont
Business Fac.: Copiers, Audio-visual, Conf. rm. cap.: 100
Sports Fac.: Pool, Tennis, Croquet, Hiking trails
Location: Napa Valley
Attractions: 140 wineries, mineral baths Calistoga, Balloons

Course: Meadowood Resort
Distance: 4,130, Par: 62
Rating: 61.0, No. of holes: 9
Guest Policy: Not specific, Dress code
Phone Club-House: 707-963-3646
Pro's name: Joe Roberts
Reservations: 24 hours in advance
Season: Year round
Guest Carry Club: Yes

The Broadmoor

Address: 1 Lake Circle, Colorado Springs, 80901
Phone: 303-634-7711   800-634-7711
Innkeeper: Douglass C. Cogswell
No. rooms: 550
Rates: $$, Credit Cards: Visa, MC, Other CC
Services: Valet, Barber shop, Beauty shop, Garage and Parking, Car hire, Inter. currency exchange, House doctor, Babysitting, Laundry, Room service
Restrictions: Pets ltd.
Restaurant: Penrose Room, Charles Court
Bar: Terrane Lounge
Business Fac.: Translators, FAX, Conf. rm. cap.: 2,600
Sports Fac.: Pool, Tennis, Handball, Croquet, Biking
Location: El Paso County
Attractions: Cheyenne Mt. Zoo, Cog Railway, Air Force Academy

Course: East Course
Distance: 7,218, Par: 72
Rating: 73.9, No. of holes: 54
Guest Policy: Must be staying at Broadmore or a member, Dress code
Phone Club-House: 719-577-5790
Pro's name: Mike Tayer
Reservations: May be made 11 months in advance
Season: Open all year
Guest Carry Club: Yes, Caddies: Yes

Breathe deeply, inhale the rich forest scent of firs and pines. Contemplate Cheyenne Mountain's mysteries. Feel the crisp evening air nip your cheek as you savor the old world charm of an institution famed for its unique blend of grace and modern convenience. At home in the Rockies since 1918, the Broadmoor is a pivotal landmark of tradition, steeped in European elegance, and offering year round activity in fabulous weather.

The Broadmoor diner enjoys a full circle of renowned and award-winning restaurants from the haute cuisine under gilt-encrusted cherubs of the Penrose Room to the rollicking fun of an authentically-constructed 18th century English pub. A new menu promises lighter entrees with a hint of nouvelle cuisine. An outstanding wine list featuring some of Napa Valley's and Europe's finest, invites your deliberation.

There are literally 101 things to do in this Shangri-la of recreational facilities and contemporary comfort. Should I shoot skeet and trap? Line up a tennis game, swim, rent a paddle boat, join a bicycling tour, ice skate, go trout fishing, head for a wicket on the croquet lawn, hike up, or think about, Pike's Peak, play squash, or try shuffleboard? If you're one for spectator sports, you'll find everything from the Men's Regional Playdown in Curling to the Annual Pike's Peak Auto Hill Climb in July. The resort is crawling with activity and interests. Where else can you visit an Olympic Training Center, a Rodeo Hall of Fame, and top it off with a massage in your room?

Championship golf has had a colorful history at Broadmoor since the first course, designed by Donald Ross, opened in 1918. During World War II, Bing Crosby, Bob Hope, Ed Dudley and L. B. Maytag played an exhibition match here and all the proceeds were used to build a driving range at nearby Peterson Field for military personnel. The golf is demanding and enjoyably hilly on all three courses. West Course was designed by Robert Trent Jones, and completed in 1965, while the third championship course (South) by Ed Seay, was ready for play in 1976. The greens on all courses are treacherously fast, and a subtly undulating requiring deft touch and keen eye.

Tamarron

This is today's conveniences amidst the charm and rusticity of a mountain getaway. A scenic 18 miles north of Durango, a name synonymous with the Old West's gold rush, and tucked away in a 20-mile valley guarded by the San Juan National Forest, Tamarron's focal point is a main lodge perched on a stone cliff overlooking rolling alpine meadows. The lodge houses 140 suites, with 270 additional Townhouse suites scattered in adjacent buildings. Guest activities center around the main lodge, and here is where you'll find elegant Le Canyon, and the San Juan Dining Room, as well as the Caboose Cafe for afternoon and evening snacks. Nightly entertainment livens up the San Juan Lounge. A car isn't a necessity here, as an extensive transportation system services the airport, local sights such as historic Durango, and shuttles guests around the property.

A full range of outdoor sports facilities including tennis courts, an indoor swimming pool, plus horseback riding, jeep tours, and a spa and health club await family vacationers and those coming for meetings.

Southwestern Colorado, near the only point in the country common to four state corners, is ideally situated for exploring the area's history and culture. A short trip will bring you to Chimney Rock, and the Navajo State Recreation area. Railroad buffs can journey 45 miles up the Animas River Gorge to the 1874 mining town of Silverton, on one of the oldest coal and steam-powered narrow gauge trains anywhere.

The golf course, an Arthur Hills design, opened in 1975, and at 7,650 feet offers a little of everything. Number 10 is one of Tamarron's more interesting holes. Try for about 210 yards on your drive. Any more and the ball and you will be in the rough of a steep embankment that drops far below the fairway's upper level. Although the green is large, it's almost totally surrounded by monstrous sand traps, plus water to the left rear. This is ranked as one of Colorado's more difficult courses.

Address: 40292 U.S. Hwy. 550 N, Durango, 81301
Phone: 303-247-8801   800-525-5420
No. rooms: 400
Rates: $, Credit Cards:
Services: Spa & health club, shops, Unisex hair salon, Free movies
Restaurant: San Juan, Le Canyon
Business Fac.: Conf. rm. cap.: 500
Sports Fac.: Tennis, Rafting, Fishing, Pool
Attractions: Bus Tours, Four Corners, Sleigh rides, Cookouts

Course: Tamarron Resort
Distance: 6,885, Par: 72
Rating: 69.9, No. of holes: 18
Guest Policy: For owners, members, and resort guests, Dress code
Phone Club-House: 303-259-2000
Pro's name: Steve Nichols
Reservations: 24 hours in advance if not on package
Season: May 1–November 1
Guest Carry Club: No

Sheraton Steamboat Springs Resort

Address: P.O. Box 774808, Steamboat Springs, 80477
Phone: 303-879-2220   800-325-3535
Innkeeper: Dermot McKeown
No. rooms: 440
Rates: $, Credit Cards: AmEx, Visa, MC, Other CC
Services: Valet, Beauty Shop, Underground parking, Inter. currency exchange, House doctor, Babysitting, Card/game area, Laundry, Room service
Restrictions: Pets ltd.
Restaurant: Cipriani's
Bar: H.B.'s
Business Fac.: Secretarial, Fax, Conf. rm. cap.: 785
Sports Fac.: 2 pools, Tennis, Ice Skating
Location: Rocky Mountain Park
Attractions: Natural hot springs, Routt National Forest

Course: Sheraton Steamboat
Distance: 6,276, Par: 72
Rating: 69.0, No. of holes: 18
Guest Policy: Call for availability, Dress code
Phone Club-House: 303-879-2220
Pro's name: Henry Franks II
Reservations: Tee time given with room reservation
Season: Late May–Late Oct.
Guest Carry Club: No

Named for its hissing thermal springs, this family resort area, known primarily as a wintertime haven is now being rediscovered for it's summer recreational opportunities. Located 150 miles northwest of Denver, and surrounded by Rocky Mountain National Park, and Routt National Forest, the town, more than 100 years old, attracts those seeking superb conference facilities, and quiet sophistication. This is the perfect place for those seeking dry heat, moderate temperatures, and alpine vistas. Statistic buffs will note that the Continental Divide, separating the river systems which flow to opposite sides of the continent, is a stone's throw away.

There's plenty of room here—400 rooms, 3 suites, and Thunderhead Lodge with 58 rooms plus 75 condominium units. Complete conference facilities and a concierge, 4 lively bars and 5 restaurants insure a good time for everyone. Cipriani's is the signature restaurant and features northern Italian cuisine with specialties such as Funghi Genevese and Salmone Alle Nocciole. Your meal isn't complete without hazelnut souffle with zabaglione.

Hot air balloon enthusiasts can get a bird's eye view of the area, and hikers will have the trails virtually to themselves. White water rafting is at your doorstep, just ask the concierge to arrange it. You'll find 2 outdoor pools, tennis, nearby sailing, hot tubs, sauna and massage, horseback riding and some of the best trout fishing anywhere.

This is mountain high golf for all abilities, designed by Robert Trent Jones, Jr. in 1972. When the wildflowers burst forth in spring, and the only sound is Fish Creek babbling, you'll know the meaning of a Rocky Mountain High. This par 72 course is characterized by some great water holes, large greens, and spectacular fall colors. Greens are bentgrass while fairways and tees are bluegrass. #10 is a par 5, requiring length and accuracy off the tee to reach the green in two. Lay up shot is generally recommended, as a clear Colorado stream protects the green.

Amelia Island Plantation

Imagine a 1250 acre island of undisturbed primeval marshlands and lagoons where egrets and herons nest, towering sand dunes, lush foliage draped in Spanish moss, all bordered by a four mile wide white beach. This is Amelia Island, where Indians fished and hunted, where pirates roamed to bury treasure, and where the flags of eight different nations have flown in the past four hundred years. This unspoiled paradise is the northern most barrier island on Florida's east coast, just twenty-nine miles northwest of Jacksonville.

Dining at Amelia Island Plantation can be as elegant as candlelight, champagne and Pheasant with Wild Mushrooms and Walnut Sauce in the Dune Side Club overlooking the Atlantic, or as casual as a hamburger at the Coop. Should you choose dinner at the Verandah, you'll find the freshest seafood the coastal waters offer. Cocktails and after-dinner drinks are served in the Admiral's Lounge, featuring live music, or try the Beach Club's lively disco.

In addition to the wide, breeze-swept beach, there are twenty-five tennis courts, horseback riding, a fully-equipped Health and Fitness Center, swimming pools, and paddleboats. The island's waters are teeming with gamefish, and arrangements can be made to set up sailing, historical river cruises and fishing trips for sailfish and marlin. Whiting, sea trout and bluefish can be caught from the beach. Jogging trails entice you to explore marsh edges, sea oats and pine forests.

You'll want to combine play at Long Point with a round or two at Amelia Links, Pete Dye's 27-hole masterpiece (its the only resort in the world with golf courses by both Tom Fazio and Dye.) The setting challenges and captivates. Long, winding fairways are framed by vivid moss-draped forests. Paddleboats glide by on mirror-smooth lakes, and holes four, five and six hug the Atlantic to keep you on your tees.

Long Point's eighteen championship holes beckon with unusual natural hazards, highly elevated fairways, large bodies of water and more marshland and beachside play. PGA greats Ben Crenshaw, Davis Love, Mark O'Meara, Hal Sutton and Peter Jacobsen have played the course; and all agree that it's outstanding.

Address: Highway A1A South, Amelia Island, 32034
Phone: 904-261-6161   800-874-6878
Innkeeper: Jack B. Healan, Jr.
No. rooms: 1300
Rates: $178.00, Credit Cards: AmEx, Visa, MC, Other CC
Services: Beauty shop, Car hire, Babysitting, Card or other game area, Laundry, Room service
Restrictions: No pets
Restaurant: Dune Side Club
Bar: Admiral's Lounge
Business Fac.: Secretarial, Copiers, Conf. rm. cap.: 500
Sports Fac.: Pool, Tennis, Riding, Full Health Spa
Location: Nassau County
Attractions: Historic fishing village, St. Augustine

Course: Long Point
Distance: 6,740, Par: 72
Rating: 72.5, No. of holes: 45
Guest Policy: Open to members & resort guests only, Dress code
Phone Club-House: 904-261-6161
Pro's name: Steve Waugh
Reservations: May be made at any time
Season: All year
Guest Carry Club: No

Boca Raton Hotel & Club

Address: 501 E. Camino Real,
Boca Raton, 33432
Phone: 305-395-3000   800-327-0101
Innkeeper: Carlo Bicaci
No. rooms: 1000
Rates: $$$$, Credit Cards: AmEx,
Visa, MC, Other CC
Services: Valet, Library, Barber shop,
Beauty shop, Parking, Car hire, Intl.
currency exchange, Nurse, Baby-
sitting, Card/game area, Laundry,
Room service
Restrictions: No pets
Restaurant: Patio Royalle, Cathedral
Bar: El Lago Lounge
Business Fac.: Secretarial,
Audio-vis., Conf. rm. cap.: 1,500
Sports Fac.: Pool, Tennis, Full
health spa, Sailing
Location: Palm Beach County
Attractions: Historical Society Tours,
Lion Country Safari

Course: Boca Raton Club
Distance: 6,695, Par: 71
Rating: 71.5, No. of holes: 18
Guest Policy: Call for availability,
Dress code
Phone Club-House: 305-395-3000
Pro's name: Ron Polane
Reservations: Call for starting times
Season: Year round
Guest Carry Club: No

Located on southeast Florida's Gold Coast, Boca
Raton's distinctive pink color and Spanish-
Moorish architecture are the legacy of architect-
eccentric Addison Mizner. Built in 1926 as the
centerpiece of Mizner's dream city, the resort
was restored to its original decor last year. Hand-
made rugs from India now cover new French
terra-cotta floors, and even the Mizner Fountain
is again in operation.

Carrying on Boca's tradition of history, Chauncey's Court, the latest addition to the resort's
dining services, was named in memory of Boca's
long time concierge Chauncey Cottrell. Experi-
ment with Chauncey's unusual breakfasts—try
Crabmeat Benedict or Smoked Salmon. For dinner, head for The Shell, where the sophisticated
elegance of soft white leather and sparkling
white lights makes the French cuisine especially
good.

Take advantage of Boca's Tennis Center, boast-
ing 22 Har-Tru courts, and The Boca Beach
Club, the watersports center providing everything from snorkeling to windsurfing. Or, go Gulf
Stream fishing for plentiful sailfish, marlin,
tuna, barracuda, and dolphin.

Enjoy the shopping nearby or participate in the
popular tours offered by Boca Raton Historical
Society. Explore the Mizner Museum, walk
through the giant columns of a 13th century log-
gia, and view antiques brought from Spain by
Mizner.

Designed by William Flynn in 1926, and redesigned thirty years later by Robert Trent Jones,
the 18 hole championship course has become an
attraction for golfers from all over the world.
The Club has had only two pros prior to Ron
Polane—but what names! Tommy Armour
reigned from 1926-1955, and Sam Snead between 1956 and 1970.

The eighteen hole course winds throughout the
grounds of the resort, with a couple of ponds in-
terspersed among a variety of palms, unusual
ferns and tropical foliage. The resort also offers
its guests golfing privileges at Broken Sound Golf
Club—which maintains two 18-hole championship courses designed by Joel Lee.

South Seas Plantation Resort

Once the hideaway of 16th-century pirates and, later, a flourishing citrus plantation, South Seas Plantation ranks among today's premier resorts. South Seas sits on 330 acres of unspoiled tropical island on the northern tip of Captiva Island, 3 miles out in the Gulf of Mexico. The tranquility of its two-mile stretch of white beach and the natural beauty of the island has won this resort its reputation as "Florida's Tahiti."

Three award-winning restaurants provide a different dining experience for every meal of your vacation . . . in surroundings that range from candlelight to casual.

Not only will you have access to 22 Laykold tennis courts scattered throughout the resort and 17 fresh-water pools—a myriad of water sports that take full advantage of the beautiful surroundings await you at South Seas. Windsurfing, sun canoes, waterskiing, jet skiing, and aquacycles are all available to guests, including Steve Colgate's Offshore Sailing School.

Also popular are the many island excursions, including the Captiva Island breakfast cruise, lunch and dinner cruises to Cabbage Key or Useppa Island, cocktail cruises through Pine Island Sound, and sightseeing cruises to Boca Grande and Cayo Costa. And for shoppers, Chadwick's Square Shops, the newly-opened gallery of fine boutiques modeled after the award-winning Periwinkle Place on Sanibel Island, is ideal.

You'll have the azure Gulf waters around you as you play this scenic nine holes built in 1973. The course is flat with a couple of lakes and a pretty stretch of fairway bordering the beach. This is the site of the annual South Seas Plantation Golf Traditional Tournament benefitting the Big Brothers/Sisters of Lee County. Haven't had enough golf? Take a short jaunt over to neighboring Sanibel Island where you'll find an additional 18 holes at the Dunes Country Club.

Address: P.O. Box 194, Captiva Island, 33924
Phone: 813-472-5111   800-237-3102
Innkeeper: Austin L. Mott III
No. rooms: 650
Rates: $$$, Credit Cards: AmEx, Visa, MC, Other CC
Services: Valet, Beauty shop, Car hire, International currency exchange, Babysitting, Card or other game area, Laundry, children's rec. program, Room service
Restrictions: No pets
Restaurant: Chadwick's, King's Crown
Bar: Chadwick's
Business Fac.: Audio-visual, Telex, Conf. rm. cap.: 625
Sports Fac.: Pool, Tennis, Waterskiing
Location: Lee County
Attractions: Cruises to Cabbage Key & Useppa Island, Shopping

Course: So. Seas Plantation
Distance: 3,300, Par: 36
Rating: , No. of holes: 9
Guest Policy: Call for availability, Dress code
Phone Club-House: 813-472-5111
Pro's name: Jerry Heard
Reservations: May be made one day in advance
Season: Year round
Guest Carry Club: Yes

Grenelefe Resort

Address: 3200 State Rd. 546,
Grenelefe, 33844
Phone: 813-422-7511   800-237-9549
Innkeeper: Michel Leidermann
No. rooms: 950
Rates: $, Credit Cards: AmEx,
Visa, MC, Other CC
Services: Valet, Barber shop, Beauty
shop, Garage and parking, Car hire,
Intl. currency exchange, Babysitting,
Card/game area, Laundry, Room service
Restrictions: No pets
Restaurant: Camelot
Bar: Lancelot
Business Fac.: Complete serv.
center, Conf. rm. cap.: 2,000
Sports Fac.: Pool, Tennis, Sailing,
Fishing
Location: Polk County
Attractions: Disney World, Cypress
Gardens, Sea World

Course: Grenelefe West
Distance: 7,325, Par: 72
Rating: 75.0, No. of holes: 54
Guest Policy: Possible to play any
time, Dress code
Phone Club-House: 813-422-7511
Pro's name: Dave Leadbetter
Reservations: Up to 90 days
in advance
Season: Year round
Guest Carry Club: No

At the center of Florida's wonderland of world-famous attractions, is the Grenelefe Resort and Conference Center. The resort embraces 1,000 lush, wooded acres along the shores of Lake Marion and remains part of a self-contained community that has its own post office, fire department, service station and convenience store.

Grenelefe dining comes in a variety that will suit every taste. Enjoy Grenelefe's 13-court world-class tennis complex, including the 1,700-seat Centre Court Stadium where national tournaments, as well as the Grand Prix Circuit, take place annually. There are also five pools, plus plentiful water sports and fishing on 6,400-acre Lake Marion, where largemouth bass and speckled perch are abundant.

More non-sport activities have been added recently, including arts and crafts classes, cooking schools and bridge tournaments. There's easier access to Florida's famous attractions as well, with the initiation of daily shuttle bus service from Grenelefe to Walt Disney World's Magic Kingdom/EPCOT Center and Cypress Gardens.

With 54 holes of championship meticulously-landscaped golf on three challenging courses ranking among Florida's best, the Grenelefe Resort and Conference Center offers a varied menu of golfing. The West Course has been ranked number one in Florida consistently, and, like all Robert Trent Jones designs, claims long, tight fairways lined with tall pines and monstrous bunkers. Many players tout the ninth and 14th as being the best holes. They're each a long par 4 with plenty of trees and sand traps, but each is more negotiable from the middle markers.

Ed Seay's East Course is much shorter and tighter at 6802 yards. Depending on your mood or your gall, you'll want to tee off the Championship first tee, positioned on the second story of the Conference Center, just outside the golf pro shop.

The newest course, the South, designed by Ronald Garl and PGA touring pro Andy Bean, is no pushover. It incorporates a variety of length, terrain, and hazards. But between the 8th and 9th hole hydrophobes beware!

The Diplomat

This has been one of Florida's big resorts for years, and now with millions being spent on public rooms, landscaping, the pool area, restaurants, lounges, and meeting rooms, this 300 acre resort offers fun-in-the-sun in a most convenient location. Less than a half hour from Miami's airport, with the Atlantic's beach on one side, and the intracoastal waterway on the other, the spruced-up Diplomat glitters in a world of its own. With 1,001 rooms and 69 suites, the resort has its own marina, nine restaurants and lounges, two health clubs, 12 tennis courts, three swimming pools, and an arcade of boutiques. Nearby is another shopping complex, and all the attractions of this popular stretch of playland fifteen minutes from Fort Lauderdale. You can bet the ponies or the greyhounds, watch Jai Alai, visit Lion Country Safari, the Burt Reynolds Theatre in Jupiter, or drive south to Miami, all within a short distance. This is the place to windsurf, rent Hobie Cats, Aqua Bikes, power boats and water skis, or relax at the pool and contemplate how many gallons of water are being recycled through the waterfalls.

The course here is the Diplomat, a par 72 flat course with plenty of water hazards and bunkers, built in 1958. Diplomat is the work of Red Lawrence, credited also with Desert Forest in Carefree, Arizona, and West Course, The Wigwam in Litchfield Park, Arizona.

Address: 3515 S Ocean Dr., Hollywood-By-The-Sea, 33019
Phone: 305-457-8111   800-327-1212
Innkeeper: Kent Olsen
No. rooms: 1001
Rates: $, Credit Cards: AmEx, Visa, MC, Other CC
Services: Valet, Barber shop, Beauty shop, Garage and parking, Car hire, Babysitting, Card or other game area, Room service
Restrictions: No pets
Restaurant: Celebrity Room
Bar: The Distillery
Business Fac.: Secretarial, Telex, Conf. rm. cap.: 4,000
Sports Fac.: Pool, Tennis, Sailing, Full Health Spa
Location: Broward County
Attractions: Race Track, Miami Seaquarium, Everglade Safary

Course: The Diplomat Country Club
Distance: 6,625, Par: 72
Rating: 70.6, No. of holes: 18
Guest Policy: Call for availability, Dress code
Phone Club-House: 305-457-8111
Pro's name: Nick Bersan
Reservations: May be made any time
Season: Year round
Guest Carry Club: No

Mission Inn Golf & Tennis Resort

Address: Box 441,
Howey-In-The-Hills, 32737
Phone: 904-324-3101   800-874-9053
Innkeeper: Bob Beucher
No. rooms: 147
Rates: $, Credit Cards: AmEx,
Visa, MC, Other CC
Services: Valet, Garage and parking,
Car hire, Babysitting, Card or other
game area, Laundry, Room service
Restrictions: No pets
Restaurant: El Conquistador
Bar: La Margarita
Business Fac.: Secretarial, Telex,
Conf. rm. cap.: 350
Sports Fac.: Pool, Tennis, Sailing,
Fishing
Location: Lake County
Attractions: Walt Disney World, Sea
World, Cypress Gardens

Course: Mission Inn
Distance: 6,354, Par: 72
Rating: 70.1, No. of holes: 36
Guest Policy: Call for availability,
Dress code
Phone Club-House: 904-324-3101
Pro's name: Jim Muszak
Reservations: May be made one year
in advance
Season: Year round
Guest Carry Club: No

Would you like to know about a secluded, one-of-a-kind family-operated retreat? One whose staff remembers returning guests names, offers a full program of children's activities, and even maintains a restored 1930's river yacht for cocktail cruises? Mission Inn is the place. Its a country-inn hideaway, 45 minutes from Walt Disney World in the foothills of Orlando, and it happens to be sitting on one of Florida's largest lakes, bass-filled Lake Harris. Spanish in style reminiscent of Florida's early days, the Inn has 160 rooms, suites and condominiums. Fountains, gardens, birds and waterfalls line the covered walkways. From screened balconies, rooms overlook velvety fairways, tennis courts, towering palms, and placid Lake Harris. Guests gather at La Margarita for cocktails and conversation, while two dining rooms El Conquistador, and El Patio tempt diners with menus featuring continental fare. The Nineteenth Hole also offers lunch and dinner. What to do in a town called Howey-on-the-Hills? Start with fishing, sailing, speedboating, tennis, swimming, or relaxing after a workout in the spa.

This is an older golf course, still in excellent shape. Built in 1924 by Scottish designer, Charles E. Clark, it had a facelift in 1970 by Lloyd Clifton. Florida Mini Tour plays here twice a year, and the Tallahassee Open Qualifier sought this course recently, as did the Florida Junior Invitational. It is a hilly layout—with an 85 feet elevation difference tee-to-green. The fourth hole is billed as "Devil's Delight," with more obstacles than many courses claim on 18. Our favorite is number six, "Pine Valley." At 472 yards, it's a short but extremely tight par five which squeezes in even tighter as you approach the green. Lots of water frames the green, and numerous bunkers starting from 80 yards out create a bottleneck for the second shot. Thirteen of 18 holes have water, and the landscape varies from hole to hole—some are wooded, and some have an abundance of tropical foliage.

Indian River Plantation

Getting to this 200 acre friendly self-contained resort of secluded beaches, water sports, and great golf and tennis is easy. Drive about forty miles north of Palm Beach, cross the St. Lucie River, and follow signs to Hutchinson Island, OR have your private jet land at Stuart's Witham Field, OR if you're cruising the Intracoastal Waterway, check Nautical Chart #11472, proceed to Marker 229 and cruise in the St. Lucie Inlet. The Island has conveniences such as a bank, gourmet market, service station, and shops, yet, there are a plenty of diversions within a short distance, should you want to explore Florida's Treasure Coast.

Accommodations are in one and two bedroom suites, all with kitchens, balconies and ocean views. In addition, there's a new 200 room hotel adjacent to the full-service 77-slip marina.

The resort has five restaurants, ranging from the elegant Inlet, whose menu is devoted to International specialties and fresh fish, to the casual Emporium, a turn-of-the-century ice cream parlor.

Recreation at this old pineapple plantation centers on the outdoors—all sorts of water sports, swimming pools, dinner and day cruises, sailing and snorkeling. Marlin, sailfish, and wahoo abound in the ocean while pompano and flounder flourish in rivers, lakes and bays. Elsewhere on the Island are historical attractions, and a museum. Flanked by the ocean and a river, the island is a stopping-off place for migrating birds, and roving security patrols watch for injured fliers so they can be treated.

Those who like a less lengthy round will come back for more on the par 61, 4,042 yard short course designed by Charles Ankrom. River Course, and Plantation Course are both relatively flat (everything is in these parts), have terrific bunkering, undulating greens, ocean breezes, and seem to have water everywhere.

Address: 385 NE Plantation Rd., Hutchinson Island, 33996
Phone: 305-225-2700   800-327-4873
Innkeeper: Bill Pullen
No. rooms: 257
Rates: $, Credit Cards: AmEx, Visa, MC, Other CC
Services: Cable TV, VCR, Radio, Hair dryer, Wet-bar & refrigerator
Restrictions: No pets
Restaurant: Scalaways
Bar: Gilbert's Lounge
Business Fac.: Audio-visual, Fax, Conf. rm. cap.: 525
Sports Fac.: Pool, Tennis, Bicycling, Waterskiing
Location: Hutchinson Island
Attractions: Elliott Museum, Burt Reynolds Dinner Theatre

Course: River & Plantation Course
Distance: 4,042, Par: 61
Rating: 56.9, No. of holes: 18
Guest Policy: Open to hotel guests & members only
Phone Club-House: 407-225-3700
Pro's name: Bob Erikson
Reservations: Not accepted outside 24 hours
Season: Year round
Guest Carry Club: Yes

Longboat Key Club

Address: 301 Gulf of Mexico Dr.,
Longboat Key, 34228
Phone: 813-383-8821   800-237-8821
Innkeeper: David Glass
No. rooms: 224
Rates: $120.00, Credit Cards: AmEx,
Visa, MC, Other CC
Services: Valet, Library, Garage and
parking, Babysitting, Card or other
game area, Laundry, Room service
Restrictions: No pets
Restaurant: Orchid Room
Bar: Orchid Lounge
Business Fac.: Secretarial, Telex,
Conf. rm. cap.: 200
Sports Fac.: Pool, Tennis, Fitness
course, Biking
Location: Longboat Key
Attractions: Ringling Museum,
Disney World, Botanical Gardens

Course: Islandside
Distance: 6,890, Par: 72
Rating: 74.2, No. of holes: 36
Guest Policy: Call for availability,
Dress code
Phone Club-House: 813-383-8821
Pro's name: Jim Owen
Fees: $35.00, Carts: 22.00
Reservations: Hotel guest—2½ days
in advance
Season: Year round
Guest Carry Club: Yes

What was once a vision of circus king, John
Ringling, who had a view of Longboat Key from
his mansion on luxurious Sarasota Bay, is now an
island resort amid the many cultural and recreational activities of Florida's west coast. Wealthy
patrons attracted to the area created a burgeon-
ing real estate market, and the region became
a winter refuge for the affluent during the 20's.
It's off the beaten track, retaining its character
of decades ago, yet major attractions are within
easy reach.

The resort's chef, Charles Vosbrugh, is a member of the prestigious Chaine des Rotisseurs.

Sporting facilities include thirty Har-Tru tennis
courts, a swimming pool, and twelve miles of
unspoiled beach. Explore the deep as you are
searching for tarpon, kingfish, and cobia in the
Gulf. Sailors know these are some of the finest
cruising waters Florida offers. Don't miss shelling after a new tide, or birdwatching along man-
grove habitats, then return to your island via an
historical park such as Egmont Key or Desoto
Point. The resort is in a wildlife sanctuary, giving it an "away-from-it-all" atmosphere, while
affording simple, understated elegance.

You'll have a myriad of choices near the resort.
The sumptuous Ringling residence, the Museum
of the Circus, the remarkable architectural landmark housing his Baroque art collection. Care to
bet on the greyhounds? A short excursion to
St. Armand's Key reveals a fashionable community of stately homes, international shops,
restaurants, and galleries.

The two championship courses at Longboat Key
Club, Islandside Course and Harbourside Course,
rank among the top. Islandside overlooks the
Gulf of Mexico and offers a rolling, palm tree-
lined adventure of 6,890 yards. Designed by
Billy Mitchell, the par 72 "watery challenge" is
an acknowledged test of accuracy with long,
sinuous fairways threaded throughout lakes
and lagoons.

The par 72 Harbourside is a somewhat longer
layout providing a completely different golfing
experience. The course is wrapped around Sarasota Bay and cuts through a lush sub-tropical
jungle of live oak, sabal palm and strangler fig.
Sixty bunkers await the golfer who also has to
negotiate lagoons, canals and the bay itself.

Nearby is The Meadows Country Club in Sarasota, and The Palm Club in Palmetto.

The Doral

The sheer size, scope and pace of this ultra-posh sportsman's paradise bordering the Everglades is enough to boggle the mind. 650 rooms are in eight lodges, including a Corporate Lodge with separate check-in. Consider opulent restaurants, bars and lounges, 2,400 beautifully landscaped acres of tennis courts, a heated Olympic-size pool, an equestrian center, jogging, fishing, bicycling, volleyball and game rooms. Stay here and you'll have privileges next door at the new $28 million Doral Saturnia International Spa, a lavish Tuscan-inspired hedonistic pleasure palace where American techniques are combined with renowned therapies. And if you're yearning for the beach, head for the sister Doral on Miami Beach via shuttle. Don't overlook local attractions such as the Bass Museum of Art with a permanent collection of Old Masters and Impressionists, and the Miami Beach Garden and Conservatory, with its beautiful display of native flora. Art Deco lovers should streak for the southern end of Miami Beach, designated a National Historic District.

Golf is king here, and you have 99 holes including a par 3 executive course at your disposal. The Blue Monster is on everybody's list as the epitome of a challenging course. It's a watery, sandy, long expanse that is the site of the annual PGA Doral-Ryder Open. Billy Casper captured the title in 1962, and the list of winners includes Doug Sanders, Raymond Floyd and Jack Nicklaus. The 18th hole here has been consistently ranked as one of the toughest on the PGA tour, a par 4 unless you're bunkering it or al lago. Count on 22 lakes stocked with large-mouth bass, tarpon and a couple hundred Top-Flite IIs.

Address: 4400 N.W. 87th Ave., Miami, 33178
Phone: 305-532-3600   800-327-6334
No. rooms: 650
Rates: $$, Credit Cards:
Services: Guest and children activity program, Valet Parking
Restaurant: Clubhouse
Bar: Rousseau's
Sports Fac.: Tennis, Pool, Saturnia Intl. Spa
Attractions: Museum of Art, Miami Beach Garden-Conservatory

Course: Blue Course
Distance: 6,597, Par: 72
Rating: 70.4, No. of holes: 99
Guest Policy: Call for availability
Phone Club-House: 305-592-2000
Pro's name: Jimmy Ballard
Reservations: When you make resort reservations
Season: Year round
Guest Carry Club: No

Turnberry Isle Country Club

Address: 19735 Turnbury Way, Miami, 33180
Phone: 305-932-6200   800-327-7028
Innkeeper: Eberhard Linke
No. rooms: 117
Rates: $$, Credit Cards: AmEx, Visa, MC, Other CC
Services: Valet, Barber shop, Beauty shop, Garage and parking, Car hire, Intl. currency exchange, House doctor, Babysitting, Card/Game area, Room service
Restrictions: No pets
Restaurant: Monaco Dining Room
Bar: Monaco Lounge
Business Fac.: Secretarial, Telex, Conf. rm. cap.: 700
Sports Fac.: Pool, Tennis, Handball, Health Spa
Location: North Dade County
Attractions: Aventura Mall, Gulfstream Race Track, Jai Alai

Course: South Course
Distance: 6,985, Par: 72
Rating: 72.9, No. of holes: 36
Guest Policy: Call for availability, Dress code
Phone Club-House: 305-932-6200
Pro's name: Julius Boros
Reservations: No starting times
Season: Year round
Guest Carry Club: No

Where is there a lush, tropical island of waterways, pools, gardens, a helipad, an unrivaled marina, an extravagant health spa and Country Club? Where is this playground to the wealthy, these four soaring residence towers, and this intimate private hotel? It's all in a private, guarded refuge called Turnberry Isle Yacht and Country Club, along the Intracoastal Waterway in North Miami Beach.

The Country Club dining room, which overlooks the golf course is a favorite for American and Continental specialties, while the Yacht and Racquet Club prides itself on northern Italian and new American cuisine. If you're in the mood for dancing, the Celebrities Lounge has the stars and sounds, and the lively Discotheque is where you'll want to rock out.

Sporting facilities leave no whim unfulfilled. 24 tennis courts featuring four different surfaces are available, as well as a full European spa with Nautilus equipment. You may leave your boat (if its under 150 feet) berthed at the marina, or charter from a variety of glorious yachts, fully stocked and crewed for an unparalleled adventure on Florida's gleaming waters. Deep-sea fishing is just a marlin away, and water sports are featured on a private beach at the Ocean Club.

Adjacent to the Country Club is Aventura Mall, largest shopping center in Florida. Have a limousine whisk you to Jai Alai, nearby galleries and restaurants, or the ponies.

Julius Boros heads the Professional Golf staff which, combined with the climate and setting, make it the masterpiece that it is. Two of Robert Trent Jones' creations provide 36 challenging holes, featuring the largest triple green in the world. The South course has been the site of the Elizabeth Arden Classic and the PGA Senior Championship, as well as numerous celebrity and private tournaments.

Grand Cypress Golf Club & Villas

Orlando, barely more than a mid-size citrus center until Walt Disney's World and Cape Canaveral were launched, is more than the fantasy kingdom that attracts over 25 million visitors annually. Easily, accessible, Orlando's attractions are diverse, well-planned and aesthetically pleasing. The recipient of numerous accolades and awards, this 1500-acre resort offers lodging options in a 750-room Hyatt Regency, and two and four bedroom Mediterranean-style villas nestled among the waterways and fairways. A tour of the extensive grounds turns up a 21-acre lake fringed by a white sandy beach, an Equestrian center, a gargantuan swimming pool, a 45-acre nature preserve, an Executive meeting center, and four turn-of-the-century Belgian trolley cars to whisk guests around.

Guests can unwind in the Regency Health Club, or head for the racquet club which has both clay and hard tennis courts, two racquetball courts, and a proshop. No need to cook if you're staying in a villa. Restaurants run the gamut from the Black Swan in the Gold Clubhouse for steaks and assorted seafood, to Ballybunion, and the Clubhouse Lounge which features live entertainment often, and the Hyatt Regency has six other restaurants. Try The Hurricane Bar in Hemingway's for a tall cool one amidst memorabilia and photos of the late outdoorsman and author.

Drop in to the Morse Gallery of Art in Winter Park, a lovely neighboring suburb, for a glimpse of fine Tiffany stained glass, or sample the five course meal served in Elizabethan style (don't wait for a fork) while Romeo romances Juliet at King Henry's Feast.

Jack Nicklaus designed the courses, and his touch is evident on all 45 holes—shaggy mounds that define the terraced fairways and undulating greens, and visibility of target areas and hazards. The courses appeared in stages, with the North and South opening in 1984, followed by East's nine holes in 1985. The "New Course," an eighteen hole gem, was ready in January, 1988. This is also the home of the Jack Nicklaus Academy of Golf, an instruction center with three Academy holes, bunkers, greens and everything conceivable to aid novice and pro to put that small ball in that very small hole. The Academy retains the services of specialists in golf technology and psychological conditioning to help you to get in shape.

Address: One North Jacaranda, Orlando, 32819
Phone: 305-239-4700 800-835-7377
No. rooms: 798
Rates: $$$$, Credit Cards:
Services: Catering, Valet service
Restaurant: Black Swan
Bar: Hurricane Bar
Business Fac.: Audio-visual, Conf. rm. cap.: 200
Sports Fac.: Tennis, Pool, Health Club, Racquetball
Attractions: Disney World, Sea World, Spaceport USA

Course: "New Course"
Distance: 6,181, Par: 72
Rating: 69.4, No. of holes: 45
Guest Policy: Open to resort guests only, Dress code
Phone Club-House: 407-239-4700
Pro's name: Paul Celano
Reservations: One week in advance
Season: Year round
Guest Carry Club: Yes

The Breakers

Address: One South County Rd.,
Palm Beach, 33480
Phone: 407-655-6611   800-833-3141
Innkeeper: James G. Kenan
No. rooms: 528
Rates: $, Credit Cards: AmEx,
Visa, MC, Other CC
Services: Valet, Barber shop, Beauty
Shop, Car hire, International currency
exchange, Nurse, Babysitting, Card or
other game area, Room service
Restrictions: No pets
Restaurant: Florentine Room
Bar: Alcazar Lounge
Business Fac.: Secretarial, Telex,
Conf. rm. cap.: 1,200
Sports Fac.: Tennis, Pool, Croquet,
Full Health Spa
Location: Island of Palm Beach
Attractions: Deep sea fishing, Worth
Avenue shopping, Dog race

Course: West Course
Distance: 7,101, Par: 71
Rating: 70.1, No. of holes: 36
Guest Policy: Course open to
members and hotel guests, Dress code
Phone Club-House: 305-659-8470
Pro's name: Bill Arnold
Reservations: 4 p.m. 2 days
in advance
Season: Year round
Guest Carry Club: No, Caddies: Yes

Palm Beach has, for generations, been synonymous with the socially elite; the playground
of the beautiful people, and much of this life
centered around the grand old landmark, The
Breakers. Designed in the Italian Renaissance
style, the exterior, with its Belvedere towers
was inspired by Rome's Villa Medici. The main
lobby, accented by frescoes and vaulted ceilings
overlooks the Mediterranean Courtyard, resplendent with fountains and cascading plants,
resembling the inner gardens of an Italian villa.
The opulent Mediterranean and Venetian Ball-
rooms, off the loggias, provide the setting for
some of society's most elegant charity and debu-
tante balls. Built by millionaires in 1926, The
Breakers, with its Flemish tapestries, crystal
chandeliers and marble floors, sits on 140 acres
of rambling lush tropical gardens. Guests can
enjoy 19 tennis courts, a private beach with
cabanas, an Olympic-size swimming pool, fitness
center, patio bar and grill, dance studio, shuffleboard, table tennis, sailing, croquet, and a
unique kids' summer camp where boys and girls
aged 10–15 learn the basics of investments and
personal finance.

Donald Ross fans will be delighted with the
Ocean Course, designed around the turn of the
century. A short course with tight fairways and
small, elevated greens, this classic is home to
many amateur events including American
Seniors, International Seniors, and the Winter
Gold League and Breakers Seniors. It's also here
that many golf celebrities come for the Palm
Beach Golf Classic with 4 tour pros. #14, a figure
"S" hole uphill, is typical of Ross' designs, with
deep bunkers and small elevated greens. The
Breakers West championship course, a twenty-
five minute drive from the hotel, was originally
designed by Willard Byrd in 1971, and has
recently been updated by renowned golf course
architect Joe Lee. Situated in West Palm Beach,
players are promised more challenges, improved
drainage, and a re-designed #9. The new hole
has a distinct dog leg requiring a second water
shot onto the new three-tiered green. The
course wasn't changed dramatically, rather, the
original layout has been refined to give the
course more character and make play more
enjoyable. A new clubhouse featuring a golf pro
shop, an elegant restaurant, saunas and steam
rooms, bar and grill, is the ideal spot to relax
while overlooking the course.

Waterville Lake Hotel, Waterville, Ireland

Bali Hyatt, Indonesia

Tryall Country Club, Jamaica

Palm Beach Gardens Sheraton Resort

Here it is, the golf resort that has everything and then some. Serious golf aficionados and/or hedonists will think they've gone to heaven as they immerse themselves in this utopia that is invigorating, exciting, relaxing, and luxurious.

Sheraton's self-contained destination, set amidst towering palms on 2340 acres fifteen miles north of Palm Beach, is the home of the Professional Golfer's Association, with four championship 18-hole courses, pollution-free air and first-rate staff waiting to treat your mind and body with the best of everything.

Don't count on ordinary fare in the Explorers dining room, as Chef Vincente Garcia, a native of Spain, has discovered recipes from far-off lands that are both interesting and delectable.

Palm Beach County is the heart of croquet in this country, and the United States Croquet Association's home is here, claiming the largest facility in the western hemisphere. As the home of the Women's Tennis Association, the spirit of Martina Navratilova moves around the 19 Fast Dry clay courts. There's also racquetball, a Nautilus fitness center, and a white sand beach on a 26-acre lake.

Area activities include Jai Alai, polo, thoroughbred harness and dog racing, horseback riding and charter fishing boats. The fabulous shops of Worth Avenue are a short ten minutes from the resort, in case you forgot your tennis bracelet.

The four courses were designed by top professionals George and Tom Fazio, and legend Arnold Palmer. While each course is distinctive in design, the longest and most challenging is the par 72 Champion: Home of the Grand Slam, and the PGA Seniors Championships. Palmer gave it a Scottish personality with more than 100 bunkers, long Bahia grass valleys, and water on 17 holes, which provide hazards to test the most accurate shotmaker.

In addition to daily clinics, individual and group lessons, the resort is celebrated for its Three Day "Killer Golf School." Whether you're new to the game, or a seasoned veteran, this intense golf instruction, grouped by ability levels, is bound to improve your game.

Address: 400 Ave. of the Champions, Palm Beach Gardens, 33418
Phone: 305-627-2000   800-325-3535
Innkeeper: Stephen P. Stearns
No. rooms: 336
Rates: $, Credit Cards: AmEx, Visa, MC, Other CC
Services: Valet, Barber shop, Beauty shop, Parking, House doctor, Babysitting, Card or other game area, Room service
Restrictions: No pets
Restaurant: Explorers
Bar: Legends
Business Fac.: Copiers, Audio-visual, Conf. rm. cap.: 900
Sports Fac.: Tennis, Pool, Full Health Spa, Croquet
Location: Palm Beach County
Attractions: Burt Reynold's Dinner Theatre, Mansion Tours

Course: Champion
Distance: 7,066, Par: 72
Rating: 74.0, No. of holes: 72
Guest Policy: Guests & Members; non-members once a yr., Dress code
Phone Club-House: 407-627-1800
Pro's name: T. Antonopoulos
Reservations: Time of reservation–2 days
Season: All year
Guest Carry Club: No

Palm Aire Hotel & Spa

Address: 2501 Palm Aire Dr. N.,
Pompano Beach, 33069
Phone: 305-972-3300   800-327-4960
Innkeeper: Elisabeth A. Bludau
No. rooms: 194
Rates: $, Credit Cards: AmEx,
Visa, MC, Other CC
Services: Valet, Barber Shop, Beauty
Shop, Parking, Car hire, House doctor,
World class spa with all amenities,
Room service
Restrictions: No pets
Restaurant: Peninsula Dining Room
Bar: Peninsula Lounge
Business Fac.: Audio-visual, Fac,
Conf. rm. cap.: 500
Sports Fac.: Tennis, Pool, Racquet
Ball, Spa
Location: Broward County
Attractions: Harness track, Jai-alai,
Greyhound race, Fishing

Course: Palmaire Resort, Palms
Distance: 6,371, Par: 72
Rating: 70.1, No. of holes: 18
Guest Policy: Open to public, call for
availability
Phone Club-House: 305-972-3300
Pro's name: Tom Malone
Reservations: Nov-April, 2 days
in advance
Season: Year round
Guest Carry Club: No

Palm-Aire is a total destination resort, 1,500
acres big 45 minutes north of the Miami International Airport, with an emphasis on golf, tennis and a major world-class fully equipped spa.
There are 194 hotel rooms, each having a private
terrace, and 21 suites overlooking fairways.

The Peninsula Dining Room, romantic with
etched, lighted mirrors, and the Peninsula Bar,
mirrored with suede padding, set a tone of tropical opulence, and the Tiki Bar poolside is great
for unwinding after a day's activities. Amenities
include tennis courts, swimming pool, racquetball courts, a jogging trail, and use of the private
beach a couple of blocks away. If you opt for the
spa, plan to luxuriate in a sanctuary of total
rejuvenation from whirlpools, steam rooms and
saunas to massages and the hand-rubbed salts of
a loofa scrub.

You can tee up at any of three courses; Palms,
Pines or Sabals. Chosen for three Florida Opens,
and the Florida PGA in 1978, the courses are
first-rate. Palms course, was designed in 1960 by
William Mitchell, an early advocate of courses
designed specifically for women. #12 takes a
demanding drive, playing about 400 yards, with
water guarding both sides of the narrow fairway.
Second shot is played into a long narrow green
surrounded by water and trapped on both sides.
Pines is a shorter course, ranked one of the
country's best public courses, and Sabals at 3401
yards is an unintimidating "executive course"
with all par 3's and 4's.

Marriott at Sawgrass

Here on the white beaches of northern Florida, where sugary dunes are covered with tall sawgrass, wild flowers and sea oats, Marriott presides over a special world of golf and tennis. 650 rooms, plus beach and golf villas overlook a lake or golf course, and the windows actually open! You'll have miles of beach to explore, several swimming pools, and two excellent restaurants. For cocktails, try Cascades in the lobby or Champs, offering live entertainment nightly. The Cabana Club Restaurant serves fresh seafood for lunch or dinner, and for breakfast and lunch you have 4 golf club dining rooms from which to choose. You can play tennis, work out, swing a croquet mallet, ride horseback, fish in 350 acres of lakes stocked for fishing, or charter a boat at a nearby marina. Shopping at Sawgrass Village will certainly help the economy. Jacksonville's International Airport is 37 miles north. If you love challenges on the course, you'll find them here, especially when the winds pick up. There are 99 holes of championship golf, including the famous par 3, 17th floating hole of the PGA Tournament Player's Club. This is the original stadium course designed by Pete Dye. The new TPC Valley Course, with hills, mounds, elevated greens and expansive waste areas is rated as one of the all-time great courses. There's also Ed Seay's Marsh Landing Course, and his Oceanside Course, plus Oak Bridge. This short and narrow course is the most forgiving. Good luck!

Address: P.O. Box 600, Ponte Vedra Beach, 32082
Phone: 904-285-2261   800-874-7547
No. rooms: 650
Services: "Marsh Monsters" and "Grasshopper Gang"— Children's programs.
Restaurant: Augustine Room, Cabana Club
Bar: Champs
Business Fac.: Conf. rm. cap.: 700
Sports Fac.: Pools, Tennis, Croquet, Horseback Ride
Location: Northern Florida
Attractions: Fishing, Sawgrass Village Shopping

Course: TPC Stadium Course
Distance: 5,761, Par: 72
Rating: 70.6, No. of holes: 18
Guest Policy: Must be hotel guest to play
Phone Club-House: 904-285-7777
Pro's name: Larry Collins
Reservations: May be made with room reservation
Season: Year round
Guest Carry Club: Yes

Burnt Store Marina Resort

Address: 3150 Matecumbe Key Rd.,
Punta Gorda, 33955
Phone: 813-639-4151   800-237-4255
No. rooms: 45
Rates: $85.00, Credit Cards: Visa,
MC, Other CC `
Services: Welcome gifts, turn down
service, complimentary newspaper,
Cable TV
Restaurant: Salty's Harborside
Bar: Castaways Lounge
Business Fac.: Audio-visual,
Copiers, Conf. rm. cap.: 250
Sports Fac.: Driving range, Boating,
Bicycling
Location: Charlotte Harbor
Attractions: Boca Grand island
excursions, Cayo Costa.

Course: Burn Store Marina
Distance: 5,809, Par: 60
Rating: 59.3, No. of holes: 18
Guest Policy: Call for availability
Phone Club-House: 813-637-1577
Pro's name: S. Johnston PGA
Fees: $10.00, Carts: 7.50
Reservations: Call for tee times
Season: All year
Guest Carry Club: Ltd

The Marina Inn provides one, two and three
bedroom condominiums with full service kitchens, private lanais, and comfortable living and
dining rooms. The real lure is the quiet sheltered
cove a few miles from the Gulf on Florida's west
coast. The password is uncrowded, as in
beaches, waterways, even the roads. With golfing, tennis, restaurants, fishing, and all sorts of
water activities, life proceeds at a slower pace
here. Salty's Harborside is the ideal spot for
dinner—try the catch of the day, shrimp, and
the melt-in-the-mouth key lime pie, as you
watch the dolphins play. Then move into the
Oar Room Lounge for live entertainment. The
Gasparilla Conference Center has the capacity
for up to 300. With the Gulf at your doorstep,
you can literally cruise the local scene. Visit
Cayo Costa, Cabbage Key and Boca Grand, or
charter a boat for deep sea fishing. Landlubbers
might want to visit Fisherman's Village with
over 40 boutiques and specialty shops.

The 18 hole par 60 executive golf course designed by Ron Garl is a flat layout with plenty of
water. You can visit the driving range or putting
green before teeing off, and lessons are available
from the pro. A second nine, par 29, was designed by Mark McCumber, also credited with
Dunes Country Club on neighboring Sanibel
Island.

Innisbrook

Hills? In this part of Florida? You bet. Innisbrook, sister resort of Durango's Tamarron, also operated by Golf Hosts, is a woodsy kaleidoscope of citrus groves, perfumed hibiscus, lakes and moss-laden pines. It's also a well-respected golf and tennis resort, plus it has a noted health and sports institute where professionals assess your overall athletic abilities, then tailor a program to help you meet your goals. The thousand acre estate is located a few miles south of the fishing and Greek sponge diving town of Tarpon Springs, on the Gulf of Mexico coast. Tampa International Airport is a 25 minute limousine drive away, and for those coming by Amtrak, Clearwater station is closest.

Guests stay in condominium complexes, the largest being a 2,000 square feet two-bedroom suite which can sleep up to six.

Tennis is big here, and the facilities are geared to the serious player, as well as we mortals who love a recreational game or two. 18 tennis courts, 11 of which are Vel-Play composition clay, and 7 faster, firm-surfaced Laykold courts are available. This is the home of the Australian Tennis Institute, featuring an individualized program of small-group clinic instruction. The large tennis and racquetball center has four racquetball courts, and a well-stocked shop carrying every accessory imaginable.

Catfish, blue gill and bass are stocked in the resort's lakes, and you can rent the rods needed to reel in the big ones. Other diversions include a fitness center, miniature golf, bicycles, 6 swimming pools, charter fishing and sailing, and a pretty beach just minutes away. Suggested area attractions include the Dali Art Museum in St. Petersburg, sports events at Tampa Stadium, the live sponge diving show at Spongeorama in Tarpon Springs, and shopping excursions to nearby St. Armand's Key.

Lucky is the golfer who can play all 63 holes here. Copperhead, rated the state's #1 course in 1986, is three nines. A tough tournament course, its fairways are bordered by towering native pines, with plenty of water coming into play. Sandpiper, shortest of the three, requires accurate iron play as each hole is well defined by bunkers and water. Island, first course to open, in the fall of 1970, is a par 72 hilly layout with many heavily wooded areas.

Address: P.O. Drawer 1088, Tarpon Springs, 34286
Phone: 813-937-3124   800-237-0157
Innkeeper: Susan Dunlop
Rates: $$, Credit Cards:
Services: Babysitting, Car hire, Beach Shuttle, Hair Salon, Tanning salon, Valet, Laundry, Safety deposit, Massage therapy, Room service
Restaurant: Copperhead Clubhouse
Business Fac.: Audio-visual, Typing, Conf. rm. cap.: 1,200
Sports Fac.: Tennis, Fitness Center, Pool, Bicycle
Location: Tampa area
Attractions: Fishing, Dali Art Museum, St. Armand's Key shopping

Course: Copperhead Course
Distance: 6,440, Par: 71
Rating: 70.8, No. of holes: 63
Guest Policy: Open to guests of resort, Dress code
Phone Club-House: 813-942-2000
Pro's name: Jay Overton
Reservations: May be made 48 hours in advance
Season: Year round
Guest Carry Club: No

Palm Beach Polo & Country Club

Address: 13198 Forest Hill Blvd.,
W.Palm Beach, 33414
Phone: 407-798-7000   800-327-4204
Innkeeper: Gary Avise
No. rooms: 135
Rates: $$, Credit Cards: AmEx,
Visa, MC
Services: Valet, Garage and parking,
Car hire, Intl. currency exchange,
comp. shoe-shine, House doctor,
Babysitting, Card/game area, Laundry,
Room service
Restrictions: No pets
Restaurant: Four dining rooms
Bar: Players Club
Business Fac.: Sec. Svc.,
Audio-visual, Conf. rm. cap.: 60
Sports Fac.: Tennis, Handball, Polo,
Health Spa
Location: Palm Beach County
Attractions: Worth Avenue, Dog
Track, Jai Alai

Course: Dunes Course
Distance: 5,516, Par:
Rating: 73.4, No. of holes: 45
Guest Policy: Call for availability
Phone Club-House: 407-798-7000
Reservations: Must be made
48 hours in advance
Season: Year round
Guest Carry Club: No

This is the international home of polo: we mean white breeches, mallets, 7½ minute-long chukkers and the Piaget $100,000 World Cup Championships. The Club is recognized as the international headquarters for the sport of kings, with ten polo fields, club house and an equestrian center. Guests stay in contemporary Florida-style condominiums with fairway of lake views, and have the use of a tennis center with 24 courts, (all three surfaces), two croquet lawns, numerous swimming pools and a full health spa. Additional amenities include rowing clinics, bicycle rentals, squash and racquetball. Three clubhouses scattered about the grounds house four dining rooms. Prince Watchers, be alert! Prince Charles has visited here four times, as have other assorted royalty.

Bring your credit cards because Worth Avenue is only 20 minutes away. The ocean is a half hour away, and the concierge will be glad to help you arrange a deep sea fishing excursion.

If you're coming for golf, you won't be disappointed. Three top designers have had a hand here. 1976 U.S. Open winner Jerry Pate teamed up with Ron Garl to design the Dunes—a Scottish style links course with treacherous pot bunkers, extensive mounding, grass traps and fairways full of swales and ripples. There's also Cypress Course by Pete and P. B. Dye. There's still another nine, the fabulous Fazio holes from 1978. Site of the PGA Chrysler Team Championship held annually in December, all 45 holes are in excellent shape.

Saddlebrook Golf & Tennis Resort

What was once orange grove in the lush Land O' Lakes area approximately twenty-five miles north of Tampa, and later a residential golf and country club community created by touring pro Dean Refram, is now a 480 acre world class golf and tennis resort. California contemporary in style, with shake roofs, manicured gardens, and paths meandering through gardens, the resort sprawls through countryside dotted with tall cypress, pines, palms, lakes and rolling hills. Guests stay in privately owned hotel rooms, and one and two-bedroom condominium suites clustered around the resort's Superpool.

Dining options include The Cypress Room, the charming lounge and greenhouse known as the Little Club, or the three tiered Polo Lounge.

Home of the national headquarters of the United States Professional Tennis Association, the tennis complex boasts a total of 37 courts; 27 Har-Tru (five lit for night play) and ten Laykold. The Superpool complex, the length of a football field, can't be ignored; it is practically a resort by itself. Surrounded by sundecks, and gardens, the free-form creation features racing lanes, a diving area, children's wading area and play area. Supervised programs for children are available during holidays and in summer.

The Jockey Club Health Spa lacks nothing. With separate facilities for men and women, guests have access to the latest equipment and amenities while following a personalized fitness program.

Busch Gardens is a 20 minute drive from the resort, with Cypress Gardens and its acres of botanical flamboyance approximately 40 minutes away.

The Saddlebrook Course and the Palmer Course are the resort's magnets. Saddlebrook, while not as hilly, was designed by Dean Refram and Arnold Palmer, and built in 1975. A swampy area naturally, the championship course utilizes water on 13 holes. Greens are large, with open approaches, and more than enough pine and cypress trees. Palmer's layout was completed in 1985, and as a par 71, players concur that with its rolling, undulating terrain, level lies are a rarity. Native Indian burial grounds are said to lie under several greens, an easy explanation for that four putt. Should you desire a thirst-quencher, a refreshment cart is usually within chipping distance.

Address: 100 Saddlebrook Way, Wesley Chapel (Tampa), 34249
Phone: 813-973-1111   800-237-7519
Innkeeper: Dick Boehning
No. rooms: 700
Rates: $, Credit Cards: AmEx, Visa, MC, Other CC
Services: Valet, Barber/Beauty Salon, Valet parking, Babysitting, Card or other game area, Laundry, Airline ticket office, Room service
Restrictions: No pets
Restaurant: Cypress Room
Bar: Polo Lounge
Business Fac.: Secretarial, Telex, Conf. rm. cap.: 1,800
Sports Fac.: Pool, Tennis, Full health spa, Fishing
Location: Tampa Bay area
Attractions: Busch Gardens, Walt Disney World, Cypress Gardens

Course: Saddlebrook Course
Distance: 6,642, Par: 71
Rating: 71.5, No. of holes: 36
Guest Policy: Call for availability, Dress code
Phone Club-House: 813-973-1111
Pro's name: Tom Cosmos
Reservations: May be made one week in advance
Season: Year round
Guest Carry Club: No

Stouffer PineIsle Resort

Address: Holiday Rd. Lk. Lanier
Island, Atlanta, 30518
Phone: 404-945-8921   800-HOTELS-1
Innkeeper: Jerry Phelps
No. rooms: 250
Rates: $, Credit Cards: AmEx,
Visa, MC, Other CC
Services: Valet, Library, Parking,
Car hire, Complimentary shoe-shine,
House doctor, Babysitting, Card
or other game area, Laundry,
Room service
Restaurant: The Gazebo
Bar: Champions Lounge
Business Fac.: Secretarial, Telex,
Conf. rm. cap.: 500
Sports Fac.: Pool, Tennis, Handball,
Sailing
Location: Lake Lanier Islands
Attractions: Horseback riding,
Twin-flume water slides, Beach

Course: Pineisle Course
Distance: 6,003, Par: 72
Rating: 69.8, No. of holes: 18
Guest Policy: Call for availability,
Dress code
Phone Club-House: 404-945-8921
Pro's name: Tommy Aaron
Reservations: The earlier the better
Season: Year round
Guest Carry Club: No

Just south of the Chattahoochee National Forest
in northwestern Georgia is sparkling Lake
Lanier, and Stouffer PineIsle Resort, a contemporary five story design, is perched in a lush
pine forest surrounded by this stunning recreational area. The lakeside setting provides a special opportunity for guests, particularly families,
to indulge in just about any recreational whim.

You'll find the food at PineIsle lives up to
Stouffer's fine reputation. The Pavilion charms
you with seafood and continental favorites while
you enjoy Lake Lanier's views. For an informal
setting, The Gazebo offers tempting selections
ranging from salads to heartier fare. The Club-
house Restaurant is the spot for a cold beer and a
mile-high sandwich after a round of golf or tennis. Kids will want to head for the great hamburgers and cookouts at the scenic Marina Grill.
You'll welcome the famed Southern hospitality,
and PineIsle knows how to serve it.

If you're an avid fisherman, or have fantasized
about Striped Bass, the creeks, quiet coves and
inlets of the deep clear lake are waiting for you.
Sailboats, dinghies, motor boats, you name it—
they're all available at an excellent marina.
Don't overlook water skiing, hiking, tennis,
horseback riding, and the twin-flume water
slides. An unbeatable white sand beach for
unlimited castle-building and a special Kids
Krew program ensure that children will have the
time of their lives.

Listed as one of Georgia's Top Ten, this 12 year
old scenic, tough course annually hosts the
Nestle World Championship of Women's Golf, a
tournament that pays the highest first place
money on the LPGA. Gary Player and Ron Kirby
and Associates designed the course, which is
very tight, with eight holes calling for drives
across sections of the lake. Hilly, rolling and
pine-scented, with elevated tees and views of
the lake and the Blue Ridge Mountains, the
course is 6,003 yards from the white tees. #5 is
similar in design to Pebble Beach's 18th—a long
drive over water, and the second shot is anywhere from a 160–250 yard shot with an inlet
guarding the front part of the green. What's
guarding the rest of it is more of lovely
Lake Lanier.

Pine Mountain Callaway Gardens

This is the spot for you if wildflowers, flamboyant greenhouse displays, a 175-acre fishing lake, quail hunting on a 1,000 acre preserve, and skeet and trap shooting appeal to you. Add sixty-three holes of golf, horseback riding, tennis, racquetball, and a smorgasbord of lakeside activities for all ages, three swimming pools, a choice of good restaurants, a variety of accommodations, and you have the ingredients for a memorable vacation in a horticultural paradise about seventy miles southeast of Atlanta. Pine Mountain is home of the famed Callaway Gardens, where hundreds of acres of gardens and woodlands bloom all year. Pathways weave through splashes of magnolias, azaleas, camellias, gardenias, rhododendrons, hollies, and special gardens cultivated with an array of indigenous trees and plants.

Spring is awesome here, but each season brings its own pleasures. A few items from the resort's calendar show water ski team exhibits, outdoor concerts, the Chet Atkins Country Gentlemen Golf Tournament, a Triathlon, a steeplechase, Beaujolais festival, traditional Thanksgiving feast, an antiques show, a "Country Christmas," and a festive New Year's Eve Dinner Dance.

Energy conservationists will want to check out the new 5-acre multi-million dollar John A. Sibley Horticultural Center, where collections of exotic plants blend into a climate-controlled setting to create a marriage of rich floral specimens and a two-story waterfall.

The names of the four golf courses are easy enough to remember: Mountain View, Garden View, Lake View, and Sky View, an easy-going 9 hole executive course. Mountain View is the Grand Daddy, with five National PGA Club championships, 2 Junior PGA tournaments, and 8 Celebrity Tournaments under its belt. The course rating is 71.4, giving one an idea of its difficulty, but no rating can be given the sheer beauty of fairways and wooded glens ablaze with magentas, roses and salmons of azaleas and rhodendrons in bloom. Gardens View course features bent grass year round on tees, fairways and greens. Lakes and streams characterize Lake View course, a par 70, 6,009 yard test where #5 is tricky. It's a short par 3 over a lake, but entrance to the green is blocked by bunkers, and the green.

Address: U.S. Highway 27, Pine Mountain, 31822
Phone: 404-663-2281   800-282-8181
Innkeeper: Ted Robison
No. rooms: 800
Rates: $, Credit Cards: AmEx, Visa, MC
Services: Beauty shop, Garage and parking, Car hire, Babysitting, Laundry, FOTO, Room service
Restaurant: The Georgia Room
Bar: The Patio Bar
Business Fac.: Secretarial, Telex, Conf. rm. cap.: 900
Sports Fac.: Pool, Tennis, Water skiing, Sailing
Location: Harris County
Attractions: Masters Water Ski Tournament, Azalea Festival, Shop

Course: Mountain View Course
Distance: 6,605, Par: 72
Rating: 71.4, No. of holes: 63
Guest Policy: Call for availability, Dress code
Phone Club-House: 800-282-8181
Pro's name: Jimmy Ballard
Reservations: Guest at resort play anytime
Season: Year round
Guest Carry Club: Yes

The Cloister

Address: Sea Island, 31561
Phone: 912-638-3611   800-732-4752
Innkeeper: Ted Wright
No. rooms: 264
Rates: Credit Cards: N, N, N, N
Services: Valet, Barber shop, Beauty shop, Garage and parking, Car hire, Babysitting, Card or other game area, Laundry, Room service
Restrictions: No pets
Restaurant: The Cloister
Bar: 4 bars
Business Fac.: Sec. Svc., Audio-Vis, Conf. rm. cap.: 450
Sports Fac.: Pool, Tennis, Croquet, Skeet & Trap
Location: On Atlantic Ocean
Attractions: Historic Retreat Plantation, Artists Colony, Shops

Course: Seaside Nine
Distance: 3,333, Par: 36
Rating: 35.9, No. of holes: 54
Guest Policy: Call for availability, Dress code
Phone Club-House: 912-638-3611
Pro's name: Davis Love, Jr.
Reservations: Day in advance, some season longer
Season: Year round
Guest Carry Club: No, Caddies: Yes

A massive fireplace and a grand piano set in a romantic Spanish-style lounge with chandeliered high ceiling and stained glass windows will greet your arrival at this exclusive island resort. Opened in 1928, The Cloister has maintained its historic charm of years gone by while providing all the modern amenities that guests appreciate.

Southern tradition is nowhere better expressed than in the food served here. An exciting Friday night treat is the plantation supper, lighted by torches and bonfire. Savor steaming clam chowder, hush puppies and picnic favorites Cloister style, to the music of the Sea Island singers.

Or, experience the expertise of chef Franz Buck in the luxury of a plush carpeted dining room overlooking gardens.

You can work off the dessert with an invigorating swim at the Sea Island Beach Club, or take advantage of the resort's 18 tennis courts. For a more relaxing sport, take a leisurely horseback ride on the beach and trails, or go boating the broad waterways beside River House.

Splashy azaleas, a quaint covered bridge, lagoons guarding tight fairways, sharply elevated greens, gargantuan deep bunkers, unpredictable ocean breezes, holes hemmed by marshes, an insouciant pelican gazing at your grip. These are The Cloister's 54 holes of legendary golf, which include four nines by four different architects at the Sea Island Golf Club, and an additional 18 at adjacent St. Simons Island Club.

Seaside Nine, opened in 1929, plays like the legend it is. #7, at 424 yards requires a powerful carry from the tee across 200 yards of tidal creek and marshes, then a tremendous bunker blocks a shorter drive to require a dogleg. Add a stiff Atlantic prevailing wind, and any birdie here will most likely be in the bush. Plantation Nine is characterized by sweeping fairways and the lagoon that lurks around four holes. Dick Wilson designed Retreat Nine in 1960, emphasizing huge lakes and the Atlantic itself which borders fairways. Marshside Nine was created to be wholly different, yet happily complementing the other Sea Island nines. The name tells you a lot about the layout. Here's hoping you learn about the marsh wrack and ghost crabs from the "Field Guide to Sea Island" instead of figuring out how to play out of it.

Kapalua Bay Hotel & Villas

Nestled in a 23,000 acre plantation on the west coast of Maui is Kapalua, one of Hawaii's most exclusive resorts. You'll get a taste of island luxury the minute you step into the hotel's grand, vaulted main lobby which opens to outdoor ocean vistas and tropical breezes.

Kapalua's variety of restaurants and gourmet menus featuring international cuisine and local specialties will please every palate. Below the hotel lobby, set amid a black marble waterfall and meandering waterways, The Garden offers everything from Maui's most tempting breakfast to gourmet dining with the sunset as its first course. Just a short stroll down the beach is The Bay Club, perched atop the promontory fronting Kapalua Bay. Here, spectacular ocean panoramas and outstanding island cuisine al fresco provide a most pleasurable diversion.

On land and sea, the sporting life is given high priority. Not only is there golf and a complete tennis complex at The Tennis Garden, there are also three secluded white-sand beaches at Kapalua where sailboating, scuba, surfing, and deep-sea fishing are available.

As if the resort's other amenities weren't enough, this is a golfer's Elysium. The Kapalua Golf Club comprises two championship courses illustrating the variety and diversity in the design work of Arnold Palmer and Ed Seay. The Bay Course, with lush tropical vegetation, and ocean vistas framed by historic Cook pines, rewards players of all levels. Village Course climbs higher in the hills, through eucalyptus and ironwood trees, past sparkling lakes and alongside ridges, then plunges dramatically into deep green valleys. A truly exhilarating visual feast, golfer's are often treated to the sight of whales cavorting in the strait.

The fifth is Kapalua's signature hole. The hole will vary in length depending on the tee used, and you may be hitting anything from an 8 iron to a fairway wood. While carrying the blue Pacific is first order of business, the green is well bunkered and offers varying pin placements.

This is the home of big-name tournaments, which the golfing staff handles with ease. The Isuzu Kapalua International happens here as well as The Nissan Cup and the 1987 World Cup of Golf. Golfing greats who have birdied and bogeyed here include Norman, Langer, Simpson, Crenshaw and Wadkins.

Address: One Bay Dr., Kapalua, Maui, 96761
Phone: 808-669-5656   800-367-8000
Innkeeper: Karl Rathgeb
No. rooms: 194
Rates: $$$, Credit Cards: AmEx, Visa, MC
Services: Valet, Barber shop, Beauty shop, Garage and parking, International currency exchange, Babysitting, Room service
Restrictions: No pets
Restaurant: Garden Restaurant
Bar: Bay Lounge
Business Fac.: Complete Conf. Fac., Conf. rm. cap.: 200
Sports Fac.: Pool, Tennis, Sailing
Location: NW corner of Maui
Attractions: Lahaina, Shopping

Course: Bay Course
Distance: 6,731, Par: 72
Rating: 73.0, No. of holes: 36
Guest Policy: Resort guests have priority, Dress code
Phone Club-House: 808-669-8044
Pro's name: Gary Planos
Reservations: One week in advance
Season: Year round
Guest Carry Club: No

Maui Prince Hotel

Address: 5400 Makena Alanui, Kihei, Maui, 96753
Phone: 808-874-1111   800-321-MAUI
Innkeeper: Chris von Imhof
No. rooms: 300
Rates: $$$, Credit Cards: AmEx, Visa, MC, Other CC
Services: Valet, Garage and parking, Car hire, International currency exchange, House doctor, Babysitting, Laundry, Yukata robes, newspaper, Room service
Restrictions: No pets
Restaurant: Prince Court
Bar: Molokini Lounge
Business Fac.: Secretarial, Telex, Conf. rm. cap.: 80
Sports Fac.: Pool, Tennis, Sailing
Location: Makena, Maui
Attractions: Kihei town, Haleakala National Park, Iao Valley

Course: Makena
Distance: 6,739, Par: 72
Rating: 72.2, No. of holes: 18
Guest Policy: Call for availability, Dress code
Phone Club-House: 808-879-3344
Pro's name: Lou Ishikawa
Reservations: May be made at any time
Season: Year round
Guest Carry Club: No

The dry leeward southwestern coast of Maui is the ideal spot for a grand luxury resort—and it's here—the Maui Prince Hotel, located in the 1,000 acre Makena Resort. Opened in 1986 and nestled in a secluded cover south of Wailea, the 300-room resort destination is a modern V-shaped structure of white tile and marble, accented inside with teak, brass and tropical foliage. A creation of Designers of Tokyo, the focal point is the inner courtyard, almost an acre in size, which artfully harmonizes local flora with a traditional Japanese watergarden. The lobby, cool, simple and elegant, is highlighted by massive displays of orchids and palms. Rooms and suites face the ocean, with a rose-toned motif.

Two of the hotel's dining rooms, the Prince Court, and the authentic Japanese Hakone, are listed in "Who's Who in American Restaurants." The chef's "Menu of the Evening" at the showcase Prince Court is an exercise in wonderfully innovative and eclectic fare combined with the freshest seasonal ingredients. An evening repast might begin with poached fingers of Opakapaka served on corn cakes with julienne of fennel and saffron hollandaise. For an entree, try the marinated loin of lamb served on grilled pumpkin squash with rosemary potatoes and blueberry relish. Assuming you are still with us, don't pass up the banana bread pudding with Jack Daniels bourbon sauce, and, to top it all off, why not sample a freshly made petit four?

This is sunbathing and swimming territory, with a long stretch of white sand beach fronting the hotel, and fairly good snorkeling grounds near the hotel. Horses are available to rent for an unforgettable beach ride, and the concierge can help you with plans for scuba diving, catamaran sailing, windsurfing, and nearby shopping. Bring your racquet, for you'll find six laykold tennis courts which have received *Tennis Magazine's* 5-star award. Or jump in one of the two swimming pools.

Robert Trent Jones, Jr. designed Makena Golf Course, which is built on volcanic cinder and winds around the hilly terrain. This is one of the most beautifully maintained courses anywhere, with 16 ocean front holes affording spectacular views of outer islands, narrow fairways and some fairly difficult uphill pitches between trees. The fast, velvety greens, often with the sparking ocean backdrop are not soon to be forgotten.

Mauna Lani Bay Hotel

Nestled in a 16th century ebony lava flow, this six-story 351 room resort, is the newest of the great golf and tennis destinations along this breathtaking coast. The atrium lobby is the most incredible feature, with six stories of lush rain forest foliage, waterfalls and a fish-filled lagoon. Acres of King Kamehameha I's ancient spring-fed fishponds and gardens provide solitude, picnic grounds and even a private swimming hole. 15th century rock shelters were left untouched during construction.

Ocean and mountain views highlight large light rooms, decorated in tones of burgundy and ivory. The Third Floor is the signature restaurant here. Opening onto a seaside garden, the casually elegant award-winner boasts one of Hawaii's most extensive and impressive wine cellars. Don't miss the famous escargot soup. The other eateries, too, deserve applause.

Flanked by the island's four great mountains, the showpiece resort's recreational facilities are excellent. The Racquet Club has two grass courts and 6 plexi-plave outdoor courts, while the Tennis Garden, with a five star rating, has ten 3 speed outdoor courts. A large freeform pool, and jogging and bike trails are guaranteed to tempt a confirmed couch potato. The white sandy beach is slide show perfect, plus you can scuba dive, sail, fish for marlin, snorkel, or try an outrigger canoe.

The magnificence of the Francis H. I. Brown Course has moved players and naturalists to praise the vast lava sculpture whose green fairways snake through a treasure trove of ancient cave-homes, shrines and petroglyphs as well as the historic King's trail. The Homer Flint design, a 6,259 yard par 72, features four ocean holes, three lakes, 43 fairway bunkers, plenty of green traps, and a spectacular ocean shot from the 6th tee. A second 18 hole course is under construction and due to open in 1990.

Address: P.O. Box 4000, Kohala Coast, Is. of Hawaii, 96743
Phone: 808-885-6622   800-367-2323
No. rooms: 351
Rates: $$, Credit Cards:
Services: Medical clinic, Beauty/Barber shop, Hawaiian Quilting, Hula Lessons, Lei making, Weaving, Historic Tour, Hawaiian Massage Demonstration, Floral
Restaurant: The Bay Terrace
Bar: The Bar
Business Fac.: Audio-visual, Conf. rm. cap.: 600
Sports Fac.: Tennis, Pool, Windsurfing, Aerobics
Attractions: Mauna Kea, North Kohala Tour, Historic Tour

Course: Francis H. I. Brown
Distance: 6,259, Par: 72
Rating: 70.5, No. of holes: 18
Guest Policy: Call for availability, Dress code
Phone Club-House: 808-885-6655
Pro's name: Jerry Johnston
Reservations: Telephone for tee times
Season: Year round
Guest Carry Club: No

Westin Mauna Kea

Address: P.O. Box 218, Kohula Coast Amuea, 96743
Phone: 808-882-7222   800-228-3000
Innkeeper: Adi W. Kohler
No. rooms: 310
Rates: $$, Credit Cards:
Services: Clinic, Fitness center, Barber/Beauty shop, Beach Service Center, Safe Deposit Boxes, Room service
Restaurant: Cafe Terrace, Batik Room
Bar: Gazebo Bar
Business Fac.: Conf. rm. cap.: 180
Sports Fac.: Tennis, Pool, Volleyball, Snorkeling
Attractions: Helicopter tours, Archaeological sites

Course: Mauna Kea
Distance: 6,365, Par: 72
Rating: 70.7, No. of holes: 18
Guest Policy: Call for availability, Dress code
Phone Club-House: 808-882-7222
Pro's name: JD Ebersberger
Reservations: Call for tee times
Season: Year round
Guest Carry Club: No

A vision of Laurance Rockefeller, and now under the helm of Westin, this splendidly understated vacation destination welcomed its first guests in 1965, as the most luxurious hotel ever constructed in Hawaii. The renowned hotel sits on a hillside overlooking a white sandy beach and crystal waters. Landscaping and architecture are imaginative, with lofty palms towering over public areas where gentle breezes play. But what's most memorable here is the antique art displayed in public areas. A majestic seventh-century Buddha, Japanese tansu chests, and a remarkable collection of Hawaiian quilts are just a few of the treasures from Pacific Islands. Rooms are large, fanned by tradewinds, with attractive wooden shutters, wooden ceiling fans, private lanais, polished brick floors, and wicker furniture. Large floral lithographs in bright island colors by Hawaii's Lloyd Sexton inspire the decor. There are also 10 suites and 8 villas. Expect impeccable service, handsomely appointed tables and an innovative menu in the exotic, split-level Batik Room with its Ceylonese motif. There are five other restaurants, and five lounges scattered about the main building. Don't miss the weekly luau, with traditional roasted pig and local favorites such as guava and poi palau, and the music of Hawaii. There is excellent snorkeling, windsurfing and boogie boarding from the beach. And of course, a beautiful pool, thirteen tennis courts, and badminton courts. Also available are Lasers, and Scuba and deep sea fishing excursions aboard the resort's 58 foot catamaran. Try horseback riding, play volleyball, go hunting, or take a sightseeing helicopter trip and look down on the rivers of lava created by the Kiluea volcano. Or relax under a palm tree and ask yourself where else you can snow ski down a dormant volcano in the morning, and body surf in 75 degree clear water in the afternoon.

The Robert Trent Jones, Sr. 18 hole course is something to behold. Ready for play in 1964, the challenging course has won numerous awards. With lush grass growing on ancient lava that spills dramatically into the sea, the par 72 layout was recently toughened and softened, with four tees to challenge all playing levels. The spectacular par-three third hole carries 200 yards over the ocean from the blue tees. Hook it and you can kiss that little ball good-bye.

Kiahuna Plantation Resort

Devotees of Kiahuna, the beautifully landscaped low-key condominium resort on Poipu Beach's sandy shore, have more to rave about since Hurricane Iwa ripped through in 1982. The reef-sheltered beaches, long considered the garden island's best for snorkeling and surfing, are now three feet wider. The resort is plantation-style, with buildings no higher than the coconut palms, blending into the mature tropical gardens which were originally planted in the 1930's. Tropical decor, high ceilings, wooden shutters, rattan furniture and natural fabrics are blended to create a casual, tasteful atmosphere. Dining options range from barbecuing and picnicking to the casual Courtside Bar and Grill and Clubhouse Restaurant. The creme de la creme here is the luxurious Plantation Gardens, where seafood and local delicacies are served in the original charming 19th century plantation house. 10 tennis courts, a large pool with a snack bar and acres of gardens for strolling will keep you busy. Beach sports are fantastic here—if you've never snorkeled, it's a must. Waimea Canyon, a 12-mile long chasm more than 3,000 feet deep is a mind-boggler when viewed through a rainbow spanning the river below. Spouting Horn, and historic Hanalei, too, are worth a visit. Next to the resort is one of the best snorkeling and body surfing beaches anywhere. This is where everyone over 10 wants to be, and lava rocks have created a shallow pool for small children.

The course here is an 18 hole championship Robert Trent Jones, Jr. links course. It covers flat terrain and mingles with several important Historic Hawaiian village sites. A nicely maintained course, the fairways are bordered by lava gardens, and cloud-veiled Mount Waialeale, the world's wettest spot, serves as a backdrop.

Address: Rural Route One, Box 73, Koloa, Kauai, 96756
Phone: 808-742-6411   800-367-7052
Rates: $$, Credit Cards:
Services: Valet, Laundry, Children's program
Restaurant: Plantation Gardens
Sports Fac.: Tennis, Organized beach activity
Location: South shore Kauai
Attractions: Helicopter tours, Whale watching cruises, Shopping

Course: Kiahuna
Distance: 5,631, Par: 70
Rating: 67.5, No. of holes: 18
Guest Policy: Call for availability
Phone Club-House: 808-742-9595
Pro's name: Charlie Ortega
Reservations: May be made one week in advance
Season: Year round
Guest Carry Club: No

Hyatt Regency Maui

Address: 200 Nohea Kai Dr., Lahaina, Maui, 96761
Phone: 800-228-9000
No. rooms: 815
Rates: Credit Cards: AmEx, Visa, Mc, Other CC
Restaurant: Swan Court, Lahaina Prov.
Bar: Weeping Banyan
Business Fac.: Conf. rm. cap.: 1,400
Sports Fac.: Health Club, Tennis
Attractions: Whalers Village Museum, 55-foot catamaran

Course: Royal Kaanapali, North
Distance: 6,305, Par: 72
Rating: 70.0, No. of holes: 18
Guest Policy: Open to public
Phone Club-House: 808-661-3691
Pro's name: Ray DeMeno
Reservations: Up to 2 days
Season: Year round
Guest Carry Club: No

The Kaanapali strip of hotels, condominiums and cottage colonies was the first planned resort complex on Maui, home of the sweetest onions, biggest protea, and potato chips like no others. Now, more than twenty-five years later, its centerpiece, the Hyatt Regency, is nothing short of spectacular. Tourists flock in droves to gawk at the multi-million dollar's worth of Asian art adorning lobbies and promenades, swans gliding on tranquil waters, and 20 acres of Japanese and tropical gardens. The eye-popper here is a two-acre water garden that incorporates grotto bar, waterfalls, streams, pools, a free-form swinging footbridge, a 130-foot water slide and exotic birds everywhere.

815 luxurious rooms in subdued tones of peach, beige and mauve overlook this jungle kingdom. Recreational diversions include a 55-foot catamaran, health club, tennis courts, popular restaurants and a disco.

The strip hops with activity night and day. Jump on the complimentary Kaanapali trolley that serves the resorts, Whalers Village Museum, shopping complex and golf courses. Join bodies sunning, sip a mai tai in a dazzling Polynesian bar, or sign the kids up for a snorkeling lesson. Hula or go scuba diving, sailing, swimming or visit historic sites.

The Royal Kaanapali Golf Courses, North and South, offer a pair of 18 hole championship courses with sweeping ocean views, blue sky, emerald fairways, and green mountains dominating the verdant landscape. North Course was designed by Robert Trent Jones, the golf course architect who has had more influence over the game than any other man. Bing Crosby played the opening holes here in 1962, and its been attracting celebrities ever since. You'll find undulating elevated greens, and generous bunkers, reflecting Jones' tenet that a well-designed course should be difficult to par, yet easy to bogey.

South Course, an Arthur Jack Snyder design, can be even trickier, with its own quirky hazards. It's a gem imbued with Snyder's strategic approach to the game—narrow fairways and small greens. As it winds from sea to mountain, the player faces a variety of holes, probably the most challenging being the ear-piercing whistle of the turn-of-the-century sugar train whose camera laden sightseers haven't developed an appreciation for concentration on the game.

Hotel de Frade, Portugal

Hotel Dona Filipa, Vale do Lobo, Portugal

St. Andrews Old Course, Fife, Scotland

The Westin Kauai, Kauai Lagoons

This new resort on the Garden Isle is only a mile and a half from Lihue, county seat, and home of an operating sugar mill. Billed as a "world unto itself", the resort takes the form of towers and wings surrounding a circular Kubla Khanesque enormous pool with dramatic waterfalls spilling over marble walls, a crystal chandelier and five jacuzzis awaiting gleaming bodies. Rooms here are large, and number more than eight hundred, in addition to suites and 49 deluxe Royal Beach Club rooms. Decor is by Hirsch-Bedner, and features coral, pinks and off-white—all with views of beach, gardens, or the aquatic fantasyland unveiled below. Public areas are open, and evenings here around the lagoons resemble a lavish Hollywood production. Twelve tennis courts, racquet ball courts and a fully equipped European spa are guaranteed to help you work off the calories ingested in one of the many restaurants and lounges. Visit the Paddling Club for high-energy adult entertainment featuring videos and exciting sounds. If you happen to be car-less, you can opt for 19th century carriages drawn by Clydesdales, or cruise the 100 acres of lagoons and wildlife refuge in an outrigger canoe or a Venetian launch. Beach activities range from sunning and surfing to the usual sailing, snorkeling, scuba diving, and boogie boarding. But you'll probably want to don a designer bikini and watch the activity at what some statisticians consider the world's largest resort pool.

Jack Nicklaus is the Director of Golf here, where you'll find two eighteen hole courses making their debut in an incredibly picturesque setting. Kiele Course, nestled above the Pacific, is a stadium course created for tournament play. From the men's white tees, its 6164 yards, with lots of water. Hole #13 is a par 3 cliff-to-cliff toughie that's all carry across the pounding surf. Kiele touts many mesmeric vistas, and with time, it can only improve. The Kaui Lagoons Course was designed in the traditional links style, offers all levels of players the ultimate in shot-making opportunities.

Address: Kalapaki Beach, Lihue, 96766
Phone: 808-245-5050   800-228-3000
Innkeeper: Larry Scheerer
No. rooms: 847
Rates: $$$ Credit Cards
Services: Beauty/Barber Salon, Safety deposit boxes, Car hire, Valet and self-parking, Room service
Restaurant: Royal Boathouse
Bar: Verandah
Business Fac.: Secretarial, Conf. rm. cap.: 1,850
Sports Fac.: Tennis, Pool, Health Club
Location: Kauai Lagoons
Attractions: Horses and carriages, wildlife island tour

Course: Westin Kaui, Kiele Course
Distance: 6,164, Par: 72
No. of holes: 18
Guest Policy: Call for availability
Phone Club-House: 808-246-5061
Pro's name: Kim Worrel
Reservations: Guests—up to a month in advance
Season: Year round
Guest Carry Club: No

Sheraton Makaha Resort

Address: 84-626 Makaha Valley Rd., Makaha, Oahu, 96792
Phone: 808-695-9511   800-325-3535
Innkeeper: David Kochi
No. rooms: 189
Rates: $, Credit Cards: AmEx, Visa, MC, Other CC
Services: Cable TV, Radio, Smoke detectors, Handicapped (8 rooms)
Restrictions: No pets
Restaurant: Kaala Room
Bar: Lobby Lounge
Business Fac.: Audio-visual, Copiers, Conf. rm. cap.: 500
Sports Fac.: Tennis, Scuba, Snorkeling, Fishing
Location: Rural country side
Attractions: World famous surfing center

Course: West Course
Distance: 6,398, Par: 72
Rating: 71.7, No. of holes: 18
Guest Policy: Resort guests have priority tee times
Phone Club-House: 808-695-9511
Pro's name: R. Kiaaina, PGA
Reservations: Required, check with pro shop
Season: All year
Guest Carry Club: No

Heading out the Farrington Highway on the dry, leeward side of the island, about an hour's drive from Honolulu, you'll find one of the island's most stirring natural wonders, the Makaha Valley. Here on a magnificent plain, reposing in grandeur under Mt. Kaala, the highest peak on Oahu, is a golf and tennis getaway minus the hype of other areas. 189 guest rooms in clusters of wooden low-rise Polynesian-inspired architecture are enveloped by tropical vegetation and well-maintained lawns. History buffs will want to visit the beautifully restored Kaneaki Heiau, a 17th century chief's temple, complete with sacrificial altar and prayer towers. A large swimming pool, four tennis courts, and a croquet lawn provide on-premises recreation. Count on an abundance of beach activities and watersports, even though the ocean is a fair hike from the hotel. If you like to "hang ten," head for the Makaha surfing beach, where world famous surfing contests are held.

Host to the annual Ted Makalena Hawaii State Open in 1983 and 84, and the annual NFL March of Dimes Invitational, the William Bell championship course is practically an old-timer for the islands. Ready for play in 1969, the country-like setting has rolling hills, Bermudagrass greens, 107 bunkers, 11 water hazards, and dazzling ocean views. A note from the pro shop reads: "We do our best to accommodate resort guests *whenever* they want to play, morning or afternoon."

Kaluakoi Hotel and Golf Club

As Hawaii's last outpost, the "Lonely Isle," was practically ignored after missionaries in the eighteenth century settled. Then came the big pineapple operators and cattle ranchers whose heirs were responsible for preserving the wilderness, glorious west end beached, (often unswimmable) waterfalls and secluded valleys. While the island lacks public transportation and traffic lights, capuccino bars, and Elvis look-alikes hula contests, it offers some spectacular views of deep jungle valleys, good hunting, hiking and bumper stickers asking "Wouldn't you rather be riding a mule on Molokai?"

The 288 rooms, in one and two story clusters, plus condominiums, are furnished with rattan, and are cooled by the trade winds and ceiling fans.

A large free-form swimming pool, four plexipave tennis courts, shops, croquet, and restaurants and lounges are all here for your enjoyment. For a succulent, well-aged melt-in-your-mouth steak, try the Paniolo Broiler, where Hawaii's famous Kiawe charcoal imparts its flavor. And if you're on the run, hit the 15-kilometer jogging course, where the scenery, if not your pace, will leave you breathless. This is a marvelous spot for a meeting, as the facilities are well-maintained, and the resort can handle up to 300 in conference rooms. Exploring the oblong-shaped island can be in a rental car, by helicopter, van, or on the back of a mule winding its way down the steep cliffs to the Kalaupapa National Historical Park. See the Molokai Ranch Wildlife Park, where barbary sheep, Rhea, oryx, and other endangered species thrive in the dry brush.

The island might be slightly sleepy, but the Ted Robinson 18 hole championship course which opened in 1977 is no sloth. The course has hosted the Kaluakoi Open for four years, the Aloha section of the PGA High School State championships, and the Airline Executives tourney. Its an experience bound by seaside holes, and an inland sojourn where fairways fringe the open rangeland blending with virtually untouched wilderness. You might spot an occasional wild turkey or axis deer. #16 is a thriller—from the white tees it's 182 yards over a deep gorge for a par three. Contoured greens, deviously placed bunkers, and even lakes contrast with briskly low shrubs, and as your head comes up in the follow-through, you can see Oahu across the channel.

Address: P.O. Box 1977, Maunaloa, Molokai, 96770
Phone: 808-552-2555   800-367-6046
Innkeeper: Dale Stetson
No. rooms: 288
Rates: $$, Credit Cards: AmEx, Visa, MC, Other CC
Services: Parking, Babysitting, Card or other game area, Laundry
Restrictions: No pets
Restaurant: Paniolo Broiler
Bar: Ohia Lounge
Business Fac.: Audio-visual, FAX, Conf. rm. cap.: 300
Sports Fac.: Pool, Tennis, Croquet, Fishing
Location: Maui County
Attractions: Wildlife Park, Kite Factory, Island Tours, Fishing

Course: Kaluakoi Golf Club
Distance: 6,211, Par: 72
Rating: 70.5, No. of holes: 18
Guest Policy: Call for availability
Phone Club-House: 808-552-2739
Pro's name: Cliff Lawson
Reservations: Groups should book in advance
Season: Year round
Guest Carry Club: No

Sheraton Princeville Hotel

Address: P.O. Box 3069, Princeville, 96722
Phone: 808-826-9644   800-826-1166
Innkeeper: Fred Matti
No. rooms: 300
Rates: Credit Cards: AmEx, Visa, MC, Other CC
Services: Valet, Barber shop, Beauty shop, Garage and parking, Car hire, International currency exchange, Babysitting, Card/game area, Laundry, Room service
Restrictions: No pets
Restaurant: Cafe Hanalei, Hale Kapa
Bar: Ukiyo
Business Fac.: Secretarial, Telex, Conf. rm. cap.: 750
Sports Fac.: Pool, Tennis, Health spa, Croquet, Polo
Location: Kauai
Attractions: Waioli Mission House, Kilauea Light House

Course: Sheraton-Lake/Ocean
Distance: 5,378, Par: 72
Rating: 72.6, No. of holes: 36
Guest Policy: Resort guests have preferred tee times, Dress code
Phone Club-House: 808-826-3580
Pro's name: R. Martinez
Reservations: Up to one year in advance
Season: Year round
Guest Carry Club: Yes

High above the lava rock tongues which stretch to meet the pounding surf, with jagged mountains covered in lush blue-green vegetation as a backdrop, is a planned resort community encompassing a mixture of home, condominiums, and the 300 room Sheraton Mirage Princeville. The unhurried North Shore of Kauai is still an uncrowded fertile valley of taro fields, exquisite beaches, and wilderness areas. The self-contained premier resort has everything from top notch tennis, golf and athletic clubs to a rare chance to see some of the Pacific's seabirds at close range. The white sandy beach below is secluded and inviting, while surfers, windsurfers, scuba divers, sailors and snorkelers, too, will think they're in heaven.

Sightseeing is a big attraction here, and what sights! Hiking to Kilauea Point, under the protection of the US Fish and Wildlife Service, visiting Hanalei Valley Lookout to see endangered koot and stilt, helicopter flightseeing, trail riding or raft trips along the Na Pali Coast, checking out the shopping, polo matches, or the occasional hukilau all contribute to the haole's vacation.

Makai, meaning "toward the sea" Golf Course consists of four nine hole courses; Ocean, Lake, Woods, and the newest, which will eventually be a full 18 hole course, Prince Course. Home of the 1978 World Cup, the Kauai Open, and the LPGA Women's Kemper Open, these Robert Trent Jones, Jr. wonders have attained high marks in their 17-year existence, and as such, it is the only course in Hawaii to have been listed within the *Golf Digest's* Top 100 for the past fifteen years. #3 on the Ocean Course, a par 3, is world-renowned as an achingly beautiful sight, as well as a formidable one. Only 125 yards, with dense grass on the left, a green protected on the left side and rear by threatening sand traps, a placid lake in front, and a thicketed canyon beyond, the player prays for respite from looking for a wayward ball. Lake Course boasts ocean views, jungle caverns and plenty of water coming into play, and Woods Course heads inland, graced with regal Norfolk pines and rock garden bunkers. The Prince, operated as a separate course from the other 27 holes, will offer the golfer natural waterfalls cascading down behind a lush green, deep verdant ravines, jungle, rocks galore, ancient mango trees, and vision of a machete to hack one's way back to the fairway.

Elkhorn Resort At Sun Valley

A short distance from the world-famous winter playground of Sun Valley, lies Elkhorn Resort—secluded, yet accessible, family-oriented, yet fun and exciting. Elkhorn is like a college town—a self-contained community with every conceivable outlet for self-indulgence. With the mighty Sawtooths as a backdrop, the contemporary Alpine resort has 130 rooms, 12 suites and 136 condominium units. The swinging bar, the Lobby Lounge provides all sorts of entertainment and is a favorite meeting place all year. Tequila Joe's, Papa Din's and Jesse's, all on the premises, offer an array of tempting entrees for every kind of palate.

Five swimming pools, eighteen Laykold tennis courts, croquet, and a spa are among the recreational facilities. Nearby are stables and some great riding trails. Sailing, windsurfing, whitewater rafting, hiking and fishing in some of Idaho's most trout-blessed streams are here to be enjoyed.

This is an outdoorsman's Utopia. The Sun Valley area, part of the Wood River Valley, boasts some magnificent wilderness. Photographers, wildflower enthusiasts and bird watchers will have a field day in these parts, as will Hemingway aficionados. He lived in neighboring Ketchum, hunted in the area, wrote part of *For Whom the Bell Tolls* here, and is buried in the town's cemetery.

Past host to Idaho's Open, Danny Thompson Memorial, and Governor's Cup, the resort's golf course was built n 1973. Robert Trent Jones, Jr. designed this lengthy scenic treat nestled under majestic snow-capped peaks. Top rated course in Idaho. A very hilly course with a lot of water, antelope, fox, hare, and deer.

Address: P.O. Box 6009, Sun Valley, 83354
Phone: 622-208-4511   800-635-9356
Innkeeper: Michael White
No. rooms: 130
Rates: $, Credit Cards: AmEx, Visa, MC, Other CC
Services: Valet, Garage and parking, Card or other game area, Laundry, Day care for kids, Babysitting, Room service
Restrictions: No pets
Restaurant: T.J.'s, P.D.'s, Jesse's
Bar: Lobby Lounge
Business Fac.: Audio-visual, FAX, Conf. rm. cap.: 400
Sports Fac.: Pool, Tennis, Croquet, Skiing, Polo
Location: South Central Idaho
Attractions: Jazz on the Green, Music Festival; Mt. Baldy

Course: Elkhorn
Distance: 6,575, Par: 72
Rating: 73.2, No. of holes: 18
Guest Policy: Call for availability
Phone Club-House: 208-622-4511
Pro's name: Jeff Steuty
Reservations: May be made with reservations
Season: May 1–Oct.
Guest Carry Club: Yes

Sun Valley Lodge

Address: Sun Valley Rd., Sun Valley, 83353
Phone: 208-622-4111   800-635-8261
Innkeeper: Wallace Huffman
No. rooms: 600
Rates: $, Credit Cards: AmEx, Visa, MC, Other CC
Services: TV, VCR, Radio, Children's program, Clinics in tennis and golf
Restrictions: No pets
Restaurant: Lodge Dining Room
Bar: Duchin Room
Business Fac.: Complete Conf. Fac., Conf. rm. cap.: 1,500
Sports Fac.: Health Spa, Pool, Riding, Tennis
Location: Central Idaho
Attractions: Shopping Village, Hiking, Ketchem, Galleries

Course: Sun Valley
Distance: 6,057, Par: 71
Rating: 71.1, No. of holes: 18
Guest Policy: Call for availability
Phone Club-House: 208-622-4111
Pro's name: B. Butterfield
Reservations: May be made 7 days in advance
Season: April-Oct.
Guest Carry Club: Yes

Sun Valley was a vision of Averill Harriman, who wanted a ski resort accessible by train for the glamorous group of the thirties. Its still exclusive, still a challenge to reach, and enjoys a well-deserved reputation as a family resort with top-notch facilities. The Lodge itself is imposing, conveying an air of genteel luxury and understated elegance. Photographs of the beautiful people who have skied, wined and dined here line corridor walls, and you are aware that the aura of the Hemingway years still lurks. Guests stay in the lodge, an inn, or condominiums. While there are several bars around the premises, the favored one seems to be what returning guests lovingly refer to as the "Doo-Dah Room," known as the Duchin Room in the brochures. The Lodge Dining Room, wood paneled and sedate, serves fresh-from-the-stream trout, inspired desserts, and has an accompanying wine list considered impressive, with a lot of California treasures represented.

A Bavarian-looking mall adjoins the Lodge, offering a lot of irresistible shops and eateries.

The nonstop activities schedule gets an A+ in quality. Wine connoisseurs await the Sun Valley Wine auction every summer, and the month-long Music Festival attracts people from Europe. You might be lucky to be here for the big rodeo, or Wagon Days in nearby Ketchum. Everybody looks healthy and fit here, probably because they've been bicycling, running, swimming, ice skating, or gone to the spa. Or just breathed the clean mountain air. Hiking in the Sawtooths, and white water rafting are activities you won't forget. One can also ride horseback, play tennis or soak up the rays around one of three outdoor pools. Free buses shuttle guests to and from Ketchum, a five minute ride away, where the flavor of the Old West lives in its bars, galleries, shops and laid back attitude.

A round of golf here is visual delight. Originally laid out in 1937 by William Bell, and redesigned by Robert Trent Jones, Jr., the hilly terrain, surrounded by aspen and evergreen, offers unobstructed views of the mogul's mansions. This is one of the west's truly beautiful mountain settings, and has hosted the Idaho Governor's Cup, Danny Thompson Memorial Celebrity Golf Tournament, and numerous others. The fifteenth hole, a 244 yard par 3 is singled out as a challenger.

Eagle Ridge Inn & Resort

Looking for a conference center or family vacation spot a couple of hours from Chicago? Hoping for a quiet rustic retreat coupled with tennis, a lake for fishing and sailing, and two championship golf courses? Search no more. Check out Eagle Ridge Inn & Resort, perched on a bluff above a lake surrounded by rolling hills and valleys, an easy 2 hour drive from the Quad cities through bucolic Illinois farmland and towns.

Lodgings range from Inn rooms to 1, 2, and 3 bedroom resort homes scattered among the fairways and tree-covered hills, or townhouses. This is a year-round resort with a range of activities including hay rides nature walks, boating, horseback riding, and cross-country skiing when the time comes. During summer, a children's program offers swimming, arts and crafts, paddleboat rides, and special field trips. You'll find a fine restaurant, a couple of fitness trails, and an indoor pool with sauna and whirlpool in addition to a fitness center.

Galena, a historic lead-mining town, and once home to U.S. Grant, gives you a glimpse of midwest Americana in the 19th century. Visit Victorian mansions, cruise the Mississippi on an old fashioned paddlewheeler, tour a winery, or enjoy a performance at Timber Lake Playhouse.

Golf is two hilly courses with plenty of water, wildlife and isolation. This is no-hassle golf with long wooded fairways, plenty of sand, and courses in top-notch condition. South Course, newer of the two, is an award winner. An innocent meandering stream and thick groves of trees have prompted a time limit of 5 minutes to search for lost balls. Both courses are par 72, with two full service pro shops, full-time professionals, and a large practice fairway and green.

Address: Box 777, Galena, 61036
Phone: 800-323-8421   800-892-2269
Innkeeper: Barbara Hocker
Rates: $$$, Credit Cards: AmEx, Visa, MC, Other CC
Services: Children's program
Restrictions: No pets
Restaurant: Yes
Business Fac.: Audio-Visual, Conf. rm. cap.: 200
Sports Fac.: Tennis, Fitness Center, Volleyball
Attractions: Historic Tour, Mississippi River Boat, Winery Tour

Course: Eagle Ridge—North
Distance: 6,401, Par: 72
Rating: 70.9, No. of holes: 18
Guest Policy: Call for availability
Phone Club-House: 815-777-2500
Pro's name: John Schlaman
Reservations: 7 days in advance for the public.
Season: April–Nov.
Guest Carry Club: No

French Lick Springs Golf Resort

Address: French Lick, 47432
Phone: 812-935-9381   800-457-4042
Innkeeper: Gaston Correa
No. rooms: 485
Rates: $$, Credit Cards: AmEx,Visa, MC, Other CC
Services: Valet, Barber shop, Beauty shop, Garage and parking, Babysitting, Card or other game area, Room service
Restrictions: Pets ltd.
Restaurant: Hoosier Dining Room
Bar: Derby Bar
Business Fac.: Copiers, Audio-visual
Sports Fac.: Pool, Riding, Full Mineral Spa
Location: Patoka Lake Region
Attractions: Tour Kimball Piano Factory, House of Clocks Museum

Course: Country Club
Distance: 6,629, Par: 70
Rating: 70.0, No. of holes: 36
Guest Policy: Call for tee times, Dress code
Phone Club-House: 812-935-9381
Pro's name: Dave Harner
Reservations: Any time up to a year in advance
Season: Mar 15–Nov 15
Guest Carry Club: Yes

Indians, French, then American explorers followed ancient buffalo through this rich valley of mineral springs. French settlers, in the late 1660's, found their cattle benefitted by licking the mineral deposits at the springs—thus the name given to this part of the Indiana territory by Americans pushing westward. The current hotel, built in the early 1900's became an attraction for prominent visitors who came to take the cure and sip minerals, as well as the rich and famous who visited the opulent casinos and clubs to gamble. In 1986 new ownership acquired the adjoining villas and set about restoring the property to its original grandeur while adding new vitality and modern touches.

The grand lobby has come alive, and the mosaic floor and ceiling moldings, the seating areas overlooking the veranda, and the marbleized columns all recall an era of graciousness and quiet charm. Guests will find five full service dining rooms, and a high tea served in the lobby on Friday and Saturday afternoon. Today's European Mineral spa features a complete beauty and health regimen. Choose from eighteen a la carte treatments—from herbal wraps and facials to a relaxing mineral bath.

This is a popular place for conventions—because of the golf and tennis facilities, and because the Meeting Planners offer a Guarantee of Service. Recreational activities include an indoor and an outdoor swimming pool, croquet, skeet and trap shooting, and six bowling lanes. For video fans, the game room boasts 25 electronic video games and two pool tables. Settle in for an evening of dollar beer, popcorn and sports on the big screen TV. Riders can arrange for horses and a day on the scenic southern Indiana woodlands, and tennis players will be able to play on 10 lighted outdoor courts, or on 8 indoor-all lighted.

Golfers look forward to coming here for many reasons, and certainly the Country Club Course is high on the list. Designed by Donald Ross, architect of Pinehurst No. 2, and Oak Hill Country Club, site of the 1989 U.S. Open, this course is extremely hilly, with large undulating greens, and plenty of mature trees. It was here, on a course reminiscent of the Scottish links, that Walter Hagen claimed the 1924 PGA National Championship, and here that the LPGA Championship tournaments of the 60's were played. Valley Course, the other 18 holes is on more level terrain.

Marriotts Griffin Gate Resort

Situated in the heart of legendary bluegrass country, this gracious Lexington resort offers a unique alternative vacation destination. Surrounding Griffin Gate, thoroughbreds graze in lush pasturelands bordered by miles of white rail fences. A tranquil environment, punctuated by the excitement and intrigue of nearby horse-racing parks and world-famous thoroughbred farms are all part of what has been called the "Horse Capital of the World."

From the spectacular, five-story lobby of the main building with its dramatic fountain and cascading walls of water, to the charming, stately mansion that has graced the property for more than 130 years, everything at Griffin's Gate speaks of the romance of the past.

The Mansion, built in 1873, now houses one of the resort's many fine restaurants. Decorated in 19th century motif, with elegant chandeliers, fireplaces, and rich mahogany furnishings, dining at The Mansion is a classic experience. Begin a perfect meal with escargot and a Caesar salad. Choose Chef Rocco Valentino's Steamed Salmon with Strawberry Sauce as your entree. And finish with his irresistible New York Style Cheese Cake. Nothing could be more perfect

Complete sports facilities are available to all guests. And plenty of sightseeing attractions are nearby at Keeneland and the famed Kentucky Horse Park, home of more than two dozen breeds. There's also Shaker Village and scores of historic homes, including the Mary Todd Lincoln House, open for touring.

The adjacent Rees Jones 18 hole championship golf course which opened in 1981, annually hosts the University of Kentucky Johnny Owens Intercollegiate Invitational, and the Bank One PGA Senior Golf Classic. Players tell of a rambling, tree-lined layout with large rolling greens, long bluegrass fairways, more than 65 sand bunkers and water coming into play on twelve holes. The number ten hole is traditionally the beginning for the Senior PGA tourney—with out of bounds right and water to the left, what's left Arnie?

Address: 1800 Newtown Pike, Lexington, 40511
Phone: 606-231-5100   800-228-9290
Innkeeper: George Cook
No. rooms: 409
Rates: $$, Credit Cards: AmEx, Visa, MC, Other CC
Services: Valet, Barber shop, Beauty shop, Garage and parking, Car hire, Babysitting, Card or other game area, Laundry, Room service
Restrictions: Pets ltd.
Restaurant: Mansion at Griffin Gate
Bar: Pegasus
Business Fac.: Audio-visual, Telex, Conf. rm. cap.: 1,400
Sports Fac.: Pool, Tennis
Location: Fayette County
Attractions: Horse Park, Shaker Village, Natural Bridge

Course: Griffin Gate Golf Club
Distance: 6,019, Par: 72
Rating: , No. of holes: 18
Guest Policy: Call for availability
Phone Club-House: 606-254-4101
Pro's name: Dan Ruffing
Reservations: Can be made up to 1 year
Guest Carry Club: No

Chatham Bars Inn & Cottage

Address: Shore Rd., Chatham, 02633
Phone: 508-945-0096
Innkeeper: Paul Ronty Jr.
No. rooms: 150
Rates: $$, Credit Cards: AmEx, Visa, MC
Services: Children's activities, Library
Restrictions: No pets
Restaurant: Main Dining Room
Bar: Inner Bar
Business Fac.: Sec. Svc., Audio-visual, Conf. rm. cap.: 300
Sports Fac.: Pool, Tennis, Sailing, Windsurfing
Location: Cape Cod
Attractions: Deep sea fishing, Galleries, Shopping

Course: Chatham Bars Inn
Distance: 2,325, Par:
Rating: 61.8, No. of holes: 9
Guest Policy: Register to play, Dress code
Reservations: Same day except for groups
Guest Carry Club: Yes

Built in 1914 as a hunting lodge for a Boston family, the Inn has received guests continuously, retaining its tradition of service befitting an elegant seaside landmark. The weathered main inn sits high on a knoll and from the wide veranda, guests enjoy views of the Outer Bar and the Atlantic. The lobby and lounges sport soft gray walls, wicker furniture with chintz coverings, and palms in huge Chinese urns. A cozy bar, library, large dining room and a living room that is transformed into a dance floor after dinner, radiate from the lobby. Guests are housed in large traditionally-appointed rooms upstairs, or choose from 26 Cape-Cod style houses dotting the grounds. The guest rooms, recently redone in Laura Ashley soft colors, have fireplaces, antiques, rag rugs and porches overlooking the water so you can sniff that salty air. Awaiting you is a secluded private beach, five tennis courts, heated swimming pool, sailing, windsurfing, clambakes, and water activities for every age and interest group. The Inn is open year-round, and offers an American plan with a traditional menu in the main dining room, and a New England version of nouvelle cuisine in the refurbished Beach House Grill. Can you resist the likes of red pepper pancakes, lobster and seafood sausages? But wait until you sink your teeth in the doughnuts.

In 1914, seven years after Pinehurst Number Two opened, Donald Ross' nine holes here were ready for play. Definitely short, the 2,325 yards are quite challenging as the course winds through rolling terrain, with views of the harbor and the ocean from the 7th and 8th holes. Close to the Inn are two championship courses. Cranberry Valley, is a 1974 creation with credit going to Bornish and Robinson. A par 72 course, the 6300 yard layout is known for large greens and tees. Nearby in Brewster is a superb public course, aptly named Captains Golf Course. This award winning course was designed by Geoffrey Cornish and Brian Silva.

New Seabury Cape Cod

An hour and a half from Boston or Providence, on Cape Cod's southern tip, is a family resort comprised of privately owned villas and offering a fantastic New England vacation. From a few model homes begun in 1964, the community has evolved into a 2,000 acre premier recreational resort of where guests may opt for accommodations ranging from oceanfront suites, seaside villas or golf-front patio homes. Full housekeeping services are provided in all of the villas. Decor ranges from 19th century Nantucket style with antiques, wide plank floors and French doors to cool California contemporary. Most have exhilarating ocean and/or golf course views, and all are fully furnished. Restaurants are coordinated under the same management, and each caters to families. The Popponessett Inn is the essence of New England dining, specializing in traditional tureens of chowders, clam and oyster fritters, and succulent lobsters dripping in lemon butter. Who could resist the flavors at the Ice Cream Scoop, a dozen clams at the Raw Bar, or the intimacy of the Gallery?

There's something for every age here, starting with three miles of sandy white beach. Children's activities are numerous—should it be movies, a waterbug slalom race, or beach blanket bingo. Sixteen all-weather tennis courts and expert instruction, in addition to miles of jogging and bicycling trails, plus swimming pools and a health spa with Nautilus equipment add up to variety and healthy appetites.

Boutique shopping is popular during summer months, as well as the Sandwich Glass Museum, and nearby Heritage Plantation. Fishing excursions can be arranged, and the well-known outlets of the Cape are a short drive.

Golf here comes in the form of two championship courses, which are rated among of the best in the nation. Dubbed Oceanfront and Challenger, or Blue and Green, these 36 holes treat golfers to dramatic seascapes, manicured greens, salt marshes splashed with Rugosa roses and the misty expanse of Nantucket Sound. Thanks to the warming Gulf Stream, a Thanksgiving Day round isn't that unusual. Home of the New England Intercollegiate Championship, and the Massachusetts Mid Am Championship, the New Seabury Country Club was called the "Pebble Beach of the East," by Francis Ouimet, the 20-year old winner of the U.S. Open in 1913.

Address: P.O. Box B, New Seabury, 02649
Phone: 617-477-9111   800-222-2044
Innkeeper: Stephen V. Frisbee
Rates: $, Credit Cards: AmEx, Visa, MC, Other CC
Services: Garage and parking, Babysitting, Card or other game area, Laundry
Restrictions: No pets
Restaurant: New Seabury
Business Fac.: Sec., Audio-Visual, Conf. rm. cap.: 125
Sports Fac.: Pool, Tennis, Sailing, Nautilus
Location: Upper Cape Cod
Attractions: Popponesset Marketplace, Sandwich Glass Museum

Course: Oceanfront
Distance: 6,909, Par: 72
Rating: 72.7, No. of holes: 36
Guest Policy: Limited tee times for non-guests, Dress code
Phone Club-House: 617-477-9111
Pro's name: Daniel H. Coon
Reservations: 24 hours in advance
Season: May 1–Oct. 10
Guest Carry Club: Yes

Sugarloaf Inn Resort

Address: Sugarloaf/USA, Carrabassett Valley, 04947
Phone: 207-237-2000   800-457-0002
Innkeeper: Tor Brunvand
No. rooms: 136
Rates: $, Credit Cards: AmEx, Visa, MC
Services: Beauty shop, Garage and parking, Car hire, Babysitting, Card or other game area, Laundry, Room service
Restrictions: No pets
Restaurant: Seasons
Bar: Cirque Lounge
Business Fac.: Secretarial, Copiers, Conf. rm. cap.: 750
Sports Fac.: Pool, Tennis, Skiing, Full Health spa
Location: Maine Mountains
Attractions: Shopping, Hartford Ballet Residency

Course: Sugarloaf Inn Resort
Distance: 6,800, Par: 72
No. of holes: 18
Guest Policy: Guests at resort have preferred tee time, Dress code
Phone Club-House: 207-237-2000
Pro's name: Ken Everett
Reservations: May be made one week in advance
Season: Mid-May thru mid-Oct.
Guest Carry Club: Yes

For some, it's the superb skiing on Sugarloaf Mountain that draws them to the resort that includes 200 contemporary condominiums on the 100 acre high mountain property. For others it's the spectacular Robert Trent Jones Jr. designed Sugarload Golf Club. And there are those who come for exciting whitewater rafting on the nearby Kennebec River.

At the Seasons Restaurant, fine dining will be a special treat after a hard day of playing. Amidst spectacular views of Sugarloaf Mountain, you'll feast on prime rib and lamb. And be sure to order their most celebrated desert, Top of Sugarloaf. With a choice of 13 restaurants within the resort complex, there's sure to be something to please any appetite.

Besides golf, swimming, tennis, riding, and fishing are favorite pastimes at Sugarloaf. But for the ultimate adventure, one of the most popular and exciting experiences at Sugarloaf is whitewater rafting down the Kennebec River. For a relaxing wind down after all that activity, take advantage of the exclusive Sugartree Club, one of the most complete facilities of its kind in the East. The 15,000 square foot club features a 20' x 40' lap pool, four hot tubs, two racquetball courts, and a full fitness center that includes an ergometer and bicycle. The Club also offers certified aerobics and swimnastics.

For many who prefer a quieter, relaxing vacation, the mountain air and the peaceful atmosphere of Maine's wilderness are enough to keep them coming back again and again.

Two things come to mind when Sugarloaf Golf Club is mentioned—one is the striking mountainous setting, particularly in full autumn bloom, and the other is its award-winning design balance (how well the holes vary in length and configuration).

Robert Trent Jones Jr.'s wilderness golf course was literally carved from the Maine woods, resulting in spectacular holes that begin in the white birch and pine forests and play downhill. Vying for memorability honors is the par-four 10th hole that starts up high and plays up the throat of the Carrabassett River. This is wilderness golf, with the scent of pine wafting through the clear air, Crocker Mountain in the background, and holes separated from each other with tees sitting high above the greens.

Rockport Samoset Resort

The Samoset is a naturally beautiful four-story cedar resort hugging the Maine coastline in Rockport, about midway up the coast, 81 miles north of Portland. Its a region of offshore islands, heavily wooded forests, lobster traps and year-round recreational activities. 150 guest rooms, condominiums and suites with private balconies or patios overlook rocky seascapes or New England woods. The main lodge and outlying buildings are rugged looking, but interiors are comfortable and modern, with floor-to-ceiling windows affording remarkable vistas.

Marcel's Restaurant is known for relaxed dining, and at cocktail time, enjoy the Breakwater Lounge as the sun slips over the yardarm.

The Fitness center includes racquetball, an indoor and outdoor pool, whirlpools, saunas, Nautilus equipment, and a multi-purpose exercise room for aerobics. You'll also find hot tub, jogging trails, tennis courts, video game room, children's playground, shuffleboard, bicycle rentals and a lot of other diversions. The gift shop features locally made crafts, and sports accessories. Children need a vacation, too, and they'll be happy campers Monday-Saturday at Samo-camp.

While you may want to stay here endlessly, there are many attractions nearby. There's sightseeing and shopping in Camden, plus the Shakespearean Amphitheater, schooner adventures, charters and ferry trips to neighboring islands, and if you like lobster, this is the area to satisfy the craving.

The course was designed by Bob Elder, and was ready for play in 1972. With unrivalled views of sailboats and skiffs on Penobscot Bay, the seaside links has seven holes bordering the bay, and two double greens, a tradition borrowed from the Old Course At St. Andrews. The eighth and the fifteenth holes share a large green surrounded by bunkers on all sides, and the seventh and sixteenth have their flagsticks on the same green with the breakwater as a backdrop. Described as having the potential of becoming the "Pebble Beach of the East," return players note the addition of numerous bunkers over the past few years.

Address: Box 78, Rockport, 04856
Phone: 207-594-2511   800-341-1650
Innkeeper: James H. Ash
No. rooms: 150
Rates: $, Credit Cards: AmEx, Visa, MC, Other CC
Services: Valet, Garage and Parking, Card or other game area, Children's program, Room service
Restrictions: No pets
Restaurant: Marcel's
Bar: Breakwater Lounge
Business Fac.: Audio-visual, Conf. rm. cap.: 650
Sports Fac.: Pool, Tennis, Croquet, Full Health Spa
Location: Mid-Coast
Attractions: Out's Head Museum, Merryspring Gardens

Course: Samoset Resort
Distance: 6,008, Par: 70
Rating: 68.7, No. of holes: 18
Guest Policy: Call for availability
Phone Club-House: 207-594-2511
Pro's name: Bob O'Brian
Reservations: May be made with room reservation
Season: April–Oct.
Guest Carry Club: Yes

Shanty Creek-Schuss Mountain Resort

Address: Box 355, Bellaire, 49615
Phone: 616-533-8621   800-632-7118
Innkeeper: T. Schreiber
No. rooms: 650
Services: Babysitting
Restaurant: Lakeview Dining Room
Bar: Lakeview Lounge
Business Fac.: Audio-Visual, Conf.
rm. cap.: 1,000
Sports Fac.: Tennis, Health Club,
Pools, Bicycling
Attractions: Shopping Tours,
Cruises, Wine Tasting

Course: The Legend
Distance: 6,394, Par: 72
Rating: 71.5, No. of holes: 18
Guest Policy: Open to public, call
for availability
Phone Club-House: 616-533-6076
Pro's name: Thomas Weideman
Reservations: May be made
2 months in advance
Season: May–Oct.
Guest Carry Club: No

These two resorts recently merged to form a classy complex operated by Club Corporation of America, whose properties include Pinehurst Gold and Country Club, Seabrook Island, and Firestone Country Club in Akron. Bellaire is on northern Michigan's Gold Coast, known for rolling wooded country dotted with natural lakes and streams. Don't be put off by the number of accommodations and facilities—remember that this area isn't densely populated and developers worked hard to retain the open space. 650 rooms, suites and condominiums ensure lodging for everyone. Both resorts offer restaurants, extensive conference facilities, tennis courts and children's programs with a wide variety of activities.

Bring your hiking boots if you enjoy exploring the trails, as the area that's popular for skiing is even prettier on a summer day, and May brings mushroom hunts. You can fish on Lake Bellaire for perch, or try the trout streams or smelt dipping. Work it all off at the Health Club, rent a bicycle or plunge in one of the outdoor pools, or an indoor one if the weather's inclement. Families congregate for swimming and watersports at the private beach club on the lake, sometimes to discuss other nearby activities such as riding, skeet shooting, canoeing, paddleboat cruises, orchard tours, windsurfing and often to rehash that old Midwest favorite, a hayride.

Arnold Palmer joined with his partner Ed Seay to create the outstanding "Legend," one of his star creations. Playing the course is like walking solo in the north woods. There are no parallel holes, and each fairway is framed by mature pine and birch. Palmer described the course as "exceptionally pleasurable to play." Two other favorites are here—Schuss Mountain Golf Club, designed by Billy Diddel. Schuss has a marvelous clubhouse, the Ivanhof Restaurant.

Grand Traverse Resort Village

What state has the most golf courses? Michigan claims this distinction, and it is here, on the shores of Grand Traverse Bay, in northwest Lower Michigan that one finds a gem of a resort offering year-round recreational facilities. There are 750 guest accommodations, yet because it's bounded by a bay and two golf courses, a feeling of spaciousness and the pleasures of northern Michigan's forests make it most appealing as a family destination. Choose from suites, hotel rooms, or condominiums facing the bay or along the fairways of a championship course.

The Trillium restaurant offers regional American dishes and a magnificent view of the environs from its glass-enclosed 16th floor setting. The night comes alive in the Trillium Lounge, where live jazz and contemporary sounds round out a fun-filled day.

An indoor sports complex offers tennis and racquetball courts, swimming pool, and a total fitness center. Outdoor sports range from softball, volleyball, and tennis to a multitude of water sports. A lovely private beach is perfect for relaxing, playing with the children or watching the sailboards. Charter fishing expeditions can be arranged for you or your group, or maybe you'll want to test your prowess on a sailboat. Winter is magical here in the tranquil forests and hills. The resort's groomed cross-country trails are geared to all levels, or you can opt for five challenging nearby downhill skiing areas.

Jack Nicklaus' striking design of The Bear has Scottish touches. The tournament course offers a variety of terrain sculpted from the northern Michigan countryside, terraced fairways and gently tiered greens nestled among lakes, streams and cherry orchards. Home of the AAA Michigan Open, the Cadillac Cup, and the Jack Nicklaus Celebrity Pro-Am, The Bear is demanding. #3, rated as one of the best holes in the state, is a picturesque par 5 at 529 yards. With trees bordering both sides and surrounding the green, and a stream running in front, a long accurate shot is in order, should the player attempt to be on in two. Laying up in front of the stream will leave the player a short pitch shot that must carry both the stream and the large sand bunker. No two holes are similar, presenting a diverse array of targets. The Resort course, designed in 1978 by Bill Newcomb, joins The Bear, and at 6,176 yards offers challenging versatility on a gently rolling landscape.

Address: Box 404, Grand Traverse Village, 49610
Phone: 616-938-2100   800-678-1308
Innkeeper: Jim Gernhofer
No. rooms: 730
Rates: $$$, Credit Cards: AmEx, Visa, MC, Other CC
Services: Barber shop, Beauty shop, Parking, Car hire, International currency exchange, Babysitting, Card or other game area, Room service
Restrictions: No pets
Restaurant: Trillium
Bar: Trillium Lounge
Business Fac.: Concierge, Audio-visual, Conf. rm. cap.: 2,250
Sports Fac.: Pool, Tennis, Handball, Full Health spa
Location: Grand Traverse Bay
Attractions: Sleeping Bear Dunes Park, Interlochen Music Camp

Course: Bear Course
Distance: 6,440, Par: 72
Rating: 75.8, No. of holes: 36
Guest Policy: Guests have preferred tee times, Dress code
Phone Club-House: 616-938-1620
Pro's name: Ken Hornyak
Reservations: Guests may make 2 weeks in advance
Season: Mid-April thru late Oct.
Guest Carry Club: No

Boyne Highlands Resort

Address: Harbor Springs, 49740
Phone: 616-526-2171   800-562-3899
Innkeeper: Wes Swain
No. rooms: 600
Rates: $, Credit Cards
Services: Saunas, Jacuzzi
Restaurant: 2 Dining Rooms
Business Fac.: Sec. svc.,
Audio-visual, Conf. rm. cap.: 1,200
Sports Fac.: Tennis, Pool, Skeet,
Skiing, Trout Pond
Location: Northwest Michigan
Attractions: Hiking, Fishing, Charter
boat trips, Shopping

Course: Heather
Distance: 6,039, Par: 72
Rating: 74.0, No. of holes: 36
Guest Policy: Call for availability
Phone Club-House: 616-526-2171
Pro's name: Bernie Fidirich
Reservations: May be made with
room reservations
Season: May–Oct.
Guest Carry Club: No

The picturesque town of Harbor Springs, four miles from Little Traverse Bay and the shores of Lake Michigan, is the backdrop of this retreat, geared to all ages and interests. It's a casual place, lively in summer with festivals, art fairs and water-oriented activities such as regattas. The resort has touches of a quaint Austrian village, and the amenities today's vacationers seek. You will stay in single, double, family and studio rooms, or in an elegant suite. The Heather Highlands Inn, close to the main Inn, offers condominiums, and has pools, and meeting rooms. A full American plan is offered, always popular with families, and a highlight of summer evenings is the dinner performance of entertainment by Young Americans, complete with costumes, sound, lighting and staging. You can spend your time fishing, sightseeing in neighboring Petoskey, chartering a fishing boat, or playing tennis, swimming or unwinding in the sauna. A sister resort, Boyne Mountain is a short drive away, and offers a wide choice of accommodations, activities and diversions.

Between the two large resorts, golfers will eventually have a total of 90 holes. Not just golf, world class golf. Here, carved through forests of birch, maple, beech and cedar, players find undulating greens, tiered fairways, grass and sand traps, ponds, mounds and small lakes. Robert Trent Jones designed nine of Heather, an award winning par 72 course, and William Newcomb did the other nine. It's heavily wooded with blueberry marshes and ponds dotting your scorecard. Greens are vast—ranging from 7,000 to 10,000 square feet. This is a toughie to par. The Moor, also a par 72, plays a little longer with rather wide landing areas and fairways. Should you play at Boyne Mountain, you'll be teeing off on both courses at 1,400 feet and winding down a wooded mountain. Don't miss the Donald Ross Memorial Course, opening in 1989, along with a new clubhouse and driving range. Individual holes have been patterned after one of the Scotsman's most famed creations such as the 14th at Dornach, the 17th at Oakland Hills South, and the second at Scioto.

Turnberry Hotel & Golf Courses, Turnberry, Scotland

Turnberry Hotel & Golf Courses, Turnberry, Scotland

The Gleneagles Hotel, Auch terrarder, Scotland

Lodge of the Four Seasons

Why not a "treetop" getaway? Here, practically mid-way between Kansas City and St. Louis, is an extensive lakeside resort community with excellent recreation facilities. The Lodge overlooks Lake Ozark, and is surrounded by dramatic and intricate Japanese gardens, highlighted by cascading waterfalls. Buildings of stone, glass and wood blend with the surroundings providing sweeping views of densely wooded hills from porches and balconies. Secluded Treetop Village, accommodating up to eight people, is nestled high among the trees, and is available on a time share basis.

French and American fare is served in the white table-clothed Toledo Room, overlooking the lake. Other eateries include HK's for steaks, Casablanca for salads and burgers, The Fish Market, Ted's Cafe, Country Deli, or the Atrium for early morning croissants. The Fifth Season, with nightly entertainment, is a great place to see the action.

Water sports are big here. You'll have all kinds of boating, water skiing, fishing, wind surfing, and good old beach bumming. There's also bowling, billiards, horseback riding, trap-shooting and a jogging path. Tennis players are enroll in the Dennis Van der Meer Tennis University, which offers clinics, lessons and plenty of courts. The sports and social center has additional tennis and racquetball courts, and an indoor golf practice range.

If you're ready to toss the junk food, try the health and fitness evaluation laboratory. You'll receive a fitness prescription and guidelines for improving nutritional habits. You can take advantage of the property's many pools, tone up on all sorts of high-tech exercise equipment, or aerobicize till all hours at the racquet club.

Babysitting is provided, and a host of children's activities are geared for the younger set, such as cookouts, nature walks, and arts and crafts hours.

Golf here is courtesy of Robert Trent Jones' deft hand. The 18 hole course winds around a few lakes, and is quite hilly, and exceptionally colorful in the fall. Golfers praise the variety of holes here; valley ridges, and the lake coming into play, as well as scores of sand traps. Beware Witch's Cover, a 233-yard par 3 requiring a sorcerer's spell to carry the cove. There's also a clubhouse with a very good pro shop.

Address: Lake Road HH, Lake Ozark, 65049
Phone: 314-365-3001 800-THE-LAKE
Innkeeper: Mark A. Bowman
No. rooms: 350
Services: Full health and fitness center, Babysitting, Children's programs, Full service beauty salon, Massage
Restaurant: Toledo Room, Ted's Cafe
Business Fac.: Audio-visual, Conf. rm. cap.: 1,000
Sports Fac.: Tennis, Pool, Sailing School

Course: Four Seasons R. T. Jones
Distance: 6,100, Par: 71
Rating: 69.5, No. of holes: 27
Guest Policy: Lodge guests, members, property owners
Phone Club-House: 314-365-3001
Pro's name: Jack Coyle
Reservations: Call for availability
Season: March–Jan.
Guest Carry Club: No

Marriott's Tan-Tar-A Resort

Address: State Rd. K.K., Osage Beach, 65065
Phone: 314-348-3131   800-392-5304
Innkeeper: Bill Bennett
No. rooms: 1000
Rates: $, Credit Cards: AmEx, Visa, MC, Other CC
Services: Library, Beauty shop, Garage and parking, Car hire, Babysitting, Laundry, Card & game area, Summer camp for children ages 5–12 during, Room service
Restrictions: No pets
Restaurant: Windrose, Cliffroom, Oaks
Bar: Nightwinds
Business Fac.: Copiers, Audio-visual, Conf. rm. cap.: 3,750
Sports Fac.: Swimming, Tennis, Racquetball
Location: Lake of the Ozarks
Attractions: Antique shopping, Bridal Cave, Ha Ha Tonka St.Pk.

Course: Tan-Tar
Distance: 6,463, Par: 71
Rating: 71.6, No. of holes: 18
Guest Policy: Call for availability, Dress code
Phone Club-House: 314-348-3131
Pro's name: Roger Billings
Reservations: May be made 7 days in advance
Season: Year round weather permit
Guest Carry Club: No

Tucked in among the fingers of Lake of the Ozarks, near places such as Hurricane Deck, Tightwad, and Climax Springs, is a 420 acre playground carved into the hills where water sports and golf are given top priority. Approximately a three hour drive or a thirty minute flight from Kansas City, or St. Louis, this Marriott's offers 1,000 rooms, of which 250 are suites, in a range of choices. There are dining rooms, lounges, patios and poolside service catering to every whim, depending on the season. A Sunday brunch overlooking the Lake, and the romantic Windrose on the Water, specializing in fresh seafood are favorites with repeat guests. For children 5 years and older, an organized recreational program satisfies their cravings for arts and crafts, beach adventures, ice-cream-making and much more. Teens, too can make new friends and enjoy activities planned just for them including mini golf, beach and water volleyball, and video game contents. Evenings aren't dull at Tan-Tar-A; live entertainment awaits you at Nightwinds, and Mr. D's is perfect for a casual drink and watching sports on wide screen T.V.

A glance at the daily activities schedule shows such diversions as aerobic dancing, sailing lessons, teen bowling, nine-tap bowling, an evening excursion boat ride, and twilight tennis. A full health spa is available, as well as indoor and outdoor tennis courts, several swimming pools, jogging trails, fishing, horseback riding, and a variety of shops.

Golfers have two choices—the Hidden Lakes course, a hilly nine holes, and The Oaks, eighteen holes, and the newer of the two. The Club has hosted the Gateway Section PGA Championship in 1983, 1984, and 1985, the Big 8 Conference Championship, Missouri Tiger Invitational Tournament, and the 1988 NCAA Division National Championship. Hidden Lakes winds over the hills and through dogwoods, oaks, and cedars with plenty of water coming into play. The Oaks is enhanced by the beauty of thick woods, gentle hills and the sparkling backdrop of the lake. Demanding approaches, narrow fairways, large challenging greens, and well-placed hazards compel the golfer to concentrate on his game. #13 is tricky and memorable. It's a 413-yard par 4 with a narrow green, and a meandering stream which adds to the Ozark scenery.

Broadwater Beach Hotel

Drive along the tame water of Mississippi's gulf coast east of Biloxi, where the marriage of antebellum and high-tech recreation have produced a balmy sportsman's delight. Meet Broadwater Beach, a tropical garden of magnolias, camellias, wisteria, even a lily pond, surrounding a 360 room resort. Stay in a lanai room, garden cottage, or apartment, while enjoying the stretch of white beach and a complete marina. Biloxi is a shrimp town, and this is the place to feast on local versions of flounder stuffed with crabmeat, and gumbos galore. Restaurants and lounges serve a variety of specialties, and the Lanai Lounge is the Perfect place for cocktails, where bathing suits are proper attire.

Charter a boat if you'd like to go deep-sea fishing, or head for the pool, shuffleboard, badminton or volleyball. Six Omnicourts, lighted for night, will please tennis players, and those with shopping and sightseeing tendencies won't be left in the lurch.

Beauvoir, the last home of Jefferson Davis, is close, as are historic houses, Gulf Islands National Seashore, marine education center and aquarium, and scores of interesting and varied excursions via boats. Space cadets will want to see the NASA Space Technology Laboratories, where all Space Shuttle main engines are tested before launch.

There are two 18 hole courses here, plus a nine-hole, par 3 fun course. The Sea Course—recognized by lofty pines and loads of other trees—is a flat, tight layout, with a really big water hazard (called the Gulf). The Sun Course, a par 72, is more open, but don't be lulled into thinking there's no water. Word has it that the pros agree quietly to play the middle tees so they can save face. Fourteen of its holes traverse water.

Address: Biloxi, 39533
Phone: 601-388-2211   800-647-3964
No. rooms: 360
Services: Babysitting, Valet, Laundry, Barber shop, Beauty salon, Complete children's program (summer)
Restaurant: The Royal Terrace
Bar: Tack Room
Business Fac.: Steno, Audio-Visual, Conf. rm. cap.: 1,200
Sports Fac.: Tennis, Waterskiing, Volleyball
Attractions: Jefferson Davis Home, Bellingrath Gardens

Course: Sun Course
Distance: 7,200, Par: 72
Rating: 69.0, No. of holes: 18
Guest Policy: Guests, non-guests, members
Phone Club-House: 601-388-3672
Pro's name: Bob Lavacek
Reservations: Guests 6–8 mos., others 2 days
Season: Year round
Guest Carry Club: Yes

Big Sky Resort

Address: P.O. Box 1, Big Sky, 59716
Phone: 406-995-4211   800-548-4486
Innkeeper: John Kircher
No. rooms: 204
Rates: Credit Cards: AmEx, Visa, MC, Other CC
Services: Cable TV
Restrictions: No pets
Restaurant: Main Dining Room
Bar: Chet's Bar
Business Fac.: Audio-visual, Fax, Conf. rm. cap.: 500
Sports Fac.: Pool, Riding, Tennis, Bikes, Rafting
Location: Yellowstone country
Attractions: Yellowstone Park, Annual Classic Music Fest

Course: Big Sky Arnold Palmer
Distance: 6,115, Par: 72
Rating: No. of holes: 18
Guest Policy: Open to public and guests
Phone Club-House: 406-995-4211
Reservations: May be made at any time
Season: June through Sep.
Guest Carry Club: Yes

The late Chet Huntley loved Big Sky country so much that he retired from NBC to develop what he considered the "ideal resort": a complete mountain hideaway in harmony with nature's endowments. Surrounding the resort are the peaks of the Rockies—snow-clad and majestic at eleven thousand feet; lush meadows bursting with lupine and Indian Paintbrush, and alpine lakes and streams with enough trout to cause a traffic jam. Meadow Village and Mountain Village comprise the two main communities here, with accommodations for every budget at each. The Huntley Lodge, with 204 rooms, an elegant dining room, Chet's Bar, pools, tennis courts, game room and meeting rooms, is a hub of activity in the Mountain Village. A sunken lobby, gigantic stone fireplaces, natural wood interiors and floor-to-ceiling windows offering views of unspoiled pine forests project an informal mood. There are also condominiums and meeting facilities capable of handling groups as large as 600. Next to the Lodge is the Mall which houses the Lookout Cafeteria, several shops, night spots and three restaurants. You might want to head for Whiskey Jack's, the resort's hot spot, serving meals and snacks into the late hours, or catch friendly poker game.

Kids love it here. During summer, there's swimming, hiking, mountain biking, tennis, horseshoes, croquet, horseback riding, and the thrills of whitewater rafting. The scenic gondola ride gives a full circle tour of Big Sky's panorama, with nearby peaks in Yellowstone standing out. All ages will enjoy exploring the National Park, Lewis and Clark Caverns, Viriginia City and Nevada City, and Ennis, a must for art lovers. Late July brings the National College Championships in Bozeman, a first-class rodeo where SAT's don't count. Mid-November to mid-April is ski season with an average snowfall over 400″ of Rockies powder, with 40 slopes covering two separate mountains.

The Arnold Palmer Golf Course, built in 1975, sits in an alpine meadow at 6,500 feet. This is a relatively flat course, where you can't help but get the feeling of wide open spaces. Under jagged mountain peaks, its 6,748 yards meander around the West Fork of the Gallitin River, with water coming into play on six holes. You'll often see beaver, ducks, eagles, and an occasional elk as you pray for a birdie. There's a fully stocked pro shop in Meadow Village.

Grove Park Inn & Country Club

Built by hand out of boulders taken from Sunset Mountain and the surrounding area, The Grove Park Inn was modeled after the Old Faithful Inn in Yellowstone National Park which original owner Edwin Wiley Grove had visited. Today it stands as a monument to the past and a grand resort for present generations to enjoy. Set in the splendor of the Blue Ridge Mountains, natural beauty surrounds the 140-acre resort year round.

A collection of six extraordinary restaurants offers you a truly international selection of culinary delights. At The Blue Ridge Dining Room and Terrace, panoramic views and a glass-enclosed terrace set the proper mood, while Chef Zuberbuhler's fine creations will please your palate. Choose Fresh Mountain Trout of Lamb Chops "Provencal" as entree, and complete the meal with irresistible White Chocolate Mousse Cake. To satisfy a different taste, head for Dynasty.

An abundance of sporting activities are available to guests on the premises. Both indoor and outdoor swimming, seven Laykold tennis courts, and a full health spa are at your disposal. Riding, hiking, fishing, and whitewater rafting can also be arranged.

However, the many area attractions will probably be the highlight of your trip to historic Asheville. Take a tour to the world-famous Biltmore Estate, a 270-room castle with splendid gardens and its own winery. Visit Cherokee Indian Village, and adjacent to the inn, there's the Antique Car Museum and Biltmore Homespun Shops, where you'll see the dyeing, carding, and spinning of wool by hand.

Designed by Donald Ross, renowned Scottish architect of Pinehurst #2, the course offers challenge and diversity to any level player. Rolling hills, tree-lined fairways and winding streams coupled with strategically placed traps make shot placement very important. Some of the best par three's anywhere are here, and the ability to score is tested on how the player handles them. Formerly The Country Club of Asheville, the course has hosted numerous tournaments and exhibitions. Among the notables who have teed off here are Jack Nicklaus, Arnold Palmer, Gary Player, Sam Snead, Bobby Jones, Ben Hogan, Fuzzy Zoeller, Billy Casper, Doug Sanders, and Mickey Mantle.

Address: 290 Macon Ave., Asheville, 28804
Phone: 704-252-2711 800-438-5800
Innkeeper: Herman R. von Treskow
No. rooms: 509
Rates: $$, Credit Cards: AmEx, Visa, MC, Other CC
Services: Valet, Barber shop, Beauty shop, Garage and Parking, Shoe-shine, House doctor, Babysitting, Laundry, Children's program, Room service
Restrictions: No pets
Restaurant: Blue Ridge Dining Room
Bar: 3 bars
Business Fac.: Secretarial, Telex, Conf. rm. cap.: 2,200
Sports Fac.: Pool, Handball, Hiking, Health Spa
Location: Buncombe County
Attractions: Biltmore House, Chimney Rock Park

Course: Grove Park Inn & Co.Club
Distance: 6,172, Par: 71
Rating: 69.4, No. of holes: 18
Guest Policy: Call for availability, Dress code
Phone Club-House: 704-252-2711
Pro's name: Bill Krickhan
Reservations: May be made up to 60 days-advance
Season: Year round

Hound Ears Club

Address: Box 188, Blowing Rock, 28605
Phone: 704-963-4321
Innkeeper: David Blust
No. rooms: 27
Rates: $$, Credit Cards: AmEx, Visa, MC
Services: Valet, Beauty shop, House doctor, Babysitting, Card or other game area, Room service
Restrictions: Pets ltd.
Restaurant: Main Dining Room
Bar: Brown bagging
Business Fac.: Sec. svc., Audio-visual, Conf. rm. cap.: 60
Sports Fac.: Pool, Tennis, Skiing
Location: Blue Ridge Mountains
Attractions: Horn in the West Drama, Tweetsie Railroad

Course: Hound Ears Club
Distance: 6,015, Par: 72
Rating: 68.3, No. of holes: 18
Phone Club-House: 704-963-4321
Reservations: May be made 2 days in advance
Season: April 1–Nov. 1
Guest Carry Club: Yes

Hounds Ears. An intriguing name, an intriguing place. The name comes from a unique rock formation resembling huge ears that dominate the mountain ridge above the club. The Lodge has a cozy, intimate atmosphere, where the Blue Ridge Mountains of Western North Carolina seem to come right to the door. It's a rather small four-season resort, remote and secluded, yet offering an atmosphere where service and comfort are at a premium. Where the staff remembers your name, and your bed is turned down each evening.

Guests in the lodge will enjoy bedrooms opening onto balconies with panoramic views of the golf course and Grandfather Mountain beyond. Longer stays can be arranged for clubhouse suites, chalets and condominiums. The dining room is intimate, done in sea-greens and warm garden colors, but doesn't lack excitement when Gene Fleri plays the organ, and a staff of enthusiastic young people are serving tables. Rainbow trout so fresh it practically quivers is available most evenings, and the ice cream pie is decadent. Piano and organ favorites can be enjoyed in the lively Brown Bagg Lounge, and the dance floor is known as the hot spot of Blowing Rock!

Swimming at Hound Ears is an adventure not to be missed! Just finding the pool is a feat, but you'll understand why it's so remote. The huge rock grotto adjoining the pool and pavilion create a setting of unsurpassed natural beauty, no matter what the hour. Excellent stables and bridle trails, are located in Cone National Park, a few miles from the club.

This is antique and craft country, or if old railroads fascinate you, the Tweetsie is but a whistle stop away. Glendale Springs, famous for frescoes, is nearby, as is Crabtree, Tennessee, site of Roan Mountain.

Golf here is on one of the most interesting and scenic mountain courses in America. Water comes into play on seventeen holes—in the form of streams, lakes and rushing waterfalls. Expect a few hills, but its pretty flat for the area, and thirteen of the holes are dog legs. The 15th is extraordinary—a par 3 of 110 yards with a sixty foot vertical drop, and water everywhere! Four bunkers await your finesse with a sand wedge.

High Hampton Inn & Country Club

Originally the private summer home of the Hamptons, the High Hampton retains a proud history that goes back to the 19th century. Friends of the Hamptons enjoyed hunting, fishing, relaxing, and gracious hospitality on the 1200-acre estate when General Wade Hampton was head of the household. Today, guests from around the world are privy to their private get away hidden high in the Cashiers Valley of the Blue Ridge Mountains.

Under the protection of Rock Mountain and Chimney Top Mountain, the beauty of North Carolina has been preserved in this lush green valley. Even the way food is prepared is untainted here. High Hampton's menu features American cuisine with selected original recipes from their own kitchen. And fresh bread, rolls, muffins and biscuits are homemade, just as sure as the fresh vegetable and herbs that go into each dish are home grown in the Inn's own gardens.

You'll have plenty of opportunities to enjoy the beautiful outdoors. Not only is golfing plentiful, but there are eight fast-dry tennis courts ready for play. Sweeping vistas and a profusion of wildflowers enhance the joy of hiking on miles of well-marked trails. And water sports such as swimming, sailing, canoeing, rowing and pedal boating on Hampton Lake are always popular. Another favorite is fishing for rainbow trout, bass, and bream. With ample casting areas and a reputation as one of the best fly-fishing areas in the region, Hampton Lake is a mecca for fishing enthusiasts.

This par 71 course with bent grass greens is on a gently rolling plateau at 3600 feet in the Cashiers Valley of the Blue Ridge Mountains. It's a natural masterpiece with a different view of woods, or lakes, or mountains, or of all three, from every hole. And the pleasure of playing it matches its beauty—whether it's spring's blossoms and wildflowers, summer's azure skies or autumn's fiery colors.

A bird's eye view shows the 8th hole as a very narrow finger of land pointing far into a lake. Talk about a water hazard! A shot struck just a shade too lightly or a shade too firmly will drop not into the cup but into the water. The par 3, 137 yard jewel requires intense concentration. You try to ignore the sailboats skimming by like butterflies, but you don't dare admire the scenery until after you've negotiated it.

Address: P.O. Box 338, Cashiers, 28717
Phone: 704-743-2411   800-222-6954
Innkeeper: Tom Stilwell
No. rooms: 140
Rates: $$, Credit Cards: AmEx
Services: Valet, Library, Parking, House doctor, Babysitting, Card/game area, Laundry, Kennels
Restrictions: Pets ltd.
Restaurant: High Hampton Inn
Bar: Rock Mt. Tavern
Business Fac.: Secretarial, Copiers, Conf. rm. cap.: 300
Sports Fac.: Swimming, Tennis, Croquet, Sailing
Location: Jackson County
Attractions: Great shopping, many waterfalls and fishing

Course: High Hampton Inn
Distance: 6,012, Par: 71
Rating: 67.5, No. of holes: 18
Guest Policy: Call for availability, Dress code
Phone Club-House: 704-743-2411
Pro's name: Bonnie Randolph
Reservations: One day in advance
Season: Year round
Guest Carry Club: Yes

Hendersonville

Address: P.O. Box 2150,
Hendersonville, 28793
Phone: 704-891-7022   800-451-8174
Rates: $55.00, Credit Cards: AmEx,
Visa, MC
Services: Large rooms, Color cable
TV, Dressing areas
Business Fac.: Conf. rm. cap.: 75
Sports Fac.: Pool, Pro shop,
3 putting greens
Location: Asheville–45 minutes
Attractions: Peaceful countryside
near Blue Ridge Mountains.

Course: Etowah Valley Golf Lodge
Distance: Par: 72
Rating: 70.0, No. of holes: 27
Guest Policy: Open to public, guests
have priority
Phone Club-House: 704-891-7022
Pro's name: Hayes Albea
Fees: $18.00, Carts: 9.00
Reservations: May be made 5 days
in advance
Season: All year
Guest Carry Club: Ltd

This is a small (70 guests at a time) golf lodge.
All the rooms are the same—large, spacious,
each with a balcony overlooking the mountains
and fairway. The shingled buildings cluster
around a central lodge where breakfast and dinner are served. There are three putting greens,
(one lighted), driving range, heated pool, club-
house and meeting facilities for 75 people. As a
lodge guest you can enjoy the racquet and health
club facilities at a nearby club. The countryside,
between the Blue Ridge and Great Smoky Mountains, is fertile and heavily wooded. Spring and
fall are extraordinary, as soft blossoms become
lush green, then are ablaze with fall color. The
bent grass greens are probably some of the largest in the south—some as large as 9,000 feet, as
the course winds through rolling valleys. The
course is designed to eliminate ball crossover
from one fairway to another, insuring unin-
terrupted play. Golfers encounter a combination
of traps and natural hazards, such as meandering
streams and duck ponds.

The Eseeola Lodge

This part of Appalachia in the Blue Ridge Mountains is quite picturesque. And, should you be here in late June, you'll be visually assaulted by an incredible display of rhodendrons in bloom. This is a rustic old lodge with a great personality and modern facilities, all in tranquil surroundings. Most rooms have their own porch, and all are tastefully appointed. Days are warm and ideal for sports and relaxation, and at night you'll snuggle under a warm blanket. Bring your tennis racket, hiking boots, bathing suit and a hearty appetite for the exceptional food you'll be served. There's a luncheon room at the Clubhouse, a card room and a recreational program for children during July and August.

Linville's population hovers around the four hundred mark, but fear not, there are some gems to explore. Between Blowing Rock and Boone is the "Tweetsie," a narrow gauge railroad surrounded by a frontier-type village and small amusement park. The Museum of North Carolina Minerals nearby has more than three hundred kinds of gems and minerals found locally.

The 18 hole course was designed by Donald Ross, unequivocally the most prominent golf architect of his day, and one of the most respected. Dating from 1929, the course is one of the highest east of the Mississippi, at 3,800 feet. Burl Dale, the head pro, is available for lessons before or after you tackle the 6,286 yard challenge.

Address: Linville, 28646
Phone: 704-733-4311
Innkeeper: John M. Blackburn
Rates: Call, Credit Cards: AmEx, Visa, MC
Services: Electric golf carts, rooms with porches, sprinkler system
Restaurant: The Clubhouse
Sports Fac.: Tennis, Trout fishing, Pool, Hiking
Location: Blue Ridge Mountains
Attractions: Ideal for sports and relaxation.

Course: Linville
Distance: 6,286, Par: 72
Rating: 69.6, No. of holes: 18
Guest Policy: Open to guest of lodge.
Pro's name: Burl Dale, PGA
Reservations: 2 days in advance
Season: Mid-May–mid-Oct.
Guest Carry Club: No

Pinehurst Hotel & Country Club

Address: P.O.Box 4000, Pinehurst, 28374
Phone: 800-672-4644   800-334-9560
Innkeeper: Patrick A. Corso
No. rooms: 310
Rates: $, Credit Cards: AmEx, Visa, MC, Other CC
Services: Valet, Barber shop, Beauty shop, Car hire, House doctor, Babysitting, Card/game area, Laundry, Room service
Restrictions: No pets
Restaurant: Carolina Dining Room
Bar: Lobby Bar
Business Fac.: Secretarial, Copiers, Conf. rm. cap.: 600
Sports Fac.: Pool, Tennis, Croquet, Riding, Sailing
Location: Sandhills North Car.
Attractions: PGA World Golf Hall of Fame, historic tours

Course: Pinehurst, Number Four
Distance: 6,371, Par: 72
Rating: 71.5, No. of holes: 126
Guest Policy: Must be a guest in hotel to play, Dress code
Phone Club-House: 919-295-6811
Pro's name: Don Padgett
Reservations: May be made up to 60 days in advance
Season: Year Round
Guest Carry Club: No, Caddies: Yes

Nestled amidst the tall pines and oaks in the sand hills of North Carolina, the Pinehurst Hotel and Country Club has played host to business and recreation since it opened in 1900. Guests came then, as they do now, to experience the mild climate, the gracious lifestyle, fine dining and their favorite sports. Roosevelt, Rockefeller, DuPont and Morgan found it the ideal place to relax . . . and so will you.

Recreation is important; you'll choose from sporting options that include exhilarating horseback riding on 75 miles of beautiful Carolina trails, nine shooting ranges for trap or skeet, tennis amid the swaying pines on 28 top courts, sailing and boating on a private 200-acre lake, and a complete health club. Don't miss the Golf Hall of Fame.

To golf enthusiasts, Pinehurst is synonymous with the game, for here in the "Golf Capital of the World," are seven championship courses—among the finest in the world.

1. Laid out in 1899 by Donald Ross, Number One is tree-lined and very tight.

2. This celebrated legend, Number 2, features small, sloping greens, deep bunkers, loose sandy soil, and rough accented by "love grass."

3. A short (6092 yards) and sporty layout, Number 3 has the greatest variety of designs. The opening holes roll through hilly, forested terrain before opening into a more Scottish setting, complete with whins and gentle rolls.

4. The latest renovation to Ross' original design was in 1983, when Rees Jones made the course a "fairer test for high handicappers, yet still a challenging course for long hitters."

5. With new tees, bunkers and water hazards added to Ellis Maples' 1928 design, the 15th hole is perhaps the most pictured hole at Pinehurst.

6. Opened in 1979, this George and Tom Fazio creation is three miles from the main club and presents an entirely different backdrop and feel.

7. The newest addition to Pinehurst Country Club's family of courses, the par 72 beauty takes advantage of the rolling terrain and features native marshes and streams on several holes.

Green fees vary, and several courses have an additional surcharge.

Mid Pines Resort

Clarion Mid Pines is a full American Plan resort in a stately 66 year-old 3 story hotel flanked by the whispering pines and azaleas which have characterized this area for generations. About 70 miles south of Raleigh–Durham, it's a short 5 miles from the Moore County Airport. There are 118 rooms in the main building, which has a comfortable lounge, and a main dining room. A lovely luncheon buffet is served on the Terrace in warm weather. The Golf Course Villas, ranging from 1 to 10 bedrooms and overlooking the 10th fairway and green are the ideal spot for families.

A variety of shops in Southern Pines and neighboring Pinehurst invites browsers and serious shoppers alike. There are four lighted tennis courts, platform tennis, a driving range, practice greens, outdoor swimming pool, and an indoor game room within the resort.

The course was planned by Donald Ross, golf pro-turned-designer whose genius lay in his ability to adapt his expertise of the wet, windswept rugged links of Scotland to North Carolina's dry sandhills. His masterpiece at Pinehurst having opened in 1907, Ross laid out a narrow, tree-lined course in Southern Pines with small undulating greens. Mid Pines isn't particularly long or strenuous, but often the subtle undulations are difficult to read. The course has played host to several national championships, including the 1980 and 1985 Women's Southern Amateur, the 1986 Women's Western Senior Amateur, and the 1988 Women's Eastern Amateur.

Address: 1010 Midland Rd., Southern Pines, 28387
Phone: 919-692-2114   800-638-2657
No. rooms: 118
Restaurant: Main Dining Room
Business Fac.: Audio-visual, Conf. rm. cap.: 250
Sports Fac.: Tennis, Pool, Platform Tennis

Course: Mid Pines Resort
Distance: 6,500, Par: 72
Rating: 68.0, No. of holes: 18
Guest Policy: Open to hotel guests & outside play
Phone Club-House: 919-692-2114
Pro's name: Chip King
Reservations: Advised to book well ahead
Season: Year round
Guest Carry Club: No, Caddies: Yes

Mount Washington

Address: Route 302, Bretton Woods, 03575
Phone: 603-278-1000   800-258-0330
Innkeeper: Manfred Boll
No. rooms: 282
Rates: $, Credit Cards: AmEx, Visa, MC, Other CC
Services: Valet, Library, Barber, Beauty Shop, Valet parking, Car hire, Resident nurse, Babysitting, Card/game area, Laundry, Room service
Restrictions: No pets
Restaurant: Main Dining Room
Bar: Several
Business Fac.: Secretarial, Copiers, Conf. rm. cap.: 700
Sports Fac.: Pool, Croquet, Skiing, Riding, Hiking
Location: White Mountains
Attractions: Mt. Washington Cog Railway; Outlet shopping

Course: Mount Washington Hotel
Distance: 6,638, Par: 71
Rating: 70.1, No. of holes: 18
Guest Policy: Public welcome with advance tee time, Dress code
Phone Club-House: 603-278-1000
Pro's name: Dan Webb
Reservations: Day in advance
Season: Mid-May through Oct.
Guest Carry Club: Yes

Designated a National Historic Landmark in 1986, The Mount Washington has been host to princes, presidents and countless notables. Nothing could be more grand than this Spanish Renaissance inspired hotel built at the turn of the century. Ringed by Presidential, Dartmouth, and Willey-Rosebrook Ranges the 2,600 acre private preserve has maintained the elegance and graciousness of an era gone by. Step inside and you'll find a doric-columned lobby with soft couches beside a massive fieldstone fireplace.

In the octagonal Main Dining Room and in the opulent 1906 Room, the tradition of service with courtesy and style lives on. Here, the dinner menu—printed on an antique water-powered press—changes daily, but excellent selections from an extensive wine list and an orchestra to accompany your meal are always constants. Athletic pursuits are varied and plentiful. Their 12 red clay courts were the original site of the Volvo International Tournament. Today, the hotel offers a complete tennis program under the direction of Head Pro Tom Over. The tradition of riding remains at The Riding Place, a beautiful Victorian stables building, where trail rides, beginners' lessons and intensive combined training are available.

P.T. Barnum called the view here the "second greatest show on earth," and that's exactly what a round of golf is in the clean mountain air. Donald Ross, who comes in second in number of original routings among *Golf Digest*'s "architects of the 100 greatest courses," has left his mark on this championship thriller.

The Golf Club teems with history, including pros such as Lawson Little, Bill Melhorn and Dave Marr. In 1934 Little won *both* the British and the U.S. Amateur Championship, and then repeated the same feat the following year! While at The Mount Washington, he won the U.S. Open in 1940, defeating Gene Sarazen in a play-off. The 1965 PGA Tournament was captured by Dave Marr.

After you've learned to spell it, you can concentrate on staying out of the Ammonoosuc River. Holes #2 and #18 require a drive across this gift of nature, and local rules dictate a one stroke penalty should you blow it. The course winds around a fairly flat front nine, with a hillier finish. Who knows, maybe you'll find one of Thomas Edison's or Babe Ruth's balls.

Balsams Grand Resort Hotel

The Dix House opened in 1873 with a capacity of 25 rooms, and by 1918 was enlarged to "grand hotel" status. Today, the 15,000 acre private estate, with a traditional New England clapboard main building, comprises The Balsams. Located in the northern reaches of New Hampshire's White Mountains, the resort's known among many avid skiers as the "Switzerland of America."

Meals are served in the main dining room where glass chandeliers, lace curtains, linen cloths and mahogany furniture provide the perfect atmosphere to complement Chef Phil Learned's lavish meals. Don't miss his celebrated Veal Saltimbocca alla Romano with Bordelaise, and top it all off with his Chocolate Pate with English Cream.

Activities abound at The Balsams. Try your hand at fly fishing for rainbow trout in nearby Lake Gloriette, and have your catch prepared for dinner by the cooking staff. Or, explore the beautiful countryside along one of the eight Balsams trails that extend from 1.2 to 6.0 miles and range from a pleasant stroll to a rigorous workout. A nine-hole par 32 executive course, the Coashaukee, is very level and flat, making it a perfect place to practice with all your clubs. An unusually scenic 18 hole championship course, The Panorama, has perhaps the most magnificent setting of all the layouts by Scottish master, Donald Ross. Featuring teacup sand traps and bowl-shaped greens, the course affords spectacular views of the entire Upper Connecticut River Valley, Mount Monadnock in Vermont, and Quebec's rolling hills.

Nearly every shot, and especially one's putts, require that the mountainside setting be considered. Players swear their ball breaks up hill until they learn to orient themselves to the slope. Small to medium-size greens are hard to hit and hold, but Ross' bunkers serve more as definition and perspective aids than as difficult hazards. Today's layout is almost entirely intact from the 1912 design, although some of the original tee boxes are now designated as ladies tees, because the Scot designed this course to be only slightly over 6,000 yards. Every ability is challenged, and all fourteen clubs will be needed for even the best players. Play as much golf as you like on either course where it's free and unlimited while you are a guest at The Balsams.

Address: Route 26, Dixville Notch, 03576
Phone: 603-255-3400   800-255-0600
Innkeeper: W. Pearson & S. Barba
Rates: $$$$, Credit Cards: AmEx, Visa, MC, Other CC
Services: Valet, Library, Barber shop, Beauty shop, Garage and parking, Babysitting, Card or other game area, Laundry, Full resort amenities, Room service
Restrictions: No pets
Restaurant: Main dining Room
Bar: Le Cave
Business Fac.: Sec. Svc., Audio-visual, Conf. rm. cap.: 500
Sports Fac.: Pool, Tennis, Croquet, Skiing
Location: Northern White Mts.
Attractions: Antique shops, miles of very scenic country drives

Course: Panorama Course
Distance: 6,804, Par: 72
Rating: 74.5, No. of holes: 18
Guest Policy: Free & unlimited to guests of Balsams, Dress code
Phone Club-House: 603-255-3400
Pro's name: Gene DeMott
Reservations: 24 hours in advance advisable
Season: End of May–Mid Oct.
Guest Carry Club: Yes

Hanover Inn

Address: P.O. Box 151, Hanover, 03755
Phone: 603-643-4300
Innkeeper: Matthew Marshall III
No. rooms: 104
Rates: $, Credit Cards: AmEx, Visa, MC, Other CC
Services: Garage and Parking, Babysitting, Room service
Restrictions: Pets ltd.
Restaurant: Daniel Webster Room
Bar: Ivy Grill
Business Fac.: Audio-visual, Copiers, Conf. rm. cap.: 250
Sports Fac.: Pool, Tennis, Handball, Canoeing
Location: River Valley
Attractions: Dartmouth Hopkins Center, Hood Museum of Art

Course: Hanover Country Club
Distance: 6,019, Par: 70
Rating: 65.6, No. of holes: 18
Guest Policy: Hotel rep should call for tee time
Phone Club-House: 603-646-2000
Pro's name: Bill Johnson
Reservations: May be made 48 hours in advance
Season: May–October
Guest Carry Club: Yes, Caddies: Yes

This is the unspoiled Upper Connecticut River Valley, blessed with photogenic red farmhouses, fields of Queen Anne's lace and black-eyed Susans, panoramic views of green mountains, and almost unbelievable peace and quiet combined with a strong sense of the past. Founded in 1780 by General Ebenezer Brewster, the Hanover Inn occupies the site of his original home. Today's Inn, overlooking the Hanover green and the campus, is a modern, 104 room neo-Georgian brick structure, owned and operated by Dartmouth College. Emphasis is on the traditional—from the canopied beds and highboys to the arched windows and white linen, silver and crystal in the Daniel Webster Room. Menus include hearty New England dishes using regional ingredients, and an impressive and judiciously selected wine list, with offerings from around the world. The Terrace, for alfresco dining is open during warm months, while High Tea and cocktails are served in the Hayward Lounge.

Many guests like taking a picnic and exploring the Appalachian Trail, or fishing the waters of the White River. Cornish, approximately 18 miles south of Hanover, welcomes visitors to the home and gardens of Augustus Saint-Gardens, one of America's greatest sculptors, and the antiquing locally is worth the time.

The original nine holes at Hanover Country Club was designed in 1899, and later revised and expanded by Geoffrey Cornish and Bill Robinson, designers of noted Cranberry Valley in Harwich, Massachusetts. There's a lot to like about this collegiate course which has hosted state championships, NHPGA events, as well as its own tournament, the annual Tommy Keane Invitational best-ball honoring the late pro and coach. You may reserve a caddie in advance, or you can carry your own bag, and green fees are relatively low, with hotel guests receiving a discount off the weekday fee. An added attraction is the policy of waiving green fees if you book two or more weeks in advance and request the golf package. The Club has one of the most spacious practice areas in New England, including the old "four hole course" for beginners and lessons. The Ski-Jump Hole is the cornerstone of the four "gully holes." The #13 is a 350 yard par four requiring a very accurate drive to avoid "the office" on the left and "Pine Park" on the right. The tee is elevated, and the approach shot is hit into a well-protected green.

Marriott's Seaview Resort

In 1913 Philadelphia magnate Clarence H. Geist became disenchanted with having to wait to play a round of golf. He decided to build his own course, and the following year the first of his two golf courses opened, as well as the beginnings of his clubhouse. The location, easily accessible from New York and Philadelphia was key, and the quiet retreat for the affluent became quite popular. Today's guests marvel at the well-groomed 670-acre estate, four-story colonial style architecture with porte-cochere, stately lobby with oriental rugs and antiques, brick floored Grill Room, and the serene terraces overlooking Absecon Bay.

Traditional favorites are served in the Main Dining Room, which is decorated in soft green and pink pastels—all with a panoramic view of the fairways. Drop in to the mahogany-lined Grill Room for breakfast or a light snack, or the Oval Lounge with its lively piano bar, where a Transfusion comes in a tall iced glass.

Enjoy pocket billiards, ping pong or a game of five card draw in the classic game room. For recreation, the resort also has a 9-hole putting green, ten outdoor tennis courts (four lighted), an indoor swimming pool, paddle tennis courts, and a hydrotherapy pool. Guests are extended privileges at nearby Health and Racquet Club.

Historic Smithville with tours, shops and restaurants is close, as is the Brigantine Wildlife Refuge, the Lennox China factory, and Noyes Art Museum. The casinos and night life of Atlantic City are a short drive from here.

Serious golfers have always regarded Seaview as legendary. Two 18-hole championship courses, vastly different from each other, make this a golfing paradise. The Bay Course, site of the 1942 PGA Championship, is a Donald Ross "Scottish links" classic featuring windswept bunkers and panoramic seaside views. As with most layouts subjected to buffeting winds, it is relatively short in yardage and has wide openings at the front of the greens to allow run-up shots. The newer and more demanding Pines course, lined with 100 year old Jersey pines, oaks and splashy rhododendron, plays over and around a great maze of fairway and greenside bunkers. Greens are lightning quick, often undulating and do not accommodate poor putters. Due to the bay-front location, golf is available almost all year long.

Address: Route 9, Absecon, 08201
Phone: 609-652-1800   800-228-9290
Innkeeper: J. Richard Fetter
No. rooms: 298
Rates: $$, Credit Cards: AmEx, Visa, MC, Other CC
Services: Valet, Garage and parking, Car hire, Babysitting, Card/game area, Laundry, Room service
Restrictions: No pets
Restaurant: Main Dining Room
Bar: Oval Lounge
Business Fac.: Secretarial, Copiers, Conf. rm. cap.: 400
Sports Fac.: Pool, Croquet, Tennis
Location: Atlantic County
Attractions: Atlantic City Boardwalk & Casinos, Lennox Factory

Course: Pines
Distance: 6,417, Par: 71
Rating: 70.9, No. of holes: 36
Guest Policy: Call for available tee times, Dress code
Phone Club-House: 609-652-1800
Pro's name: Mike Fingleton
Reservations: Guests may call 7 days in advance
Season: Year round
Guest Carry Club: No

Inn of the Mountain Gods

Address: P.O. Box 269, Mescalero, 88340
Phone: 505-257-5141   800-545-9011
Innkeeper: Ron A. Duncan
No. rooms: 250
Rates: $, Credit Cards: AmEx, Visa, MC, Other CC
Services: Valet, Babysitting, Laundry, Room service
Restrictions: No pets
Restaurant: Dan Li Ka Dining Room
Bar: Ina Da Lounge
Business Fac.: Copiers, Audio-visual, Conf. rm. cap.: 650
Sports Fac.: Tennis, Riding, Canoes & Rowboats
Location: Otero County
Attractions: White Sands Monument, Space Hall of Fame

Course: Inn of the Mountain Gods
Distance: 6,416, Par: 72
Rating: 72.1, No. of holes: 18
Guest Policy: Open to the public
Phone Club-House: 505-257-5141
Pro's name: Jack Warlick
Reservations: Should make tee time w/reservations
Season: Year round weather permit
Guest Carry Club: No

New Mexico has a lot of wide open spaces, and this stunning mountain resort is surrounded by and engulfed in the serenity of the secluded, heavily forested Mescalero Apache Indian Reservation. At 7,200 feet in the Sacramento Mountains of south central New Mexico a few miles east of White Sands Missile Range, the Inn is a most unique spot. Owned and operated by the Mescalero Apache Tribe, the visitor will find scenic outdoor sports, fine dining and excellent shopping for tribal handcrafts, all on a pristine Alpine lake. With 250 rooms, one still has the feeling of isolation, partly because the surroundings are undeveloped, and its naturally an incredibly quiet place. The lobby is large, with a 50 foot copper sheathed fireplace dominating a warm room filled with Apache artifacts and contemporary furnishings. A lively piano bar which overlooks the mountains, Lake Mescalero and the golf course. Accommodations are shingled chalet-style with large windows facing the lake, and when you depart you have the feeling that all is well-maintained, and surprise! Everything worked!

You might choose archery, badminton, canoeing, lazing poolside, or exploring the forests on horseback. Tennis courts, and trap and skeet shooting are popular pastimes here, as are the big game hunting packages. This is definitely where the antelope play and discouraging words are seldom heard.

Off the reservation, you'll find the White Sands National Monument, art galleries, Alamogordo Space Hall of Fame, and Ruidoso Downs, renowned for the best in quarter horse and thoroughbred racing in the cool pines.

Fans of first-rate home style Mexican food will want to try the Old Road Restaurant nearby.

The golf course here is by Ted Robinson, who also is credited with Sahalee Country Club in Redmond, Washington. Its a rolling layout bordering the lake, with fairly hard fairways, giving the ball a good bounce. With fairways bordered by stands of pinyon, cottonwood, aspen and pine, its more than likely you'll see the trees up close. The front nine is narrower, and you'll need precise shots to carry the water on several holes. The second hole, with its elevated tee and dogleg left can be a devil, especially if you try to cut the corner, where huge trees will hamper progress. Greens are large, well-maintained and undulating, plus pretty slick due to the altitude.

Desert Inn Country Club & Spa

Desert glamor, big name entertainment, glitter, nightly production spectaculars, the allure of casino action, the Hughes mystique, breakfast and dinner 24 hours a day, sunshine, and a multi-million-dollar redesign concept. The Desert Inn is a Las Vegas landmark where guests experience all of this in a desert resort with luxurious amenities. Located on the Strip not far from the downtown "Glitter Gulch" area, this hotel and casino is the only Nevada property to be a member of the Preferred Hotels network. Step inside and you'll find bars, restaurants and a shopping arcade carrying everything from bathing suits to formal wear. A tour of the grounds reveal ten outdoor hydrowhirl spas scattered about, an Olympic-size pool set amidst gardens of lush foliage, tennis courts, spa, several bars and a casino highlighted by 30 brass chandeliers and some of the most attentive staff in this teeming desert oasis. The buildings are all hexagonal in shape, resulting in unique and cozy corners, and the pattern is even carried out in cement sidewalks. The 821 rooms, including 95 suites, are housed in two, three, seven, nine and 14-story buildings, each one named after a famous golf or tennis event. St. Andrews and Augusta have glass exteriors, and the seven-storied Wimbledon building is shaped like a modernized Mayan pyramid.

After opening in 1951, the Desert Inn hosted the Tournament of Champions for 13 years, and the golf world will long remember the days when 10,000 silver dollars were wheeled out to the champion in a wheelbarrow! Past winners who received the heavy metal are Gene Littler, Sam Snead, Arnold Palmer, and Jack Nicklaus. Site of PGA Tour and Senior PGA Tour events, the par-72 layout has attracted professionals, entertainers and European royalty, as well as Presidents John Kennedy, Lyndon Johnson, and Gerald Ford.

The signature hole is the par-3 seventh, traditionally one of the toughest on the PGA Tour. It stretches out to 209 yards from the championship tees, and looks innocent enough with colorful flowers and railroad ties, but that's when the trouble begins. The green is guarded by water and a brick retaining wall to the left and in front, and there are bunkers to the right and behind the difficult two-tiered green. Most players bail out to the right, hoping to make par from the sand.

Address: 3145 Las Vegas Blvd. S., Las Vegas, 89114
Phone: 702-733-4444   800-634-6909
Innkeeper: Kevin Malley
No. rooms: 821
Rates: $, Credit Cards: AmEx, Visa, MC, Other CC
Services: Valet, Barber Shop, Beauty Shop, Valet and self parking, Car hire Babysitting, Card/game area, Laundry, Room service
Restrictions: No pets, no children in casino
Restaurant: Portofino
Bar: Raffles Lounge
Business Fac.: Secretarial, Telex, Conf. rm. cap.: 990
Sports Fac.: Tennis, Shuffleboard, Health spa
Location: Center of Strip
Attractions: Hoover Dam, Grand Canyon, Death Valley, Auto Coll.

Course: Desert Inn Country Club
Distance: 7,111, Par: 72
Rating: 75.2, No. of holes: 18
Guest Policy: Call for tee times and availability, Dress code
Phone Club-House: 702-733-4488
Pro's name: Dave Johnson
Reservations: 60 days in advance w/confirm hotel
Season: All year
Guest Carry Club: No

The Sagamore

Address: On Lake George, At Bolton Landing, 12814
Phone: 518-644-9400   800-843-6664
Innkeeper: David Boyd
No. rooms: 350
Rates: $$, Credit Cards: AmEx, Visa, MC, Other CC
Services: Shoe shine, Valet parking, Games room, Laundry, Hair salon, Supervised children's program, Room service
Restaurant: Sagamore Dining Room
Bar: Van Vinkles
Business Fac.: Fax, Conf. rm. cap.: 780
Sports Fac.: Tennis, Pool, Full Health Spa
Location: Lake George
Attractions: Fort William Henry, Gore Mtn. Fort Ticonderoga

Course: Sagamore Resort
Distance: 6,810, Par: 70
Rating: 71.5, No. of holes: 18
Guest Policy: Hotel guests & members priority tee time
Phone Club-House: 518-644-9400
Pro's name: Tom Smack
Reservations: May be made with hotel reservations
Season: May 1–Oct. 31
Guest Carry Club: No

Approach the Sagamore from the waters of Lake George, in the Adirondacks and you'll see the stately white central tower and veranda with rambling clapboard wings. Like the legendary Phoenix, the hotel, listed in the National Register of Historic Buildings, has reopened as a year-round playground and conference center, under the management of Omni Hotels. The resort is steeped in local lore and tales of the Northeast's elite vacationing here. The main building, well-preserved and dating from 1923, dominates the 72-acre island, and houses 100 rooms and suites, while seven nearby lodges offer 240 additional rooms and suites with fireplaces and private balconies. Transportation around the private island is by vintage motorcars or horse and buggy. A variety of restaurants provide formal and casual dining, while cocktails can be enjoyed at the Veranda, a Victorian style lounge serving high tea, late evening coffees and piano music. There's a complete sports center with indoor tennis and racquetball, indoor pool, and a full-treatment spa. You'll also find four all-weather outdoor courts, lighted for night play. Visit the marina, which has dockage for 60 boats, and is the meeting place for activities such as water-skiing, sailing wind surfing, fishing and lake swimming. Try parasailing for a glimpse of the area, scuba diving or canoeing.

The Conference Center is by far the most flexible and comprehensive facility in the area. Connected to the main hotel by walkway, it includes three meeting rooms, and an elegant ballroom, ideal for receptions and dinners.

You'll tee off on one of America's classic championship and more entertaining courses; a Scottish style par 70 course through lovely mountainside acres overlooking Lake George. Donald Ross planned the course a year before he designed Seminole, where Ben Hogan was a member. Large and rolling with deep green side bunkers. The contours are such that a missed chip shot may roll off. The thirteenth hole is considered by many to be the most breathtaking, but also the most difficult. It's a very tight driving hole with water right and in front of the green. The second shot is uphill to "one undulating mass," Ross' reference to a very rolling green. The course has hosted New York PGA Match Play 1986–88, and 1986, '87 and '88 Challenge Cup Matches.

Nevele Country Club

Ellenville is easily accessible from The Big Apple, the western part of the state and the Philadelphia area. If you're looking for a conference or getaway site in the Catskills, consider a thousand acre resort with a full American plan and Jewish-American cuisine, elegant public areas, nice guest rooms and good recreational facilities. This is a fairly large resort—435 rooms and such amenities as tennis, an Olympic-size outdoor pool, an indoor pool, health clubs, horseback riding, an indoor game room, boating on the lake, fishing, bicycle riding, and racquetball. The main dining room offers special diets as well as an attractive menu featuring seafood and a large variety of home-baked items. A coffee shop, snackquabana at the outdoor pool, loft cafe, safari lounge, aquabar, espresso bar, and stardust room for nightly entertainment round out the picture of restaurants and watering holes.

Children of all ages are pampered here. A daycamp program that runs from breakfast to bedtime stimulates and occupies them, freeing parents to pursue their own diversions. Women love the upscale shopping at the outlet malls nearby. You'll have a pleasant course to play, one that hosts regional amateur tournaments. Look for rolling terrain with a lake and creek running throughout. Tom Fazio redesigned the layout recently, so if your grandfather always birdied the 16th hole, don't count on it running in the family. The lake surrounds the fairway and three sides of the tricky green.

Address: Ellenville, 12428
Phone: 914-647-6000   800-647-6000
No. rooms: 435
Rates: Call, Credit Cards: AmEx, Visa, MC, Other CC
Services: Supervised Day Camp, Cable TV, Luxury towels, Babysitting, Large bathrooms, Room service
Restrictions: Pets ltd.
Restaurant: Homestead-steak & seafood
Bar: Safary Lounge
Business Fac.: Audio-visual, Copiers, Conf. rm. cap.: 1,400
Sports Fac.: Tennis, Pools, Sailing, Bike, Ice skate
Location: Upstate NY–Catskills
Attractions: Upscale shops @ Woodburry Commons, Catskills Mtns.

Course: The Nevele Country Club
Distance: 6,500, Par: 70
Rating: 69.4, No. of holes: 18
Guest Policy: Call for availability
Phone Club-House: 914-647-6000
Reservations: May be made up to 2 weeks in adv.
Season: Mid-May–mid-Oct.
Guest Carry Club: Yes

The Lodge at Black Butte Ranch

Address: P.O. Box 8000, Black Butte Ranch, 97759
Phone: 503-595-6211   800-452-7455
Innkeeper: Michael J. Gallagher
No. rooms: 100
Rates: $, Credit Cards:
Sports Fac.: Pool, Tennis, Horseback riding
Attractions: Over 16 miles paved jogging/biking trails

Course: Glaze Meadow
Distance: 6,600, Par: 72
Rating: 68.0, No. of holes: 18
Guest Policy: Guests & home owners preferred tee times
Phone Club-House: 503-595-6689
Reservations: Call for starting time
Guest Carry Club: Yes

This is one of those seldom-found treasures that you hope no one else discovers—at least not for a while.

Located amid ponderosa pines in high plateau country a few miles from Sisters, the wood-and-glass resort and residential community is the kind of place people keep returning to year after year. Accommodations are in condominiums or rental homes, many with spectacular views of snow-covered volcanic peaks, a lake or well-kept lawns. Don't miss dinner in the main lodge's dining room, dubbed "most romantic restaurant in central Oregon." Children can't wait to come back—the supervised recreation center and a program in conjunction with nearby Camp Tamarack during summer deserves an A+ in quality. On the premises you'll find a general store, four swimming pools, over 16 miles of paved jogging and biking trails, 19 outdoor tennis courts, and a stable of the ranch's amiable horses.

Golfers love it here—no outside events are held on the two 18 holes course, Big Meadow and Glaze Meadow, and there are various programs available with a staff of four PGA pros. Robert Muir Graves was responsible for Big Meadow, which came after Glaze Meadow, designed by Gene C. "Bunny" Mason. They're gently rolling as they zigzag through tall pines, and aspen, and across water. You'll have ample time to gaze upward for a glimpse of geese in flight and some awesome views of the Sisters.

Salishan Lodge

The natural beauty of the central Oregon coast, dense forests, lagoons, pounding ocean, rocky beaches, is what makes this naturalist's haven special. No crowds, glitter, high tech or pollution. *Salishan* comes from salish, ancient Pacific Northwest Indian for "coming together from diverse points to communicate in harmony."

200 rooms in low-rise wooden villas overlook a most stupendous landscape of woods, fairways or the untouched Pacific coast. Rooms are designed for privacy, with fireplaces, balconies lithographs by local artists, and extra-large bathrooms.

The tri-level dining room is worthy of all accolades, stars, and recognition. Here is Pacific Northwest seafood at its best. The menu is unpretentious, reflecting the freshest and artfully prepared offerings from the sea. Salmon is the name of the game here, you'll find it everywhere, from the breakfast menu's bagels with smoked salmon to barbecued, or baked in a delicate puff pastry. The wine cellar is impressive; lengthy, well-rounded, and reasonably priced. Besides exploring the coves and trails of the property, there are tennis courts, indoor pool, a variety of classes such as woodcarving or oil painting, kite flying, horseback riding, and even basket weaving. In addition, you can try fly fishing, deep sea fishing, shell-collecting, crabbing or clamming. And imagine the thrill of seeing gray whales migrating, or harbor seals sunning themselves. Across the highway is an intriguing assortment of shops, and there are picturesque little towns down the coast.

No earth movers had a hand in this 18 hole course, patterned in the Scottish tradition in harmony with nature. Rugged and challenging, the course winds around, highlighted by ocean views, lofty pines and sparkling lakes. Resort guests have priority tee times on the course. Players who prefer to carry their clubs love to play here, carts aren't mandatory. Number 13, a 402 yard par 4, will take a straight drive between the troublesome dunes on both right and left. The green is guarded by a gargantuan H-shaped trap, and should you hook it, you'll be in Siletz Bay with the seals.

Address: Gleneden Beach, 97388
Phone: 503-764-2371   800-547-6500
Innkeeper: Hank Hickox
No. rooms: 200
Rates: $$
Services: Library, Complimentary tea service Mon-Thur in winter
Restaurant: Sun Room, Marketplace
Business Fac.: Audio-visual, Conf. rm. cap.: 150
Sports Fac.: Tennis, Pool, Jogging, Fitness Center
Location: Oregon coast
Attractions: Whale-Watching, Hiking, Guided Naturalist Tours

Course: Salishan Golf Links
Distance: 6,439, Par: 72
Rating: 71.5, No. of holes: 18
Guest Policy: Public, but resort guests have priority
Phone Club-House: 503-764-3632
Pro's name: Grant Rodgers
Reservations: May be made 2 weeks in advance
Season: Year round
Guest Carry Club: Yes

Sunriver Lodge and Resort

Address: P.O. Box 3609, Sunriver, 97702
Phone: 503-593-1221 800-547-3922
No. rooms: 360
Rates: $
Services: Kids Klub, Ski shuttle, Golf and Tennis lessons, Full beauty services
Restaurant: Provision Company
Business Fac.: Audio-Visual, Conf. rm. cap.: 500
Sports Fac.: Tennis, Pools, Nature Center, Sauna
Location: Near Bend
Attractions: High Desert Museum, Flower Arranging, Fashion Show

Course: Sunriver—North
Distance: 6,863, Par: 72
Rating: 73.0, No. of holes: 36
Phone Club-House: 503-593-1221
Pro's name: Dick Gentling
Reservations: Call for availability
Season: Mid March to end of Oct.
Guest Carry Club: Yes

This is the quintessential Oregon high desert sports resort. Located about 160 miles southeast of Portland, guests can arrive by commercial plane at Redmond, by Amtrak at Chemult, or show up in their private plane on Sunriver's 5500-foot lighted runway. Heading into its third decade, the Resort is pouring money into a major facelift, and guests will be able to choose from newly decorated condominiums, rustic cabins, private homes or rooms in the imposing main lodge.

Recreational diversions include two immense swimming pools, 18 plexi-paved tennis courts, indoor racquet club, hot tubs and sauna, and a resident naturalist to guide nature walks and explain the vagaries of river otters, owls and porcupines.

You'll find an elegant dining room for dinner and Sunday brunch, The Provision Company Restaurant for breakfast, lunch and dinner, live music at night in the Owl's Nest Lounge, and snacks and lunches at the 19th Hole on the North Course, and the Steak deck on the South Course during golf season.

Exhilarating white water rafting on nearby Deschutes River is available, as are fly fishing excursions, bicycle trips, horseback riding, sightseeing flights, and hiking on the Green Lakes Trails. Locals like to wind surf at Cultus and Elk Lakes, and calm water kayaking and canoeing can be enjoyed on many Cascades lakes.

Robert Trent Jones Jr. is responsible for the breathtakingly beautiful North Course. Selected by a group of top PGA professionals, North Course was recently ranked fourth in the "'Northwest's Best' Top 25 Courses." You'll find doglegs on nearly every hole, plentiful native shrubbery and pine trees, lush fairways and true, smooth greens set amid hilly terrain, lava rock outcrops, and bunkers that hug the edge of the green. Seven lakes dot the course, all under the watchful eye of 3,100 foot snow-capped Mount Bachelor, and it's here that the pros come yearly for the PGA Sunriver Oregon Open Invitational. South Course is longer, while a par 72, also. With its more level terrain, mid-fairway mounds and elevated greens and tees, this course winds in and out of meadows carpeted with dazzling wildflowers under the clean, sunny mountain skies. Both courses have full facilities including pro shops, club rentals, driving range, putting green, food and drinks.

Avalon Lakes Golf Course & Inn

Warren's location, equidistant from New York and Chicago, Cleveland and Pittsburg, make the Avalon Inn an ideal destination for the small or large meeting. As a bonus, there are plenty of recreational facilities for the family. Many of the resort's 144 rooms overlook the flat green expanses of a mid-western country setting. An indoor Olympic-sized pool, saunas and other health facilities, plus shuffleboard, indoor or outdoor tennis await you. History buffs can visit the McKinley Memorial nearby.

The Tall Oaks Dining Room, evoking a "tavern-on-the-green" atmosphere, serves continental favorites while piano music tinkles in the background. The Country Gardens Restaurant, on the lower level, serves snacks and lighter meals in a casual atmosphere.

Choose from two 18 hole-golf courses, Old Avalon and the newer Avalon Lakes. Pete Dye teamed up with William Newcomb to turn out the well-known Avalon Lakes course, a par 71 challenger. You'll be given a half dozen balls compliments of the pro shop when you tee off. Any way you slice it, they don't expect them back. Both courses are well-trapped with an ample water supply.

Address: 9519 E. Market St., Warren, 44484
Phone: 216-856-1900   800-828-2566
No. rooms: 144
Rates: $
Restaurant: The Tall Oaks
Bar: Terrace Patio
Business Fac.: Secretarial, Copiers, Conf. rm. cap.: 850
Sports Fac.: Tennis, Pool, Health Club, Sauna

Course: Avalon Lakes
Distance: 6,425, Par: 71
Rating: 71.7, No. of holes: 18
Guest Policy: Open to public, Dress code
Phone Club-House: 216-856-7211
Pro's name: Gordon Wagner
Reservations: 7 days
Season: April–Nov.
Guest Carry Club: Ltd

Shawnee Inn

Address: Shawnee-On-Delaware, 18356
Phone: 717-421-1500   800-SHAWNEE
Innkeeper: J. Versteegde
No. rooms: 100
Rates: $, Credit Cards: AmEx,
Visa, MC, Other CC
Services: Valet, Library, Beauty shop,
Car hire, House doctor, Babysitting,
Card/game area, Laundry
Restrictions: No pets
Restaurant: Dogwood Room
Bar: Charles Lounge
Business Fac.: Secretarial, Telex,
Conf. rm. cap.: 150
Sports Fac.: Pools, Riding, Canoeing,
Rafting
Location: Bank of River
Attractions: Delaware Trolley Tour,
Pocono Raceway

Course: Shawnee Inn-Country Club
Distance: 6,636, Par: 72
Rating: 72.4, No. of holes: 27
Guest Policy: Call for tee time,
Dress code
Phone Club-House: 717-421-1500
Pro's name: Gordon C. Neely
Reservations: May be made 7 days
in advance
Season: April–Nov.
Guest Carry Club: No

Built in 1912 of reinforced concrete, the Shawnee Inn, was one of the first fireproof structures built in the United States. Overlooking the serenely beautiful Delaware River not far from Stroudsburg, and with the Delaware Water Gap National Recreation Area as its neighbor, this venerable old Poconos landmark invites you to sit awhile on its veranda and enjoy the amenities. Once the home of Fred Waring and his Pennsylvanians, the inn offers rooms, suites or one of the 300 two-bedroom villas in the 2200 acre resort. The stately Dogwood Dining Room, with cathedral ceilings, massive wooden beams and an abundance of cascading ivy is a relaxing environment. A typical dinner might include Scotch smoked salmon filets, red leaf lettuce with raspberry vinaigrette, sorbet, veal a la siegfried, fresh asparagus, and a coupe Romanoff.

For recreational activities during any season, the Shawnee Inn has them all. The river is a playground for rafting, canoeing, or tubing. Or swim in an indoor pool, play tennis day or night, try volleyball or basket ball, or putt away on the mini-golf course. In addition, hiking, horseback riding and fishing are three things to write home about. Theatre buffs will want to check out the Shawnee Playhouse featuring popular Broadway shows with a professional New York cast. If you're an outlet fanatic, you'll have a whole complex of stores five miles away, and the Pocono Raceway is half an hour's drive.

A. W. Tillinghast, or Tillie as he was known, designed the original course—many years before his masterpieces at Winged Foot, Quaker Ridge and Baltusrol in New Jersey. This is a course to enjoy the scenery—twenty seven holes with great expanses of forested mountain greenery and the Delaware on both sides. Site of the 1938 PGA Championship, won by Paul Runyan, and the 1987 Eastern Collegiate Athletic Conference Championship, the course is the home of "The Swing's the Thing" Golf School. #7 of the blue nine is a 152 yard par 3 stretch—you tee off from the island to a green across the river. As you try to stay clear of the water and bunkers, bear in mind that it was here that many avid golfers, including Dwight Eisenhower, Perry Como, and Jackie Gleason chipped and probably prayed to carry the same river. Arnold Palmer, too, has played many rounds at Shawnee, and it was in the Shawnee Pro Shop that he met his wife.

Hyatt Regency Cerromar Beach

For some travelers, this mix-and-match sister-hood of two Hyatt resorts adjacent to each other, complete with nine restaurants, casinos, a full range of water sports, 28 tennis courts, gorgeous balmy weather, ocean views, and an incredible state-of-the-art river pool snaking around 4½ acres of tropical Eden isn't enough. But add 4 Robert Trent Jones championship courses, and a chance to explore a 100-mile island with tropical forests, 400 year old towns and a population flavored by Indian, Spanish and African influences, and you have a near-perfect vacation. Dorado Beach, a postcard-like stretch of Pristine coastal property was developed as a grapefruit and coconut plantation in 1905. Featured are 300 rooms and casitas along a two mile white crescent beach. Other attractions include a recreation program offering crab races, samba lessons and mah jongg, a health club, shops, and a full health spa. The piece de resistance at Cerromar Beach is the labyrinthian swimming pool, the world's largest, designed by water swami, Howard Fields.

The courses at Dorado Beach opened in 1958, and East Course has hosted many tournaments such as the 1961 Canada Cup, Pro-Am Invitational since 1963, and Chi Chi's Charity Classic. Some memorable holes: The 10th is a par-5 following the curve of the beach and meandering through forest; but nothing compares to the "Z" hole, that old devil #13. Its a par-5 double-dogleg of 540 yards. Reachable in two by big hitters, but you must play over two ponds to reach the green. The green has a pond in front, and the sparkling Atlantic as a backdrop. The West Course layout bobs in and out of tropical jungle, a constant reminder of plantation days. The second nine has no shortage of water hazards. #15 is a mean 405 yard, par 4 which gives you a chance to carry a lake, avoid a dense jungle and spare the swaying palms on the right from a slice.

Cerromar's North and South Courses are gems built on flat, open land minus the plantation look. Robert Trent Jones returned in the early seventies to produce a par 72 layout with wide fairways ideal for fast play. Hole #7 is a dramatic par 3 175 yard test of skill and concentration. The green sits immediately above the rocky shore, and when the tide's high, too much club will be penalized by a watery grave. This is the host site of the Annual Puerto Rico Golf Classic.

Address: Dorado, 00646
Phone: 809-796-1010   800-228-9000
Innkeeper: Hendrick Santos
No. rooms: 504
Rates: $$$$ Credit Cards: AmEx, Visa, MC, Other CC
Services: Valet, Barber shop, Beauty shop, Garage and parking, Car hire, Babysitting, Laundry, Int. currency exchange, Card/game area, Room service
Restrictions: No pets
Restaurant: Swan Cafe, Orchid Room
Bar: El Yunque
Business Fac.: Secretarial, Telex, Conf. rm. cap.: 1,500
Sports Fac.: Pool, Tennis, Bicycles, Health Spa
Location: North Coast
Attractions: Old San Juan, El Yunque Rain Forest, Race Track

Course: Hyatt Dorado Beach, East
Distance: 7,001, Par: 72
Rating: 70.2, No. of holes: 72
Guest Policy: Call for availability
Phone Club-House: 809-796-1600
Pro's name: Miguel Colon
Reservations: May be made two days in advance
Season: Year round
Guest Carry Club: No

Palmas del Mar

In some ways this sprawling Mediterranean-style resort geared to the sports-conscious is reminiscent of a sun-drenched college with an outstanding athletic program. As the Caribbean's most popular destination for tourists, you'll see why, as you head east out of noisy, crowded San Juan for Humacao, which has splendid beaches. Palmas del Mar, which calls itself "The New American Riviera" is large-all 2,700 acres of villas, a hotel, and condos clustered around a championship golf course, marina, and 20 court tennis center managed by All American Sports. Conference planners are delighted to find there is a full range of meeting facilities with amenities for every interest group.

For starters, you'll find seven restaurants. a complete water sports center, a casino and disco, an equestrian center, jogging trails, and bars and lounges for relaxing in the cool Caribbean breeze. The beach is uncluttered, long, and palm-lined—perfect for children and those of us who relish romantic sunsets. Be sure to inquire about golf packages—we found some good ones.

Open for play in 1973, the course was designed by Gary Player, and Americans Arthur Davis and Ron Kirby. Winding through coconut groves, and cane fields, with heavy tropical rough, lagoons, canals, and devilish sand traps, the par 72 layout has the toughest five successive holes in the Caribbean, according to Seth Bull, club pro. He claims the 13th is the most difficult par three around. Uphill against the wind for 250 yards to a two-level green. Then he adds, slyly, "We can make the pin placement so subtle that it's impossible to par the hole."

Address: P.O. Box 2020, Humacao, Puerto Rico 00661

Phone: 809-852-6000 800-221-4874

No. rooms: 290

Rates: $$, Credit Cards: AmEx, Visa, MC, Other CC

Services: Private Airstrip, Gift Shop/Boutiques, Beauty Salon, General Store, Wellness Center

Bar: Bar

Business Fac.: Sec.Svc, Audio-Visual

Sports Fac.: Tennis, Swimming, Sailing Equestrian Ctr

Attractions: Casino, Shopping for local handicrafts.

Course: Palmas del Mar

Distance: 6660, Par: 72, No. of holes: 18

Kiawah Island Resort

You'll be living in the midst of centuries-old buried treasures, a reputedly haunted mansion and one of the most well-preserved natural environments, all with the best that modern resort vacationing can provide at Kiawah Island Resort

Present-day visitors to Kiawah Island enjoy virtually the same breathtaking first impression that the island's original guests, the Kiawah Indians, did. Only 21 miles from Charleston the semitropical character of this haven has remained virtually undisturbed for millennia. Indeed, many of the magnificent oak trees in Kiawah's dense maritime forest have been here for hundreds of years.

Island dining takes on a unique flavor all its own as outstanding dishes are prepared to complement the island's mild climate. At the Indigo House, American cuisine features excellent shrimp, lobster and succulent beef.

Few resorts sequestered in beautiful settings have been successful in combining aesthetics, a spirit of ecological preservation, and three very different courses offering exhilarating golf. Meet an exception. The first course, Marsh Point, was designed by Gary Player, who felt that a player needs a course where there's a chance to make pars, but will require touch to recover if he goes for the green and misses. The fifth here is a short par-4 bordering the inlet, and the green is waiting for you on a platform island smack in the middle of the marsh.

The Nicklaus course, Turtle Point, is longer, wider, easier to chip to, and every hole with a water hazard has a "bail-out," but it's by no means an easier eighteen. Number 12 is a favorite. It lacks water, but it's long, and rather tight, with a foreboding bunker like a big dog's paw fronting the green.

The scenery on Tom Fazio's Osprey Point Course is absolutely awesome. Sierra Clubbers and John Audubon himself could swap tales of myrtle, magnolias, egrets, otters, deer, and the osprey, a rare hawk who makes this region his home. The course is built on a series of islands, and you cross ten wooden bridges during a round. The last hole is a roller-coaster par-5 monster encompassing water, treacherous bunkers, and a narrow landing area for your second shot that won't be charitable to a hooker.

Address: P.O.Box 12910, Charleston, 29412
Phone: 800-654-2924   800-845-2471
Innkeeper: Charles F. Daoust
No. rooms: 150
Rates: $$, Credit Cards: AmEx, Visa, MC, Other CC
Services: Valet, Parking, Room service
Restrictions: No pets
Restaurant: Jasmine Porch
Bar: Topsider
Business Fac.: Audio-visual, Telex, Conf. rm. cap.: 600
Sports Fac.: Pool, Tennis
Location: Charleston County
Attractions: Historic district, Citadel Mall

Course: Turtle Point Course
Distance: 6,889, Par: 72
Rating: 73.5, No. of holes: 18
Guest Policy: Call for availability, resort rate, Dress code
Phone Club-House: 803-559-5551
Pro's name: Tommy Cuthbert
Reservations: Call for times
Season: Year round
Guest Carry Club: Yes

Seabrook Island Resort

Address: P.O. Box 32099, Charleston, 29417
Phone: 803-768-1000   800-845-2475
Innkeeper: John Stagg
No. rooms: 330
Rates: $, Credit Cards: AmEx, Visa, MC, Other CC
Services: Planned family and children's activities, Cable TV, Radio
Restrictions: No pets
Restaurant: Island House
Business Fac.: Bohickets, Half Shell, Conf. rm. cap.: 2000
Sports Fac.: Tennis, Bicycles
Location: Charleston
Attractions: Historic tours, Carriage tours, Fort Sumter

Course: Crooked Oaks
Distance: 6,880, Par: 72
Rating: 73.0, No. of holes: 18
Guest Policy: Check for availability
Phone Club-House: 803-768-1000
Pro's name: Margo Walden
Reservations: Call in advance
Season: Year round
Guest Carry Club: No

With a year-round mild climate moderated by the Gulf Stream, a dedicated commitment to conservation and ecology, and no high-rises to mar the dazzling views, Seabrook is nearly perfect. This 2,200 acre private island (and they DO mean private, as in sentry gates) is 23 miles south of Charleston, and caters to families, as evidenced by the numerous organized activities such as pony rides and treasure hunts.

Condominiums are privately owned, and are offered in a variety of settings and sizes. Island House, with a formal dining room featuring savory Lowcountry Cuisine and a renowned wine list, is the social center. The names tell it all: Cap's Sam's, The Half Shell Raw Bar.

There's plenty going on here. You can play tennis, swim in the ocean or pools, or use a wading pool at the Beach Club, rent a bicycle, go windsurfing, join an exercise class, go fishing or crabbing, rent a Hobie Cat, or swab the decks if you're tied up at the marina. An equestrian center will provide a suitable companion for a ride on the beach.

Conference planners should note that 12 individual meeting rooms, with seating for 10–300 eager beavers. Nearby are tours of Fort Sumter, plantations and garden tours, historic Charleston, and some upscale shopping with names such as Banana Republic, Gucci, and Victoria's Secret. Designer Robert Trent Jones called Crooked Oaks Course "one of my best." The 18 holes follow a 6880 yard path around moss-draped oaks, and across treacherous marshlands. Willard Byrd designed and aptly named 18 hole championship Ocean Winds Course, the shorter of the two. Margot Walden, 1968 LPGA pro of the year, and Seabrook's golf director operates three daily clinics. There's a driving range and pro shops ready to help you.

Marriott's Hilton Head Resort

Located within Shipyard Plantation's 800 private acres, this oceanside hotel offers a wide range of family and individual activities. Guests will find two restaurants, a lounge, indoor and outdoor pools, with easy access to shops and sightseeing. Located in a tropically landscaped setting, there is a beautiful stretch of clean sandy beach for you to roam. There are tours of historic Savannah and Beaufort, browsing in Harbour Town's shops, tennis galore, musical events, and incredible fishing, both in the salt-marshes and big game fishing in the Gulf Stream 65 miles offshore. For nature lovers, Hilton Head Island is a unique and complex wonder. Expect to see the Cabbage Palmetto, beautiful white egrets and the graceful osprey, as well as the white-tailed deer, and alligators who co-habit the island with the growing population of people. Developers have let them remain in their natural habitat, and signs asking people to refrain from feeding them are common.

Marriott guests can tee off at Shipyard Golf Club, home of the Hilton Head Seniors International, and numerous Senior PGA events. It's a narrow 27 hole course with water hazards on 25 holes. You'll wander through tall pines, magnolias and moss-draped oaks, and over lagoons and ponds which must be avoided to match par.

Address: 130 Shipyard Dr., Hilton Head Island, 29928
Phone: 803-842-2400   800-334-1881
Innkeeper: Angus Cotton
No. rooms: 338
Rates: $, Credit Cards: AmEx, Visa, MC, Other CC
Services: Oversized guest rooms, Handicapped (8 rooms), Cable TV, Radio, Media rentals, Spouse programs, Full health spa, Room service
Restrictions: No pets
Room service
Restaurant: Pompanos, The Veranda
Bar: The Mockingbird
Business Fac.: Audio-visual, FAX, Conf. rm. cap.: 1,100
Sports Fac.: Tennis, Pools, Fishing, Boating, Riding
Location: Low Country
Attractions: Harbour Town, Daufuskie Island tours.

Course: Shipyard Golf Club
Distance: 6,167, Par: 72
Rating: 69.7, No. of holes: 27
Guest Policy: Check for availability
Phone Club-House: 803-785-2402
Pro's name: P. Rouillard
Reservations: Up to 2 weeks in advance.
Season: All year
Guest Carry Club: Ltd

Palmetto Dunes Resort

Address: P.O. Box 5606, Hilton Head Island, 29938
Phone: 803-785-1161   800-826-1649
Innkeeper: Mimi Helmken
Rates: $$, Credit Cards: AmEx, Visa, MC, Other CC
Services: Linens, Kitchen utensils, Washers/Dryers, Color TV, Daily or weekly housekeeping, Grocery store, Specialty shops.
Restaurant: The Hemmingway, Pralines
Bar: Club Indigo
Business Fac.: Complete bus. fac., Conf. rm. cap.: 200
Sports Fac.: Tennis, Bicycling, Canoes, Pools
Location: Waterfront
Attractions: Ten miles of man made lagoons, 25 Tennis courts

Course: Palmetto Dunes
Distance: 6,122, Par: 72
Rating: 69.3, No. of holes: 18
Guest Policy: Open to public, call for availability
Phone Club-House: 803-785-1140
Pro's name: C. Pellerin PGA
Reservations: May be made 2 mo. in advance
Season: All year
Guest Carry Club: No

This balmy, 1,800 acre relaxed development represents a unique mingling of residential and resort amenities. The resort area is highlighted by 54 holes of unsurpassed golf, the Rod Laver Tennis Center, a 505 room beachfront Hyatt Regency, and the Mariner's Clarion Inn. Pass the security gates of this attractive lowcountry private environment, and you'll find spacious condominiums and single family vacation homes. Everything is spread out and you get the feeling that the architects weren't sardine-packers. Bicycles paths cross sleepy lagoons, residences are on large lots, dolphins play offshore, while egrets, pipers, and pelicans share the broad hard-packed beach with runners and families. Shelter Cove, bordering a meandering creek, is a self-contained marine community containing shops, restaurants, office condominiums, and boat slips.

You can do as much or as little as you want—there are pages of restaurants from which to choose, nightlife, swimming pools, tennis facilities, canoe rentals, organized nature walks, theater, special events such as tournaments and festivals, and children's programs.

Golf options include three courses designed by three of the game's greatest names. The Robert Trent Jones layout is highlighted by a unique winding lagoon system which comes into play on 11 holes. Bunkers are huge, and greens are built up on the sides and back by rolling mounds. #10 is a long par 5, with a green sitting on the Atlantic's edge. The George Fazio course is a familiar name to followers of Golf Digest's list of America's 100 best. The 16th hole features a few of the course's yawning fairways and greenside bunkers. With only two par 5's, you've got a series of long par 4's that require long accurate second shots to reach the narrow greens. Opened for play in 1986, the Arthur Hills course is characterized by palmettos, dramatic elevation changes, continuous lines of dunes and some stiff ocean breezes. There's a unique seaside character here, complete with beautiful salt marshes, rolling fairways and lagoons which come into play on 10 holes. Be careful looking for your ball on the muddy banks—that placid looking alligator doesn't know a bogey from a birdie.

Sea Pines Plantation

Many people know this as Sea Pines Plantation—home of Harbour Town Golf Links, sub-tropical forests, salt marshes and sleepy lagoons zig-zagging across gentle, wide beaches, hiking, bird-watching, and fresh-from-the-dock-seafood. Meet the new Sea Pines Resorts, a re-organized giant now encompassing Sea Pines Plantation, Shipyard Plantation, and Port Royal Resort. Perched down at the tip of coastal South Carolina, just 45 minutes from Savannah. With 500 condominiums and townhouses, plus private houses, its a matter of preference—waterfront, fairway or woodland view. The island is crawling in restaurants, and at Sea Pines you can opt for prime rib and crab legs The Gold Eagle Tavern, or the Sea Pines Beach Club during the summer. More than two dozen pools, three top-notch racquet clubs are available with 50 grass, hard and clay courts, bicycle riding, beachcombing (great after a winter or fall storm) riding, croquet, and hiking on fifteen miles of quiet trails await the family vacationing here. Of course windsurfing, sailing, deep-sea and freshwater fishing, water-skiing and good old guilt-free beach-lounging is to be enjoyed.

World-famous as a golfer's paradise, Hilton Head is home of Harbour Town Links. Site of the annual MCI Heritage Classic, its course rating in a walloping 74 from the championship tees, certainly one of the highest anywhere. Pete Dye designed this classic beauty, with Nicklaus as consultant. Highly touted by tour pros, this toughie is a shot makers course—not long, but very demanding—a real pond-lovers dream, with smallish fast greens.

Ocean and Sea Marsh courses, designed by George Cobb, were the first courses to be built on the island. With holes bordering the Atlantic, egrets to admire, giant oaks draped with Spanish moss, and traps galore, these are fun courses to play. Down the way at shipyard Golf Course, the designer courses include the original Cobb 18, plus a more recent nine by Willard Byrd. Ready for more? Try Port Royal's three 18-hole courses. Willard Byrd was here, too, on the tight, winding Planter's Row. At par-72 Robber's Row and Barony, both George Cobb products, players delight at undulating greens and historic plaques on tees.

Can't you just taste the she-crab soup on a deck overlooking the water after a euphoric round on the links?

Address: P.O. Box 7000, Hilton Head Island, 29938
Phone: 803-785-3333   800-845-6131
Innkeeper: Patsy G. Hancock
No. rooms: 502
Rates: $, Credit Cards: AmEx, Visa, MC, Other CC
Services: Garage and parking, Babysitting, Laundry
Restrictions: No pets
Restaurant: Gold Eagle Tavern
Bar: Gold Eagle
Business Fac.: Conf. rm. cap.: 500
Sports Fac.: Pool, Tennis, Riding, Sail, Bicycles
Location: Hilton Head
Attractions: Historic Savannah & Beaufort, Comm. Playhouse

Course: Harbour Town Golf Links
Distance: 5,824, Par: 71
Rating: 70.0, No. of holes: 18
Guest Policy: Call for availability
Phone Club-House: 803-671-2446
Pro's name: Cray C. Corbitt
Reservations: 24 hrs.–14 days depending on season
Season: Year round
Guest Carry Club: Yes

Westin Resort Hilton Head

Address: 135 S. Port Royal Dr.,
Hilton Head Island, 29928
Phone: 803-681-4000   800-327-0200
Innkeeper: Pat Burton
No. rooms: 416
Rates: $$$, Credit Cards: AmEx,
Visa, MC, Other CC
Services: Valet, Barber & Beauty
shops, Garage & Parking, Car hire,
Babysitting, Laundry, Art Gallery,
Room service
Restrictions: No pets
Restaurant: Brasserie, The Barony
Bar: Marsh Tacky
Business Fac.: Complete bus, serv.
Sports Fac.: Pool, Tennis, Croquet,
Polo, Sailing
Location: Sea side
Attractions: Harbortown, Shelter
Cove, Savannah–45 minutes.

Course: Barony Course
Distance: 6,038, Par: 72
Rating: 68.7, No. of holes: 18
Guest Policy: Guests have priority
tee times
Phone Club-House: 808-681-3671
Pro's name: G. Duren, PGA
Reservations: Contact the pro shop
Season: All year
Guest Carry Club: No

No need for devotees of the Inter-Continental on
Hilton Head to fret. Only the name's been
changed. It's the same charm of Charleston and
Beaufort reflected in the lobby design, with
lovely antiques, oriental rugs on polished
wooden floors, and huge bouquets of fresh
flowers.

Set on 24 acres of beachfront inside the gates of
Port Royal Plantation, (plantation here is syn-
onymous with development) this luxury
horseshoe-shaped hotel has 416 rooms, pool and
ocean swimming, a health club, water sports,
tennis courts, conference facilities for the multi-
tudes, and a large variety of dining and enter-
tainment facilities. The island is a paradise for
sports enthusiasts—not only are there miles of
wide white beaches for bike riding, running, and
castle building, tennis buffs can choose from any
kind of court, shoppers will love exploring a
huge outlet mall, and seafood lovers can check
the local fleet's catch for shrimp, scallops, blue-
fish, sea trout and more.

The Kids' Korner, a well-organized compli-
mentary pleasure package for the 5-12 year-old,
offers all sorts of activities including kite flying,
arts and crafts, alligator races, shell collecting,
volleyball and more. For a modest fee, teens can
participate in organized activities such as water-
skiing, sunset cruises and trips to Harbour
Town.

You'll have access to three par 72 championship
courses: Barony, Robber's Row, and Planter's
Row. Barony has small greens that are well-
protected by deep bunkers, lagoons and Ber-
muda rough that require accurate approach
shots with shot and medium irons. Robber's
Course is on the marsh side atop what was once
Civil War grounds and the historic town of Port
Royal. Fairways are oak and magnolia-lined, and
approach shots will find relatively large, well-
trapped greens. The newest course is Planter's
Row, host of the 1985 Hilton Head Seniors Inter-
national. Greens are large, undulating and some-
times treacherous.

Los Monteros, Marbella, Spain

Los Monteros, Marbella, Spain

Son Vida Sheraton Hotel, Palma de Mallorca, Spain

Wild Dunes Beach & Racquet Club

Webster tells us a dune is a hill or ridge of sand piled up by the wind commonly found along shores. The dunes on tiny Isle of Palms just outside Charleston are Tom Fazio's award-winning.

Since the island was accessible only by boat until the turn of the century, it became a sanctuary for hundreds of species of birds and animals, and remains so today.

Lodgings are in wind-weathered one, two and three-bedroom villas and houses that look out on the never-ending stretch of sand, waves and dunes. If you've left the cooking behind, there are a myriad of restaurants from which to choose.

Fun for the family comes in the form of Island scavenger hunts, movies, wacky water sports, bingo and much more. Life (for some) centers around the water, and the amenities are first rate. Surf and creek fishing, sailboats and windsurfs are at your disposal.

Cottage clusters have pools, and there are two other 25-meter beauties. Tennis is taken seriously here, and the facilities are outstanding.

Nearly three miles of sugar-white beaches, and sprawling marshlands offer an undisturbed glimpse into the habits of Mother Nature's offspring. If you're here between April and August you can see the baby loggerhead turtles.

Wild Dunes Links is a young course by Tom Fazio where the holes are routed through moss-draped live oaks, exotic palms and magnolias onto severely rolling coastal terrain, then across saltwater marshland before the finishing holes right on the Atlantic. Relentless winds, massive dunes, deep rough and pot bunkers challenge the concentration of the most seasoned golfer. Experts highlight the fact that the course and the weather are so varied that a player can expect to use each club in his bag. Harbor Course, another Fazio layout, features a short narrow front nine holes which play adjacent to the Intracoastal Waterway. The back nine begins at the Yacht Harbor and winds along marshlands and through ancient trees. "Marsh Monster," the doglegged 13th is played from a small island fringed by an expansive marsh, and embodies all the characteristics that have made Fazio holes a true test of a golfer's skill. Sit a spell on the picturesque Clubhouse's spacious decks and ponder the question of which came first, the loggerhead or the egg?

Address: Isle of Palms, 29451
Phone: 803-886-6000   800-845-8880
Rates: $$$, Credit Cards: AmEx, Visa, MC, Other CC
Services: Children's and teen's activity programs
Restrictions: No pets
Restaurant: Island House, The Club
Business Fac.: Audio-visual, Conf. rm. cap.: 350
Sports Fac.: Tennis, Pools, Fishing, Bicyling, Fish
Location: 15 miles–Charleston
Attractions: Charleston's Widow's Walks, Fort Sumter, Museum

Course: Wild Dunes Links
Distance: 6,108, Par: 72
Rating: 69.6, No. of holes: 36
Guest Policy: Call for availability, Dress code
Phone Club-House: 803-886-6000
Pro's name: Terry Florence
Reservations: Call for tee times
Season: Year round
Guest Carry Club: Yes

Myrtle Beach Hilton

Address: Myrtle Beach, 29577
Phone: 803-449-7461   800-HILTONS
Innkeeper: Wayne D. Tabor
No. rooms: 392
Restaurant: Arcadian
Gardens-Alfredo
Business Fac.: Audio-visual, Conf.
rm. cap.: 900
Sports Fac.: Pool, Tennis, Sailing,
Jogging, Biking
Location: Grand Strand
Attractions: Amusement park,
Mini-auto race track, Ripley's

Course: Arcadian Shores
Distance: 5,974, Par: 72
Rating: 68.8, No. of holes: 18
Guest Policy: Open to public,
Dress code
Phone Club-House: 803-449-5217
Pro's name: David Huber
Reservations: Book up to year ahead
Season: Year round
Guest Carry Club: No

Approximately 100 miles north of Historic Charleston lie the Elysian fields of golfdom. Here on South Carolina's Grand Strand, a 60 mile stretch along the Atlantic, golfers will find 44 fabulous courses, with more on the drawing boards. Several things can be attributed to the reign of "King Golf." 241 annual days of sunshine and a year-round mean temperature of 71.1 degrees, well-designed and maintained courses in a bustling seaside resort environment, and first rate accommodations—all halfway between Miami and Manhattan, are what make Myrtle Beach the tourist magnet that it is.

This 14-story 392 room contemporary white hotel is strategically situated in the Arcadian Shores section of the Grand Strand, and offers newly decorated large airy rooms, each with a private balcony and view of the Atlantic.

Restaurants include Alfredo's, an elegant dining room facing the ocean, the Arcadian Gardens Restaurant for casual fare, and sandwiches and salads at the Pool Terrace. The Veranda Bar, and the Wet Whistle Bar, featuring a steel drum band, will wet *your* whistle, while the rooftop nightclub, Another World is a great spot for dancing and checking out the action.

Step outside to the pool deck and 600 foot beachfront and a world of sunning, sailing, jogging, shelling, biking and sailboarding. Tennis players will find four lighted courts, and kids find so many attractions in Myrtle Beach that they're oblivious to the fact that Dad and Mom are teeing off on a different course every day. Who can resist the outlet malls, an amusement park, mini-auto race track, skating rink, a Ripley's "Believe-it-or-Not" Museum, Guinness Hall of World Records, a wax museum, antique auto museum, and an incredible water park for thrilling, drenching rides?

Designed by Rees Jones, whose company was chosen to redesign Brookline's Country Club for the 1988 U.S. Open. Natural lakes weaving in and out of the fairways, sixty-four white sand bunkers, a variety of trees, and the salty breezes off the Atlantic offer plenty of challenge. When you make your reservation, you'll be able to choose from a slew of nearby courses, and golf package rates. You can indicate your choice of course and tee times from an extensive list which is provided by the hotel.

Fairfield Glade Conference Center

This is an understated place where you can set your own pace. Located between Knoxville and Nashville, Fairfield Glade's next door neighbor is 84,000 acres of protected forest abounding with game. You can stay in the 100 room lodge, or in a condominium. There's a feeling of spaciousness here. No wonder, the resort is on 12,000 acres of Cumberland plateau and includes 4 gold courses, three pools, a full-service marina, tennis facilities, numerous lakes, a children's playground, and miniature golf. This is a wonderful place for bicycling and horseback riding, particularly in spring and fall. Two restaurants and a couple of lively lounges offer a variety of entertainment, and a shopping complex nearby ensures the availability of everything.

Fairfield Glade is the only course in the state claiming bentgrass tees, greens, and fairways, the layout has many elevation changes with lots of natural rock outcroppings, mountain streams and lakes, and maple, laurel and rhododendron lining the fairways. #14 is a favorite—a par three that drops 90 feet from tee to green with a placid lake as backdrop. Stonehenge is closed January and February, but fear not, the kindly pro assures us that at least two of the four are open all year.

Address: P.O. Box 1849, Fairfield Glade, 38555
Phone: 615-262-6702   800-251-6778
No. rooms: 100
Rates: $, Credit Cards
Services: Shops, Beauty shop, Pharmacy, Bank, Shops, children's playground
Restaurant: Greenhouse
Bar: Inglenook
Business Fac.: Audio-Visual, Conf. rm. cap.: 400
Sports Fac.: Tennis, Pools, Miniature Golf, Riding
Location: Cumberland County
Attractions: Cumberland Co. Playhouse, Catoosa Wildlife Area

Course: Stonehenge
Distance: 6,202, Par: 72
Rating: 69.9, No. of holes: 18
Guest Policy: Must be registered guest to play
Phone Club-House: 615-484-7521
Pro's name: Tom Waltz
Reservations: 5 days in advance, or earlier
Season: Closed Jan., Feb.
Guest Carry Club: No

Hyatt Regency DFW

Address: P.O. Box 619014, DFW Airport, 75261
Phone: 214-453-8400   800-228-9000
Innkeeper: Abdul Suleman
No. rooms: 1390
Rates: $$, Credit Cards: AmEx, Visa, MC, Other CC
Services: Garage and parking, Car hire, Shoe-shine, Babysitting, Summer game room, Laundry (valet), Room service
Restrictions: Pets ltd.
Restaurant: Nonna's
Bar: O'Shaughnessy's
Business Fac.: Secretarial, Telex
Sports Fac.: Pool, Handball, Racquetball, Spa
Location: Tarrant & Dallas Co.
Attractions: Galleria Mall, Neiman Marcus, Hard Rock Cafe

Course: Hyatt Bear Creek, West
Distance: 6,677, Par: 72
Rating: 72.7, No. of holes: 36
Guest Policy: Call for availability, Dress code
Phone Club-House: 214-453-0140
Pro's name: Larry Box
Reservations: May be made any time
Season: Year round
Guest Carry Club: Yes

As a prominent attraction within the DFW Airport, the twin towers of the 1,390 room Hyatt Regency offer the elegant touches familiar to Hyatt clientele, first rate meeting facilities, and a championship golf course. Recently facelifted, guests will find all the amenities here, in addition to the convenient location. The lobby is Southwestern contemporary in decor, with an earthy palette of teal and peach. Light stained oak, exquisite chandeliers and original Texas artwork complete the picture. Two floors feature Hyatt's Regency Club, with complimentary continental breakfast, and afternoon cocktails in the private lounge. Open 24 hours, Sullivan O'Shaughnessy's Grill is reminiscent of a 1950's corner drugstore. An Irish pub of the same name is nearby, while Brighton's Express Lounge is definitely Victorian. Papayas' welcomes travelers for casual fare, and for hearty steaks, fresh seafood and mesquite-grilled specialties, you might try Mister G's. Care for a taste of northern Italy? Sit back and hear an aria sung by your waiter as you dine on tortellini and veal parmigiana at Il Nonnos, or enjoy the lobby piano bar's offerings.

The environs are worth exploring. You can drive to Southfork, home of the Ewings, or take in Six Flags Over Texas, a theme park. Try Wet 'n Wild, a Texas-sized park of waterslides and inner tube chutes, or head for some legendary names such as Neiman-Marcus, and Bloomingdale's. Old City Park, close to downtown, with its restored Victorian houses, log cabins and an old railroad depot, appeals to all ages.

Hyatt Regency DFW also manages Hyatt Bear Creek Golf & Racquet Club, a 335-acre resort, just a five-minute shuttle ride away. It's a gorgeous layout of rolling hills, mature oak and cottonwood trees, two 18 hole golf courses, a driving range, practice bunkers and 2 putting greens, 2 picnic pavilions, and a snack bar and lounge. Tennis buffs will find 7 Laykold courts. Ted Robinson designed the East Course in 1980, and it has since hosted many tournaments including the PGA Regional Qualifying, National Lefthanders, Texas State Open, National Juniors Championship, and the MDA Gatlin Brothers Tournament. #5 East Course is a picturesque par-4 that's not long, but requires 2 perfectly placed shots over water to reach the bentgrass greens. Shoppers take note: the Golf Shop is considered one of the best in the country.

Horseshoe Bay Country Club Resort

All the superlatives associated with the glamour, the good life, and the know-how to create a first-class resort with quality amenities can be applied to this private country club resort deep in the heart of Texas. Horseshoe Bay, Norman Hurd's dream-come-true of a premier golf destination, is spring-fed streams and ancient rocks, exotic gardens, miles of shoreline and coves on a lake where anglers search out perch and catfish, four thousand acres of scenic overlooks and horseback trails, meeting and group facilities, a fully equipped marina, a magnificent two-tiered pool fed by a waterfall from granite outcrops, and an airstrip, should your plans include private flight. Dining can be elegant at The Captain's Table, with gold monogrammed matches, table-side flambeau and a French staff, or the casual touches of The Keel Way at the Yacht Club.

The tennis gardens are composed of four covered courts and ten outdoor courts surrounded by lakes, waterfalls and lush gardens. Within the complex is a Fitness Program consisting of Body Shape-up classes and Aqua Aerobics, and an Equestrian Center, under the supervision of a Riding Master, offers boarding, trail rides and lessons.

This is the spot to live out your golf fantasies on three Robert Trent Jones courses. The courses are well designed and maintained—enough so that the Texas State Open, the Texas State Amateur, the Texas State Mid-Amateur, and the Southern Texas PGA have opted to hold tournaments here. Think about the name—Slick Rock—and you'll get a clue about the topography. Pampas bush is an unplayable lie, and arborists will delight at the specimens of persimmon, varnish trees, cork screw, chinese tallows and eldarica pines, as well as the outcroppings of colorful granite. The second nine is more open, with greens of Penncross bentgrass, and water coming into play on seven holes. The Ram Rock, built eight years later, plays through brooks, waterfalls and rock gardens, small greens, and much sand. Fairways are tight and you'll need some well-placed drives to stay out of the water, especially on #4. Many professionals rave about #11, which plays down a slope to a small green with water and a sand trap lurking to the left. The 150 yard par 3 12th plays across the lake to a green protected by bunkers in front and on both sides, oaks behind, and an old schoolhouse left intact.

Address: Box 7766, Horseshoe Bay, 78654
Phone: 512-598-2511   800-252-9363
Innkeeper: Jan Boswell
No. rooms: 350
Rates: $$$$, Credit Cards: AmEx, Visa, MC, Other CC
Services: Valet, Beauty Shop, Car hire, Card or other game area
Restrictions: No pets
Restaurant: Yacht Club
Bar: Anchor Lounge
Business Fac.: Copiers, Audio-visual, Conf. rm. cap.: 250
Sports Fac.: Pool, Tennis, Water Skiing, Sailing
Location: Highland Lakes
Attractions: LBJ Home, Longhorn Caverns, Falls Creek Winery

Course: Slick Rock
Distance: 6,839, Par: 72
Rating: 72.0, No. of holes: 54
Guest Policy: Must be staying at resort or w/member, Dress code
Phone Club-House: 512-598-2511
Pro's name: Mike Mahan
Reservations: May be made 7 days in advance
Season: Year round
Guest Carry Club: No

Waterwood National Resort & CC

Address: Waterwood Box One, Huntsville, 77340
Phone: 409-891-5211
Innkeeper: Don Craven
No. rooms: 83
Rates: $, Credit Cards: AmEx, Visa, MC, Other CC
Services: Weekly Exercise, Supervised park for children, TV
Restrictions: No pets
Restaurant: Garden Room
Bar: Garden Court
Business Fac.: Audio-visual, Sec., Conf. rm. cap.: 250
Sports Fac.: Tennis, Pool, Sailing, Bike, Fish
Location: Lake Livingson
Attractions: Big Thicket Ntl.Forest, Sam Houston Museum, Shops

Course: Waterwood National
Distance: 6,258, Par: 71
Rating: 69.7, No. of holes: 17
Guest Policy: Play permitted to member of USGA course
Phone Club-House: 409-891-5211
Pro's name: Eddie Dey
Reservations: Make tee time with reservations
Season: Year round
Guest Carry Club: Yes

The General Manager's note reads—"Resort to the Best of Texas!" Located on Lake Livingston in the heart of East Texas hill country, Waterwood is a world of clean air, tall pines and plenty of recreation opportunities. Accommodations are in beautifully appointed guest rooms, including four suites with patios and balconies overlooking the golf course. There are also forest lodge rooms which are a bit more secluded. The Garden Room and its adjacent Garden Court Lounge set the pace for leisurely meals and entertainment.

Lake Livingston, with a full service marine is just the spot for bass fishing, sailing or simply contemplating. Tennis players will have four lighted Laykold courts, and four swimming pools scattered about the resort await the serious lap-counters and sun-bathers. Bicycle through the pines or visit the Health Club with weight equipment, saunas and aerobics classes.

An impressive selection of meeting rooms, banquet areas and services are available to the conference planner.

Carved from the deep East Texas Piney Woods, the Pete Dye course abounds in long vistas of rolling, narrow tree-lined fairways, natural rough, deep bunkers and small well placed greens. This is the site of the PGA tour qualifying school in 1978, '79, and '81; the Women's Western Amateur in 1982, and the Women's Southern Amateur in 1984. Tall Texas tales recount #14, a par three that requires a 225 yard carry over water from championship tees to a small cliffside green. There's a sizeable practice and teaching area including driving range, putting greens and sand chipping area.

Del Lago Resort & Conference Center

This is a meeting planners dream come true. Covering more than 300 acres on Lake Conroe's edge 40 miles north of Texas, Del Lago provides complete conference facilities in a tranquil environment. You can survey it all from a one or two bedroom suite twenty-one stories above the lake. There's no lack of recreation. The spa and fitness center offers everything from a workout, tanning bed and massage therapist to work your body over, to racquetball and exercise classes. 13 hard surface tennis courts, and many other additional seasonal activities are available. Start with horseshoes and finish with swimming, a game of softball or volleyball. The marina offers a variety of party boats for private functions or you can sail solo. For larger groups, Lake Conroe has a turn-of-the-century stern wheel paddle boat.

Lago Vista is a split-level restaurant overlooking the pool area, marina and lake, and scattered about are several other eateries, as well as a hearty Texas-style barbecue in the pool area in warm months.

There are local fairs, shopping the Texas Renaissance Festival, hunting, antiquing and historic home tours all nearby, and the local theater and symphony perform in a restored theater nearby.

The championship course, built in concert with the local ecology intact, is a year-round haven. A product of Jay Riviere and Dave Marr, the course hosted the 1987 TPA tour event, Del Lago Classic. You may also remember the Palmer-Lopez vs. Player-Stephenson match here in November of 1984. Signature hole is #9, a 464 yard par 4 with narrow driving fairway. Sounds easy, but you'll need a long second shot over water to a long, narrow green. This is Texas, and everything's long. Hotel guests have priority tee times here amid eleven lakes, more than 80 sand traps, and those long fairways lined with pines and white oaks.

Address: 600 Del Lago Blvd., Montgomery, 77356
Phone: 409-582-6100   800-558-1317
Innkeeper: Alberto S. Cobian
No. rooms: 310
Rates: $, Credit Cards: AmEx, Visa, MC, Other CC
Services: Babysitter, Cable TV, Florist, Groceries, Safe deposit boxes, Room service
Restrictions: Pets ltd.
Restaurant: Cafe Verde
Bar: Fiddler's
Business Fac.: Complete bus. fac., Conf. rm. cap.: 1,000
Sports Fac.: Tennis, Pool, Hiking/Jogging, Boating
Location: On Lake Conroe
Attractions: Super sports competition, 3 local fairs

Course: Del Lago
Distance: 6,825, Par:
Rating: 70.9, No. of holes: 18
Guest Policy: Guests have priority tee times, Dress code
Phone Club-House: 409-582-6100
Reservations: May be made any time
Season: All year
Guest Carry Club: No

Woodlands Inn & Country Club

Address: 2301 N. Millbend Dr.,
The Woodlands, 77380
Phone: 713-367-1100   800-433-2624
Innkeeper: Juan Aquinde
No. rooms: 268
Rates: $, Credit Cards: AmEx,
Visa, MC, Other CC
Services: Valet, Library, Barber shop,
Beauty shop, Parking, Car hire, House
doctor, Babysitting, Card/game area,
Laundry
Restrictions: No pets
Restaurant: Woodlands Dining Room
Bar: Lobby Bar
Business Fac.: Sec. Svc.,
Audio-visual, Conf. rm. cap.: 1,000
Sports Fac.: Tennis, Pools, Health
Club, Ice Skate
Location: Montgomery County
Attractions: NASA, various Houston
Sporting activities

Course: TPC Woodlands
Distance: 6,387, Par: 72
No. of holes: 54
Guest Policy: Open to public, call for
availability
Phone Club-House: 713-367-1100
Pro's name: Gary Rippey
Reservations: Resort guests have
priority
Season: Year round
Guest Carry Club: Yes, Caddies: Yes

Think of Houston, and Philip Johnson's Pennzoil Towers, the Astros and Oilers in the Astrodome, the Lyndon B. Johnson Space Center, and the showplaces on River Oaks Boulevard. Think golf, and The Woodlands Inn, sitting on 25,000 acres of oak and pine forests 14 miles from the airport, an oasis of comfortable style. The main building and 14 guest lodges are rough cedar two-story units clustered among mature Texas pines. Designed expressly as a conference center, features include over 40,000 square feet of meeting space, a ballroom, and 20 conference rooms with state-of-the-art communication and presentation equipment.

Everything is here to promote a sense of fitness, productivity and pleasure. Among the choices are two restaurants, bar, a fully equipped men's and women's health spa, 6 swimming pools, game room, or skating at the nearby ice rink. For in-depth tennis instruction and tournament play, you may want to attend a Peter Burwash International "Tennis for Life" weekend. A unique open design in the recreation center combines lobby and game room with a view of 3 indoor courts, and four additional courts plus 17 outdoor courts offer a combination of hard court and clay. Right in the center, and meandering through the development is Lake Harrison, home to ducks, lily pads and many Titleists. Hikers and bikers have over 30 miles of trails, and shoppers can pursue the wares at The Wharf, a retail emporium adjacent to the Inn.

The highlight of the resort is the championship Tournament Players Course, one of eight currently used in the United States, and open to the public. Home of the Lee Trevino State Open, and the Annual Insurance Agents Houston Open, this is the course with the much-photographed #13 surrounded by water. You'll see permanent built-in seating in stadium-like mounds on #18—all the better to watch the pros strut and putt. Ask Hale Irwin, Curtis Strange, or Greg Norman how they played #17—its a stickler with a lake guarding the green. North Course is open for Inn guests.

The Homestead

You are in for a treat should you take the Skyline Drive of the Blue Ridge Parkway and make the Homestead your destination. Here you'll step back to an era where gentlemen open doors, piano music accompanies high tea, and coats and ties are de rigueur. You'll see no blue jeans, minis or shorts here, for the management continues to stress a standard of gracious living not often found. Amidst mountains, valleys, streams and those unforgettable hot springs, this 15,000 acre venerable resort is renowned for superb golf and tennis, thermal baths, and trap and skeet shooting, in a relaxed traditional environment.

The large Kentucky red brick hotel with its famous clock tower has 600 rooms, impressive salons, wide colonnades for strolling, rolling lawns, and diversions such as carriage riding and lawn bowling. Miles of scenic trails wind through the Virginia countryside for horseback riding, and the trout are plentiful in the resort's beautiful mountain stream. Other activities include swimming in indoor or outdoor pools, archery, bowling on eight tenpin lanes and a range of indoor games plus nightly movies.

Considered by many to be *the* best mountain course, Cascades Upper is hilly and demanding, requiring a variety of shots. The architect of the par-70 course was William Flynn, designer of Shinnecock Hills, site of the 1986 U.S. Open, and Cherry Hills, where Arnold Palmer shot a 65 to win the U.S. Open in 1960. (A young amateur named Jack Nicklaus finished second.) Sam Snead, who grew up down the road, and caddied Cascades as a boy says, "it's the most complete golf course I know of . . . the perfect place to practice for a tournament because you have to hit every shot in the bag. The drive, long irons, fairway woods, delicate pitches over water, side hill, uphill, downhill lies, long and short trap shots—everything!" The United States' oldest golf championship, the U.S. Amateur, was held at Cascades-Upper in 1988, with the Lower Cascades Course serving as the second site of stroke play qualifying. Robert Trent Jones added this last longer 18 in 1963, and players will recognize his heavily-trapped large greens and long tees. The Homestead Course, dating from 1892, with putting green and practice fairway, claims the oldest first tee in continuous use in the country. It is the shortest of the three, open year-round, while Cascade Courses are open spring through late fall.

Address: Hot Springs, 24445
Phone: 703-839-5500   800-468-7747
Innkeeper: Gordon L. Rockwell
No. rooms: 600
Rates: $$, Credit Cards: AmEx, Visa, MC, Other CC
Services: Valet, Library, Barber, Beauty shop, Garage and parking, Car hire, House doctor, Babysitting, Card/game area, Laundry, Room service
Restrictions: Pets ltd.
Restaurant: Dining room, 7 restaurants
Business Fac.: Secretarial, Telex, Conf. rm. cap.: 26 rooms
Sports Fac.: Pool, Tennis, Croquet, Riding, Spa
Location: Bath County
Attractions: Stonewall Jackson's home, Natural Bridge

Course: Cascades-Upper
Distance: 6,282, Par: 70
Rating: 70.0, No. of holes: 54
Guest Policy: Call for availability, Dress code
Phone Club-House: 703-839-5500
Pro's name: Herman Perry
Reservations: Tee time needed, make 1 week advance
Season: Spring through late fall
Guest Carry Club: No

The Tides Lodge

Address: 1 St. Andrews Ln.,
Irvington, 22480
Phone: 804-438-6000   800-446-5660
Innkeeper: E.A. Stephens, Jr.
No. rooms: 62
Rates: $$$, Credit Cards: Visa, MC
Services: Valet, Garage and Parking,
Car hire, Complimentary shoe-
shine, Babysitting, Card/game area,
Laundry, Summer children's program,
Room service
Restrictions: Pets ltd.
Restaurant: Royal Stewart Dining
Room
Bar: McD's Pub
Business Fac.: Secretarial, Copiers,
Conf. rm. cap.: 100
Sports Fac.: Pool, Tennis, Croquet,
Sailing, Bicycle
Location: Lancaster County
Attractions: Christchurch, Stratford
Hall, Yorktown

Course: Tartan—Tides
Distance: 6,566, Par: 72
Rating: 69.9, No. of holes: 45
Guest Policy: Call for tee time, Dress
code
Phone Club-House: 804-438-6000
Pro's name: Mac Main, Jr.
Reservations: As soon as possible
Season: Year round
Guest Carry Club: Yes

In the same location, the 60-room Tides Lodge offers an attractive variety of accommodations. These range from single rooms to suites for four. Or, pamper yourself with a waterfront 2 bed-room condominium on "The Green," where you can walk out your door and tee off within minutes.

In keeping with the Scottish mood, diners will appreciate the Royal Stewart Dining Room where you can sample local seasonal delicacies such as blue crabs and oysters, or sauteed fillet of fresh grouper. Rates include just about every-thing including the summer children's program and yacht cruises, tennis and use of sail boats. One of the world's last cable-drawn ferries crosses the Corrotoman River near The Lodge—a marvelous excursion for all ages. Yorktown's bat-tle fields are 35 minutes away, and Colonial Wil-liamsburg, Norfolk and Richmond are about an hour's drive.

Guests at The Lodge can play the Golden Eagle Course at The Tides Inn, or The Inn's Executive Nine. The first nine holes of the championship Tartan course were designed by Sir Guy Cam-pbell of St. Andrews, and the back nine by George Cobb, one of several architects responsi-ble for sprucing up Augusta National, home of the Masters.

Tides Inn

Poised on the shores of historic Carter's Creek and the Rappahannock River, The Tides Inn is a small family resort whose main attraction is its idyllic setting. Just over an hour's drive north of Williamsburg, this forty year old rambling clapboard Inn hosts many returning guests who seek the relaxed pace, amenities and climate of Virginia's northern neck.

Most rooms have spectacular bay or river views, many have balconies, and none has a TV! The Lee Suite, with 2 canopied beds, jacuzzi and marble counters, is accented with lovely antiques.

Lunch and cocktails are served at the Summer House, aboard the yachts, at the Beach Pavilion or at Cap'n B's at the Golden Eagle. Dinner in the Rappahannock Dining Room overlooking the river, might begin with a hot oyster cocktail and be followed by luscious sauteed soft shell crab. The Inn's policy is to offer activities on a complimentary basis, except for golf, mid-April to November. This includes yacht cruises, paddleboats, oyster roasts, bicycles, and canoes. History buffs can explore the birthplaces of Washington and Lee, the shops and lore of colonial Williamsburg, and the backroads of Lancaster County.

Two eighteen-hole courses are available for guests, the Golden Eagle, and Tartan Golf Course. Designed by George Cobb, several holes play over the lake on a course that's fairly hilly considering this is a fairly flat part of Virginia. #5 is the one to write home about—a great par 4 experience! The tee shot is difficult because the player must bite off only what he thinks he can carry on the fly. Water, again, but the carry is a shorter one—and then the green. Its guarded by water on the left and two large bunkers on the right, sloping gently towards the water. Good shots are rewarded, and poor ones penalized.

Tartan is noted for narrow tree-lined fairways, water on 10 holes, and numerous twists, doglegs and dips. Greens are large, and a gurgling stream seems to be everywhere.

Address: Irvington, 22480
Phone: 804-438-5000   800-446-9981
Innkeeper: Betty G. Dawson
Rates: $, Credit Cards:
Restaurant: Rappahannock Dining Room
Sports Fac.: Tennis, Boating
Location: Rappahannock River
Attractions: Birth places of Washington & Lee, Williamsburg

Course: Golden Eagle
Distance: 6,523, Par: 72
Rating: 70.9, No. of holes: 18
Guest Policy: Call for tee time, guests have priority, Dress code
Phone Club-House: 804-438-5501
Pro's name: Jeffrey Winters
Reservations: Telephone for reservations
Season: Year round
Guest Carry Club: Yes

Ford's Colony

Address: 101 St. Andrews Dr. Williamsburg, 23185
Phone: 800-548-2978 800-565-4340
Innkeeper: Realtec, Incorporated
No. of rooms: 20
Rates: $145.00, Credit Cards: AmEx, Mc, Visa,
Services: Bellmen, Concierge, Daily maid, Linen, Valet, CC membership, Hospitality van, Complimentary range balls
Restrictions: No pets
Restaurant: "The Dining Room"
Bar: Piano Bar and Lite Fare
Business Fac.: Available to small groups
Sports Fac.: Jogging trails, Aerobics, Weight equipment
Location: Williamsburg-4 miles
Attractions: Colonial Williamsburg, Busch Gardens, Jamestown

Golf Course: Ford's Colony Country Club
Distance: 3,371, Par: 36 Rating: 70.3, No. of holes: 27
Guest Policy: Call Pro Shop for information Dress code
Club House Phone: 804-565-4100
Pro's Name: Scott Harrill
Fees: $53.00, Carts: Included
Reservations: Accepted 30 days in advance
Guest Carry Club: No

Inspired by its proximity to the Colonial capital named for King William of Orange, Ford's Colony offers a golfing vacation in a prestigious country club community. Guests stay in luxuriously appointed condominiums located in the heart of Ford's Colony.

These 2 and 3 bedroom condominiums homes are spaciously designed to give you plenty of room to relax and stretch out. With so much to do at Ford's Colony, we know that when you play hard you want to rest easy. After a full day of golf, tennis or sightseeing in nearby Williamsburg, you'll appreciate coming home to a whirlpool tub, fully equipped kitchen and cable TV.

Beyond sports, you'll enjoy dining and entertainment at our gracious Ford's Colony Clubhouse. Renowned for its carefully stocked wine cellar, the restaurant is a drawing card for connoisseurs. An evening of impressive service and charm was capped by an Esprit de Cognac in the intimate Lounge.

The Dan Maples designed golf courses provide challenges for all caliber of golfers. Three or four sets of tees on each hole permit the golfers to accept the challenge of their choice. Each hole is distinctive with rolling bermuda grass fairways, speckled with sand and water, and lined with oak, hickory, holly and dogwood trees. Undulating bentgrass greens provide inviting targets on each hole.

Ford's Colony has the honor of hosting the qualifying rounds for the Anheuser-Busch Classic, Yamaha Cup Matches, and in 1989, the MAPGA Tournament of Champions.

Ford's Colony puts you at the center of rich and varied sightseeing, shopping and sporting opportunities. Step back into 18th century life at Colonial Williamsburg. Feel the seafaring mystique of Jamestown, or relive America's heritage on the Revolutionary War battlefield of Yorktown. For amusement, the magic of Busch Gardens awaits your active pleasure. As for shopping, browse 'til your heart's content at a myriad of quaint shops lining kthe historic streets. Or, search for bargains at the well known Williamsburg Pottery Factory and a variety of other brand-name outlets dotting the area. For sea-lovers, there's sailing, boating and fishing on the plantation-lined James River.

Colonial Williamsburg Inn

The restoration of Virginia's 18th century capital, where George Washington, Patrick Henry and Thomas Jefferson plotted revolution, is an exercise in authenticity not to be missed.

Located adjacent to the 173-acre Historic Area, the whitewashed brick rambling Regency style Inn, built in 1937, is furnished with antiques and faithful reproductions. Owned and operated by the Colonial Williamsburg Foundation, the Inn also offers accommodations in taverns and colonial homes within the Historic Area. Providence Hall, a restored home, is available for special events.

The Inn's guest list is long and impressive, and includes Queen Elizabeth II and Prince Philip, the Emperor and Empress of Japan, Sir Winston Churchill, movie personalities such as Elizabeth Taylor, John Wayne, and Ronald Reagan.

The Regency Dining Room, a study in tranquil green, Empire accents, and Chinoiserie, reflects the quiet elegance of the landed gentry of 19th century England. An exquisite afternoon tea is served daily in the East Lounge, while the Regency Lounge is a comfortable meeting spot, complete with piano music.

Recreational and sports facilities include 4 clay and 4 Hartru tennis courts, an indoor and an outdoor swimming pool, lawn bowling, croquet, and a full health spa.

Golfers will find 27 holes of challenging Robert Trent Jones' design here in Virginia's picturesque Tidewater area. Each August, the course hosts the Middle Atlantic PGA Championship, but other times guests have no trouble getting a tee time. Opened in 1963, the Golden Horseshoe Golf Course spreads over 125 acres of rolling terrain, with fairways stretching over a five-acre lake, up densely wooded ravines, and through glades of flowering trees and bushes, culminating in large sculptured greens. The hole that seems to fascinate the most is the 16th—"island green." The par-three, 168-yard hole plays without fairway to a green completely surrounded by water. As if the water isn't enough, Jones tempts the wayward ball with three menacing bunkers at water's edge. Jack Nicklaus established the course record—67 from the championship tees, in 1967. An additional nine holes, the par-31 Spotswood Course, also by Jones, has plenty of doglegs, lakes, and cushioned turf.

Address: P.O.Box B, Williamsburg, 23185
Phone: 804-229-1000   800-446-8956
Innkeeper: Russel E. Cleveland, Jr.
No. rooms: 235
Rates: $$, Credit Cards: AmEx, Visa, MC
Services: Valet, Library, Barber, Beauty shop, Outside parking, Complimentary shoe-shine, Babysitting, Card/game area, Laundry, Comp. afternoon tea, Room service
Restrictions: No pets
Restaurant: Regency Dining Room
Bar: Regency Lounge
Business Fac.: Secretarial, Copiers, Conf. rm. cap.: 65
Sports Fac.: Pool, Tennis, Croquet, Full Health spa
Location: Tidewater
Attractions: Historic area Colonial Williamsburg, Craft shops

Course: Golden Horseshoe
Distance: 6,340, Par: 71
Rating: 70.0, No. of holes: 27
Guest Policy: Non-guests pay higher fees. Call, Dress code
Phone Club-House: 804-229-1000
Pro's name: Del Snyder
Reservations: When you book your trip
Season: Usually year round
Guest Carry Club: Yes

Kingsmill On The James

Address: 1010 Kingsmill Rd.,
Williamsburg, 23105
Phone: 804-253-1703   800-832-5665
Innkeeper: Harry D. Knight
No. rooms: 300
Rates: $, Credit Cards: AmEx,
Visa, MC
Services: Cable TV
Restrictions: No pets
Restaurant: Riverview
Bar: Moody's Tavern
Business Fac.: Audio-visual,
Copiers, Conf. rm. cap.: 300
Sports Fac.: Tennis, Pool,
Racquetball, Spa
Location: Williamsburg (Col.)
Attractions: Williamsburg Pottery,
Outlets, Historic Plantation

Course: River Course
Distance: 6,776, Par: 71
Rating: 74.5, No. of holes: 18
Guest Policy: Call for availability
Phone Club-House: 804-253-1703
Pro's name: Al Burns
Reservations: May be made with
room reservations
Season: Year round
Guest Carry Club: No

There are a few places that each of us should
visit during our lifetime, and Williamsburg,
swathed in history, and basking in glorious restoration heads the list. Developed by Anheuser-
Busch, this meticulously-planned conference
center/resort reeks of quality in concept, design,
and amenities. Lodging is in condominiums
which vary in size. The 60,000 square foot conference center can accommodate large and small
meetings, and offers state-of-the-art facilities.
There are several fine restaurants on the premises, all offering expansive views of the historic
James. Don't miss the colonial atmosphere at
Moody's Tavern—a paneled cozy gathering
place. The Sports Club is fully equipped with indoor and outdoor pools, saunas and racquetball
courts, even a grill, while a game room for billiards, cards and chess occupies the top floor.
Tennis buffs appreciate a complete shop and 12
all-weather courts, plus use of a ball machine.
The marina's gorgeous—in a protected harbor
with picnic and beach area. Its here that you'll
get everything you need for saltwater and freshwater fishing, or tie up if you're cruising the
area.

You'll have all of historic Williamsburg to de-
vour, plus the wonders of adjacent Busch Gardens, a re-creation of eight European villages. In
addition, there are more than 30 rides, shopping
and live entertainment.

The accolades accorded golf facilities here are
well-deserved. Challenge yourself to Pete Dye's
River Course, home of the PGA Anheuser Busch
Golf Classic. Walk the fairways where Tom
Sieckmann, after overshooting the 18th green,
took home the money in 1988. Plenty of big rolls
and swells on the greens. Or tee off on Arnold
Palmer's Plantation Course, around ponds, lakes
and river views. Curtis Strange, a familiar figure
especially after the 1988 U.S. Open, is the Touring Pro; he frequently conducts clinics and exhibitions here. As if all this isn't enough the Golf
Shop heads the list of "friendliest and most
helpful anywhere."

The Buccaneer Hotel

What a history this family-owned and operated hotel has had. Hugging 248 acres of shore with vistas of Christiansted's harbor to the west, St. Thomas and St. John to the north, and Buck Island National Park to the east, the resort is a place where returning families are remembered and pampered. During the mid-1600's it was a hospice, under the Danes, a sugar factory, later a cotton plantation, and subsequent owners bred cattle here. De Luxe beachside rooms with private patios to "no frills" rooms (perfect for extra children provided that they are over four years) in a wide range of settings are available. The open-air Terrace Restaurant with its unimpaired view of the harbor, the beaches, tennis courts, lounges, spa, watersports, horseback riding, shopping arcade, all add up to a vacation you'll never forget. A glance at the Coconut Grapevine keeps guests apprised of such earth-shattering events such as croquet games, Jimmy Hamilton playing jazz, island tours, a scuba or royak demonstration, and should you be the lucky winner of the "World Class Hermit Crab Races" you'll win a free seaplane trip to St. Thomas for a day of duty-free shopping. Don't miss the excursion to Buck Island Underwater National Park—truly unique and worth the trip.

Tim Johnston, an amiable golf pro, gives tips on how to play the 18 hole course. An excerpt reads: "Hole #12—the island hole—this hole looks like a monster, but is actually a birdie hole! The directional flag is 165 yards from the tee. Should your tee shot "splash," the drop area is the rear of the ladies' tee. This is an enjoyable course occasionally featuring a tail wind as bonus!"

Address: P.O. Box 218, St. Croix, 00820
Phone: 800-223-1108
Innkeeper: Robert D. Armstrong
No. rooms: 147
Rates: $$$, Credit Cards: AmEx, Visa, MC, Other CC
Restrictions: No pets
Restaurant: Terrace, Mermaid, Brass Parrot
Bar: Terrace Lounge
Business Fac.: Conf. rm. cap.: 2 rooms
Sports Fac.: 3 beaches, Snorkeling, Health spa
Location: Caribbean Sea
Attractions: Buck Island Underwater National Park.

Course: Buccaneer
Distance: 5,504, Par: 71
Rating: No. of holes: 18
Guest Policy: Call for availability
Phone Club-House: 914-763-5526
Pro's name: Tim Johnstonn
Reservations: May be made with room reservation
Season: All year
Guest Carry Club: Ltd

Carambola Beach Resort Golf Club

Address: P.O. Box 3031, St. Croix, 00851
Phone: 809-778-3800   800-223-7637
Innkeeper: S. Lee Bowden
No. rooms: 157
Rates: $$$$, Credit Cards: AmEx, Visa, MC, Other CC
Services: Ceiling fans, Mini bar, Scream porches, Hammocks
Restrictions: No pets
Restaurant: Saman & Mahogany Rooms
Bar: Flamboyant
Business Fac.: Audio-visual, Copiers
Sports Fac.: Tennis, Scuba, Sailing, Horseback riding
Location: Edge of Rain Forest
Attractions: Ancient stone sugar mill ruins, Saman trees

Course: Carambola Beach Golf Club
Distance: 6,181, Par: 72
Rating: 69.8, No. of holes: 18
Guest Policy: Reservations made through golf shop
Phone Club-House: 809-778-3800
Reservations: Tee time 2 days in adv.-for guests
Season: All year
Guest Carry Club: No

On the north side of the 84 square mile island in surroundings evocative of a classic Carribbean Great House, sits the first Rockresort to open is the area since the sixties. Caramola, names for a star-shaped fruit from a tree cultivated in East India, is modeled after a traditional fishing village with red roofs, high dormered windows, raftered ceilings, and private screened porches that beckon cooling trade winds.

Your room is in a tropical garden by the sea, perhaps in the superb Davis Bay Suite, housed in its own sugar mill. Separate sleeping and sitting areas in the luxurious guest rooms blend colorful fabrics with rattan to give a feeling of spaciousness and tropical elegance. Consistent with Rockresorts' philosophy for a Carribbean resort, guest accommodations have no televisions or telephones. The restaurants here offer West Indies cuisine minus excessive spices and fats. Produce is brought from the resort's own farm, and what isn't grown here comes from local sources.

Guests can play tennis, soak up rays at the gorgeous beach, swim in the pool, relax in the jacuzzis, snorkel, or explore some of the sights on the island.

Golf is fabulous here on a Robert Trent Jones, Jr. course that opened in 1966 under the name Fountain Valley. Rolling past ancient stone sugar ruins deep in a lush valley of tall bamboo, enormous saman trees and endless varieties of palms, it's like playing in a botanical garden. Those in the know claim its string of par three holes is the best in the tropics. The par-5 13th is only 458 yards, but a sharp dogleg, a sparkling pond and a steep ravine will test your finesse. This is the home of the Annual Louise Charity Classic (major league baseball players), Shell's Wonderful World of Golf, the Eastern Caribbean Championship, and the future site of the Club Champions Championship.

Stowe Mount Mansfield Resort

Mt. Mansfield is Vermont's highest peak, and from its summit you can peer into 3 states and Canada. In this charming New England village you'll see a traditional way of life where friendliness and family activity are stressed.

The resort consists of an Inn and condominiums in varying settings. Stowe Village offers every kind of eatery imaginable—from sundaes to sushi. Guests at the resort have access to a complete Fitness Center, and the amenities at Stowe Country Club, which is operated by the resort. The Club has tennis courts, a first-rate golf shop, and an attractive New England-y Clubhouse with a dining room, luncheon patio, and meeting areas.

This is one of New England's more scenic courses, where the clear blue sky and crisp, clean air heightens the pleasure of carrying a mountain stream. It's not unusual to see a mama fox and a youngster playing on the green, or chasing a fallen crabapple. Plan on thrills in the hills here, as well as several ponds. It's spectacular here in the fall.

Address: RR1, Box 1310, Stowe, 05672
Phone: 802-253-7311   800-253-4754
Innkeeper: Wayne D. Hoss
No. rooms: 100
Rates: $$, Credit Cards: AmEx, Visa, MC, Other CC
Services: Babysitting, Programs for the young, Color TV, Room service
Restrictions: Pets ltd.
Restaurant: Toll House
Bar: Fireside Tavern
Business Fac.: Complete bus. fac., Conf. rm. cap.: 200
Sports Fac.: Tennis, Pools, Health Spa, Bicycling
Location: Mountain setting
Attractions: New England villages, Ski center

Course: Stowe Country Club
Distance: 6,163, Par: 71
Rating: 68.0, No. of holes: 18
Guest Policy: Open to the public
Phone Club-House: 802-253-7321
Pro's name: J. Hadley, PGA
Reservations: May be made 3 weeks in advance
Season: End of May to Oct.15
Guest Carry Club: No

Sugarbush Inn

Address: Sugarbush Access Rd.,
Warren, 05674
Phone: 802-583-2301   800-451-4320
Innkeeper: Tim Piper
No. rooms: 45
Rates: $, Credit Cards: AmEx,
Visa, MC, Other CC
Services: Car hire, Van service,
Parking, Valet, Laundry
Restaurant: Onion Patch, Terrace
Room
Business Fac.: Audio-visual, Conf.
rm. cap.: 225
Sports Fac.: Tennis, Pools, Sports
Center
Attractions: Skiing, Hiking, Fishing,
Soaring, Polo, Shopping

Course: Sugarbush
Distance: 5,886, Par: 70
Rating: 69.0, No. of holes: 18
Guest Policy: Inn guests have priority
Phone Club-House: 802-583-2722
Pro's name: Michale Busk
Reservations: Call for availability
Season: May–end of Oct.
Guest Carry Club: Yes

This is clean, pure, simple Vermont. Village greens with local Revolutionary War heroes flanked by aging cannons, whitewashed parsonages, wooden bridges spanning trout-filled streams, and bread fresh from 18th-century brick beehive ovens. Its also the colonial-style Sugarbush Inn, a luxurious isolated retreat in the Green Mountains, not far from Montpelier. Stay in the gracious Inn, or a condominium with one-two or three bedrooms. You'll find indoor and outdoor pools, jacuzzi, saunas, 11 tennis courts, and newly redecorated conference facilities. This is primo cross-country ski area, so you can imagine the gently rolling terrain when the Top-Flites are four feet under. The food is wonderful in the main dining room, or you may prefer the less formal greenhouse setting in the Onion Patch. Not soon to be forgotten is the nightly seafood bar on the front lawn and the 19th Hole Restaurant overlooking the golf course.

The course here is dramatic. With mountains that top four thousand feet looming in the background, and sudden bursts of red, orange and red covering the hills and valleys in the fall, the rolling course is stunning. You won't have a lot of level lies on this Robert Trent Jones course; the old timers will tell you to just play from one landing area to the next.

The Woodstock Inn & Resort

Close your eyes and imagine a small New England town whose village green is surrounded by a beautifully preserved landmark village of red and white clapboard and brick houses. The original Inn burned and a new handsome Rockresort emerged in 1969. Handcut stone, weathered timbers, patchwork quilts and a staff renowned for service are what guests will remember. Historians have noted that Woodstock has four church bells forged by patriotic night rider and hero, Paul Revere.

Not too big, this 121 room gracious establishment includes two suites and three guest houses. A ten foot fireplace dominates the hospitable lobby which is filled with antiques, seasonal floral arrangements and touches of New England. An afternoon tea is served here. Rooms are furnished in modern oak, and many have views of surrounding hills, ablaze with russets and golds of the changing seasons.

Guests can partake in a myriad of activities. Choose from indoor or outdoor swimming and tennis, handball and squash, croquet, racquetball, paddle tennis, or hiking in surrounding hills. A full health spa includes the works from whirlpool to massage to weight training.

Dinner is an occasion in the main dining room, and gentlemen are expected to don a jacket. Guests congregate in the Pine Room for cocktails or after dinner libations.

Exploring historic Woodstock, shopping for antiques and crafts, and the Billings Farm Museum, are all favorite pastimes of returning guests.

Come winter, guests can enjoy the snow either on ross-country skis or at the resort's slopes. Or try ice skating, dogsledding and sleigh rides.

Robert Trent Jones redesigned this narrow course here which was originally built in 1895. A brook meanders throughout the holes in this picturesque valley adding variety and interest to your game.

Address: 14 The Green, Woodstock, 05091
Phone: 802-457-1100   800-223-7637
Innkeeper: Laurance Rockefeller
No. rooms: 121
Rates: $, Credit Cards: AmEx, Visa, MC, Other CC
Services: Valet, Garage and parking, Car hire, International currency exchange, Babysitting, Card or other game area, Laundry, Room service
Restrictions: No pets
Restaurant: Main Dining Room
Bar: Pine Room
Business Fac.: Sec., Audio-visual, Conf. rm. cap.: 320
Sports Fac.: Pool, Tennis, Handball, Croquet, Spa
Location: Windsor County
Attractions: Calvin Coolidge Home, Billings Farm & Museum

Course: Woodstock Country Club
Distance: 6,043, Par: 69
Rating: 69.0, No. of holes: 18
Guest Policy: Call for availability
Phone Club-House: 802-457-2112
Reservations: May be made 2 days in advance
Season: May 1–Nov. 1
Guest Carry Club: Yes

Inn at Semiahmoo

Address: 9565 Semiahmoo Pkwy.,
Blaine, 98230
Phone: 206-371-2000   800-542-6082
Innkeeper: Ray Esperti
No. rooms: 196
Rates: $, Credit Cards: AmEx,
Visa, MC, Other CC
Services: Valet, Library, Car hire, Intl.
currency exchange, Babysitting, Card/
game area, Laundry, Room service
Restrictions: No pets
Restaurant: Stars
Bar: Packers
Business Fac.: Secretarial, Copiers,
Conf. rm. cap.: 10 rooms
Sports Fac.: Pool, Tennis, Handball,
Croquet
Location: West of Blaine
Attractions: Victoria, B.C.-Old
England Today, European Shops

Course: The Inn at Semi-ah-moo
Distance: 7,005, Par: 72
Rating: 74.3, No. of holes: 18
Guest Policy: Not specific, Dress code
Phone Club-House: 206-371-2000
Pro's name: Craig Griswold
Reservations: May be made with
hotel reservation
Season: Year round
Guest Carry Club: Yes

Washington's newest and finest destination resort hotel, The Inn at Semi-ah-moo, is located on the site of the historic Semi-ah-moo Salmon Cannery, at the far Northwest corner of the Continental U.S. At this natural wildlife refuge, you'll be sharing the beaches with seals, shorebirds and migratory ducks and geese. Here, great bald eagles soar overhead, and deer step lightly through the underbrush.

The elegant Stars restaurant highlights the inn's seafront location, with two levels facing the water and an open-aired decor accented by natural fir and hemlock. Under the direction of Chef David Benot, you'll experience the delights of specialties like Baked Salmon Wrapped in Parchment, accompanied by a fine Northwest wine.

Plenty of area attractions will keep the nongolfer busy. Nearly every imaginable sporting diversion is available on the resort premises, including indoor tennis, racquetball, squash and programmed conditioning. Outdoors, enjoy jogging trails, cycling lanes and paths which wind along the beach and up through majestic firs.

But, Semi-ah-moo's historic marina is probably most popular of all. A seafaring place since the 1880's when the Star Fleet sailed from the cannery docks and gold seeker shipped off to Alaska, today's Semi-ah-moo offers new excitement with trips to the nearby American San Juan Islands, the Canadian Channel Islands, Old English Victoria and cosmopolitan Vancouver.

The championship Arnold Palmer-designed golf course opened to rave reviews in July, 1986. The 7000 yards of cedar, hemlock and fir have been sculpted from the uplands forest. Generous landing areas, a profusion of white sand bunkers, and rolling fairways test every golfing ability, with water coming into play on seven holes, necessitating precise shot-making from start to finish. Bent grass has been used on tees, greens and fairways for a premium playing surface.

The Resort at Port Ludlow

To spend time at Port Ludlow on Puget Sound is to escape to an azure-colored water wonderland with snow-capped Mount Baker in the background, rugged pine and cedar forests, and cool, clear lakes.

Designed for family enjoyment, recreational activities include a heated outdoor pool in summer (indoor pool and jacuzzi fall through spring), a squash court, 7 plexapave tennis courts, saunas, a pitch and putt area, bicycles, and a supervised children's game room. Join the sailboats on Puget Sound—you can rent one or join a sightseeing tour at the 300-slip saltwater marina, and should you be anchoring here and want to play golf, the resort maintains a fleet of vans to take marina guests to the links.

The Harbormaster Restaurant, overlooking the Sound, is popular with visitors and locals. We begin our feast with stuffed shrimp before digging into a fresh whole dungeness crab for two, and finished with a luscious raspberry and chocolate truffle. The Wreckroom Lounge livened up the evening with strains of live 50's, 60's and 70's tunes. Many guests enjoy the solitude of the 3500 acres, but should you yearn to explore the environs, you'll find nature hikes, raft trips, charter fishing, and poking around historic Port Townsend.

The piece de resistance here is the magnificent golf course. Home of the annual Pro-Am tournament, the Pac Rim tournament, and the St. Patricks Day Couples Classic, the course is rarely crowded despite its notoriety. The American Society of Golf Course Architects ranks the ten-year old layout in the top one percent of the best designed courses in the nation on the basis of natural beauty, design aesthetics, drama and subtlety, fairness, and how well it plays.

Designed by Robert Muir Graves the course sits on high ground, and was created to preserve the natural beauty of the forest, streams and lakes, and above all, to take advantage of the vistas across the bay. Voted "Best in the Northwest" consistently, the course was carved from a dense forest, with towering firs flanking its fairways, and wild rhodendrons bursting forth in spring. The par-4 thirteenth hole will cause the player to exercise his patience, and certainly test his skills. The U.S.G.A. has rated the course 138 on the SLOPE system, compared to a national average of 113, giving you an idea of its difficulty.

Address: 60M # 3 Paradise Bay Rd., Port Ludlow, 98365
Phone: 206-437-2222   800-732-1239
Innkeeper: Dave Herrick
No. rooms: 188
Rates: $, Credit Cards: AmEx, Visa, MC, Other CC
Services: Garage and parking, Card or other game area, Laundry
Restrictions: No pets
Restaurant: Harbormaster
Bar: Wreckroom Lounge
Business Fac.: Copiers, Audio-visual, Conf. rm. cap.: 125
Sports Fac.: Pool, Tennis, Handball, Croquet, Bikes
Location: Olympic Peninsula
Attractions: Victorian Homes Tours-Port Townsend

Course: Port Ludlow
Distance: 6,787, Par: 72
Rating: 74.4, No. of holes: 18
Guest Policy: Call for availability, Dress code
Phone Club-House: 206-437-2222
Pro's name: L. Blackwell
Reservations: May be made one week in advance
Season: Year round
Guest Carry Club: Yes, Caddies: Yes

The American Club

Address: Highland Dr., Kohler, 53044
Phone: 414-457-8000   800-458-2562
Innkeeper: Susan P. Green
No. rooms: 160
Rates: $, Credit Cards: AmEx, Visa, MC
Services: Valet, Library, Garage and parking, International currency exchange, complimentary shoe-shine, Babysitting, Card/game area, Room service
Restrictions: No pets
Restaurant: The Immigrant
Bar: Horse & Plow
Business Fac.: Sec., Audio-Visual, Conf. rm. cap.: 600
Sports Fac.: Pool, Tennis, Ice skating, Health spa
Location: East Central Wis.
Attractions: Historic Wade House, Design Center, Arts Center

Course: Blackwolf Run
Distance: 6,068, Par: 72
Rating: 70.7, No. of holes: 27
Guest Policy: Resort guests offered lower fee
Phone Club-House: 414-457-8000
Pro's name: Mark Hagenbach
Reservations: 2 weeks in advance, or with reservation
Season: April–Oct.
Guest Carry Club: Yes

Built in 1918 as housing for immigrant Kohler Company employees, The American Club has been transformed into one of the Midwest's favorite hotels and conference centers. Set in a quiet village atmosphere, the English Tudor style building is just as breathtaking inside as outside. Handcrafted oak paneling, travertine counters, stained glass, crystal chandeliers, oriental rugs and museum-piece furnishings are pulled together with a deep blue and rich wine color scheme.

Their four sumptuous restaurants also reflect the Club's history. The Immigrant, their showcase restaurant, features such gourmet delights as smoked Irish lamb, fresh Dover sole and delicate white medallions of veal, all complemented by an impressive selection of fine wines from their own cellars.

Take advantage of the Club's Sports Core, one of the country's finest and most complete health and racquet facilities. The Parcours, a 2.2 mile woodchip jogging and exercise trail, provides a breathtaking backdrop of woodland and wildflowers for a lovely walk or jog. And to relax, try a refreshing whirlpool soak or an invigorating sauna.

Rediscover nature at River Wildlife, Kohler's unique 800-acre wilderness preserve. Charter a boat on Lake Michigan or paddle your course on the Sheboygan River; the fishing's great.

Along the banks of the Sheboygan River a few miles upstream from where chief Black Wolf led his braves against the Chippewas and Meno-minees, is a true Pete Dye masterpiece. It's a rugged, natural course with plenty of mounds, moguls, deep bunkers, a gorgeous pond, wild grasses, and yes, railroad tie reinforcements. Three nines, descriptively dubbed River, Valleys and Meadows give the player plenty of chance to see the water. Valleys nine is noted for dramatic elevation changes, and undulating tabletop greens clinging tenaciously over gullies and wild ravines. For the average player, accuracy is the challenge. Alice Dye, a tournament-level player, wanted to ensure that women and shorter hitters wouldn't feel left out, thus you'll find multiple tees, and even a hole with two greens. Two old flatcars span the creek as bridges winding through the 4th and 5th holes of Valley, and in another spot an aging rustic barn is used as a halfway house. In Pete Dye's words, ''There could not be a better natural setting for golf.''

Olympia Village Conference Center

Carefully designed to blend with its dramatic 400-acre setting of forest, hills, rivers, and lakes, this complete luxury resort of stunning modern beauty lies in southern Wisconsin lake country. The resort's decor allows nature to come inside, as you'll see when you arrive in the lobby that features a fireplace wall that sweeps to the sky, celestial windows that are massive skylights, and handsomely beamed ceilings that add a finishing touch.

The Terrace is Olympia's main dining room, where international dishes are prepared with flair and served at a leisurely pace. Candlelight makes the atmosphere elegant and glass window walls that reveal a panoramic view of spectacular sunsets and the green countryside beyond make it all the more relaxing. Don't miss the Sunday Brunch here; it's a favorite with everyone. A charming alternative is The Beach House at Silver Lake, an informal restaurant featuring fresh seafood and perfectly prepared steaks and chops.

If tennis is your game, play year round on excellent indoor and outdoor facilities at the Country Club. Racquetball, volleyball, badminton, softball, and shuffleboard are also available. After the workout, pamper yourself at Olympia's Spa, where you can relax in their magnificent Roman pools, indulge in a luxurious massage or an herbal wrap, and enjoy a tingling loofa treatment.

While the Spa rejuvenates, relaxes and pampers your body, the eighteen holes here will challenge your lower body action in another way—into the downswing for more power with your driver. This course, most of which is level or gently rolling with many crisscrossing small lakes and streams, plays longer than the yardage indicates. Both nines are very different, with the front characterized by long, narrow holes and rolling tree-lined fairways. The back is more open and flat, but water awaits you on seven holes.

The golfing facilities are pros at handling tournaments, as well as catering to many large corporate and national meetings. Its unique combination of exhilarating golf and a "full-service" health spa put it in a special class.

Address: 1350 Royale Mile Rd., Oconomowoc, 53066
Phone: 414-567-0311   800-558-9573
Innkeeper: Franklin Kumbera
No. rooms: 380
Rates: $, Credit Cards: AmEx, Visa, MC, Other CC
Services: Valet, Barber shop, Full service beauty salon, Garage and parking, Car hire, House doctor, Babysitting, Laundry, Full health spa, Room service
Restrictions: No pets
Restaurant: Terrace Dining Room
Bar: Polo Lounge
Business Fac.: Secretarial, Copiers, Conf. rm. cap.: 3,899
Sports Fac.: Pool, Tennis, Handball, Skiing, Polo
Location: Waukesha County
Attractions: Old World Wisconsin, House on Rock

Course: Olympia Village Resort
Distance: 6,567, Par: 72
Rating: 71.0, No. of holes: 18
Guest Policy: Call for availability, Dress code
Phone Club-House: 414-567-0311
Pro's name: Dave Hallenbeck
Reservations: Resort guests have priority
Season: April 1–end of Oct.
Guest Carry Club: No

The Greenbrier

Address: White Sulphur Springs, 24986
Phone: 304-536-1110   800-624-6070
Rates: $$$$, Credit Cards:
Services: Valet, Beauty shop
Restrictions: Pets ltd.
Restaurant: Ryder Cup Grille
Sports Fac.: Tennis, Pools, Bowling, Riding, Billard
Attractions: Fishing, Trap & Skeet Shooting, Carriage Rides

Course: Greenbrier
Distance: 6,311, Par: 72
Rating: 71.7, No. of holes: 18
Guest Policy: Call for availability
Phone Club-House: 304-536-1110
Pro's name: John Murphy
Reservations: May be made with hotel
Season: April–Thanksgiving
Guest Carry Club: No, Caddies: Yes

This is the Grande Dame of American tradition, rich in history and nostalgia. Long a spa for those seeking a panacea for plowman's knee or tinker's elbow, tales of miraculous recoveries spread, and it became a mecca for wealthy Southern patrons. Today's Greenbrier looks like an elegant hybrid of the White House, surrounded by 6500 acres of broad lawns, a profusion of gardens, and acres of eastern deciduous forests. Add the Allegheny Mountains as a backdrop, parlors glowing with antiques and Oriental art, and a dedication to service often touted by rarely delivered, and you won't want to leave. Guests can stay in a variety of accommodations, ranging from traditional hotel rooms and suites, to cottages and condominiums. Each is individually decorated, no two are alike.

Upon waking, your biggest problem will be choosing from the plethora of activities available. Horseback riding along miles of wooded trails, jogging, fishing for trout and bass, golf (of course), indoor or outdoor tennis, shuffleboard, table tennis, lawn bowling, bicycling, swimming, inside or out, or an invigorating hike, to name a few. Don't forget to take the horse-drawn carriage ride through the grounds. The spa beckons, and such a spa! Daylong pampering sessions offering mineral baths and the works are available to all guests. Breakfast and a six-course dinner are included in the room rate, and a lavish luncheon buffet in the Ryder Cup Grille will leave you sated.

The resort is a National Landmark, and for those curious about other historic spots, head out to some of the Civil War battlefields, such as Droop Mountain. Pearl Buck's birthplace isn't far, or you might want to check the action at Organ Caves.

Three scenic championship courses are available. Lakeside opened in 1910. Old White, was next, designed in 1914 by Charles Blair Macdonald, who had learned the game in Scotland as a youngster, and his partner Seth Raynor. Jack Nicklaus redesigned what had been a somewhat flat Greenbrier course in 1976. He added a lake, redid greens so now they're tiered, and increased the size of many traps. #14 boasts one that is nearly 80 yards long. Carved in a valley, with Kates Mountain as a backdrop, the course is heavily wooded with oak and maple. One course stays open all year, so if you should want to play a round in January, it's yours!

Jackson Hole Racquet Club Resort

Jackson Hole, often compared to Alpine Switzerland, lies at the foot of Yellowstone National Park tucked between the Grand Teton and the Gros Ventre mountain ranges in northwest Wyoming. Surrounding the valley are gleaming snow-streaked peaks which climb 7000' up from the lake-studded green valley. Here, nestled among groves of shimmering aspen. This is the home of The Jackson Hole Racquet Club Resort, a perfect example of preservation of an untouched wilderness.

Jackson Hole has a wide variety of restaurants, ranging from sophisticated Italian cuisine to dude-ranch barbeques. Guests can sample the Austrian fare at Steigler's, a renowned dining spot at the Racquet Club. House specialties include Elk Medaillons St. Hubertus, an elk schnitzel with sauce Venaison, poached pear, and red cabbage with potato croquettes.

Recreational paradise awaits you here. Virtually every form of outdoor adventure is available, in addition to a top-notch athletic club. Choose from back country bicycle tours, a breathtakingly beautiful float or raft trip, miles of trout streams, or take a horse into the real Old West and chow down at the cookout. How about a guided ascent in one of the top climbing ranges of the world? As if all this isn't enough, a John Gardiner Tennis Center, and the nationally acclaimed Jack Dennis Flyfishing School are nearby, as well as racquetball and polo.

In Jackson Hole you'll find a Ralph Lauren Polo Shop, and art galleries adjacent to boot shops, a taxidermy and even Dirty Jack's Theatre. This is rodeo country, folks, so bring your camera and be prepared for unparalleled pampering.

Golf centers around a striking Arnold Palmer-Ed Seay designed course which spells solitude cradled in the gentle hands of a mountain valley. Water comes into play on nearly every hole of the meadow-type course, which is well-bunkered with contoured greens. Players rave about the par three hole #12 (221 yards) with its "over the water" tee shot set dramatically at mountain's base. This par-72 course which opened in June, 1987 promises diversity in its layout against a splendid natural backdrop.

A few miles away in Jackson, perched under Fossil Mountain, lies another championship course, designed by Robert Trent Jones. Beware—lots of water here.

Address: Box 3647 Star Route, Jackson Hole, 83001
Phone: 307-733-3990 800-443-6931
Innkeeper: Robert A. Cole
No. rooms: 120
Rates: $, Credit Cards: AmEx, Visa, MC
Services: Baby sitting, Laundry, Health Club—complimentary, with saunas, jacuzzis, steam room, jogging track, gym, Nautilus weight room
Restrictions: No pets
Restaurant: Stieglers
Bar: Stieglers Lounge
Business Fac.: Copiers, Audio-visual, Conf. rm. cap.: 150
Sports Fac.: Pool, Tennis, Racquetball
Location: Teton County
Attractions: Tours of Yellowstone and Grand Teton

Course: Teton Pines
Distance: 7,401, Par: 72
Rating: 74.2, No. of holes: 18
Guest Policy: DNR, Dress code
Phone Club-House: 307-733-1005
Pro's name: John Godwin
Reservations: Beginning in April, for that season
Season: 1st wknd May–1st wknd Oct
Guest Carry Club: Yes

Monchs Posthotel

Address: Dobler Strasse 2, 7506 Bad Herrenalb, 7506

Phone: 49-07083-7440 800-372-1323

Innkeeper: Hubert Monch

No. rooms: 37

Rates: $$, Credit Cards: AmEx, MC, Other CC

Services: Gift Shop-Boutique, Full Health Spa

Restaurant: Restaurant Klosterschanke

Bar: Hotel Bar

Business Fac.: Secretarial Service

Sports Fac.: Swimming, Croquet, Skiing, Riding, Polo

Attractions: Hiking, Thermal Bath, Black Forest, Baden-Baden

The Monch family have tended this peaceful welcoming luxury hotel in the Black Forest for more than 125 years. Sitting amid its own park in the heart of this tranquil town, a half hour's drive from Baden-Baden, the former relais de poste has been shined and polished to show off its historic atmosphere. There are thirty-seven rooms and two suites, many with oversized bathrooms and balconies overlooking the park, a charming bar and a heated swimming pool in the garden. The restaurant is worthy of a detour, and breakfast and lunch are served under ancient trees in the garden in warm weather. Relax in the thermal baths, go riding, fishing or hunting, or practice your German so you can understand the local rules on your score card.

The Golf Club Bad Herrenalb-Bernbach is 500 meters from the hotel. This is nine holes and 5215 meters of hilly terrain, with the forest counting as a major hazard. It isn't a piece of cake—every hole is a challenge, with few level lies, and greens that are tough to read.

Course: Bad Herrenalb-Bernbach

Distance: 5215m, Par: 72

Rating: 68.0, No. of holes: 9

Pro's name: Gordon Weston

Schlosshotel Kronberg

If you are bitten by the "schlosshotel (castle hotel)" bug, this striking 19th century fairy tale hostelry in the forest should be on your list. Built in 1888 by Empress Friedrich, Queen Victoria's daughter, it has been home to aristocrats, French army officers and American soldiers. Guests are impressed by the atmosphere of art treasures and period pieces, in fact it's much like staying in a museum. Each room offers a splendid view of the rose garden and park, and the suites are spacious, with plenty of brocade, velvet and priceless rugs. A main dining room, and a smaller one, have won considerable acclaim for the chef whose specialties include breast of quail in Madeira and a sensational Bavarian duck. The wine list is good in terms of both quality and choice, with some nice French Burgundies in addition to the German offerings.

The castle isn't far from Frankfurt and its famed Palmengarten, one of the continent's most famous botanical gardens, and you also might want to pop into Bellak, for the best in German handicrafts.

An attractive eighteen hole golf course is set in the middle of the surrounding park, and during spring and fall, particularly, it is truly a delightful place. Fairways are lush and rolling, featuring several rare specimen of trees, and there are streams meandering around the holes. A driving range and putting green will help you warm up before you hit the golfplatz.

Address: D-6242 Kronberg im Taunus, Kronberg, Postfach 1326

Phone: 49-06173-701-01 49-06173-40-01

Innkeeper: H. Altoff/S. Tuchel

No. rooms: 53

Rates: $$$, Credit Cards: AmEx, MC, Other CC

Restaurant: Big Dining Room

Bar: Bar

Business Fac.: FAX 49-061-73-701267

Attractions: Frankfurt, International Fairs, Hiking, Windsurf

Course: Golf & Landclub Kronberg

Distance: 6000, No. of holes: 18

Phone Club-House: 06173-1426

Season: April-November

Sonnenalp

Address: D- 8972,
Ofterschwang/Oberallgau
Sonthofen, Bavaria

Phone: 49-8321-7229

No. rooms: 230

Rates: $$, Credit Cards: AmEx

Services: Babysitting, Sauna,
Massage, Fitness Center, Boutique

Business Fac.: Audio-Video, FAX

Sports Fac.: Smimming, Archery,
Riding, Tennis

Course: Sonnenalp

Distance: 6040m, Par: 72,
No. of holes: 18

Phone Club-House: 08321-7276

Hugging the foothills of the Tyrolean Alps in Southern Bavaria, this quiet family-run resort of sixty years welcomes visitors to an atmosphere of "sport and cure". Emphasis is on physical activity, healthful approaches to food, and family activities. This is comparable to a good BMW—everything spells quality, good workmanship and is rather chic. Lodgings are in hotel rooms, suites, apartments and small cottages, all furnished in attractive contemporary colors. There's something for everyone, whether it's yoga, hiking, bicycle trips, swimming, archery, boating, or soaking up the glorious sunshine under snow-clad peaks.

Try tennis, squash, windsurfing on the lake, or take time for a whirlpool and massage, followed by a sauna.

Fashion-conscious shoppers will be happy to part with their marks in the boutiques on the premises.

Children love it here, and so do parents who are assured they'll flourish in the myriad of activities exclusively for them.

There are 18 holes of golf, designed by Donald Harradine. As you might expect, fairways and greens are well-manicured. Between the first and eighteenth holes are 6,000 yards of evergreens, lakes and glimpses of the majestic summits. Grounds are in top shape, from the putting green and driving range to the handsome golf shop.

Instruction is available, and the course is open April to November.

Brenner's Park Hotel

This hotel, one of Europe's finest and most stately, isn't billed usually as a golf resort, but we've included it because of the close liaison the staff has with the Golfclub Baden-Baden. Occupying a premier spot in its own private park off the Lichtenaler Allee facing the River Oos, the chic hotel reminds one of a Hapsburg summer palace. The decor is elegant and tasteful, well suited to its international clientele, and the brochure is printed in Japanese and Arabic, certainly a sign of the times. A full range of spa facilities, the Schwarzwald Clinic specializing in internal disorders, elegant restaurants, and a ravishing indoor swimming pool are but part of the attraction. The tennis club and the opulent Baden-Baden Casino are nearby, as are bridle paths, and the delights of the Black Forest. The Black Forest Wine Road winds between Baden-Baden and Lorrach-Basel, and visitors can sample the local wines, or picnic near the vineyards.

You can tee off between April and the end of October at the short and challenging Golfclub Baden-Baden. It's in the heart of the forest with huge ancient trees framing the fairways. Count on hilly terrain, and from a couple of holes, you'll have some great views of the town.

Address: An der Lichtentaler Allee, D-7570 Baden-Baden, Schillerstrasse 6, Black Forest

Phone: 49-07221-3530 800-223-6800

Innkeeper: Richard Schmitz

No. rooms: 100

Rates: $$$, Credit Cards: AmEx, Other CC

Services: Beauty Salon, Barber Shop, Valet, Concierge Beauty Farm, Clinic

Restaurant: Brenner's Park-Restaurant

Bar: Oleander

Business Fac.: FAX 49-7221-353353

Sports Fac.: Tennis, Hiking, Skeet, Riding, Swimming

Attractions: Horse Racing, Black Forest, Augustinian Museum,

Course: Golfclub Baden-Baden

Distance: 4095m, Par: 64

Rating: 65.0, No. of holes: 18

Phone Club-House: 07221-23579

Of
Special Interest

ARTS, MUSIC, THEATERS

Hotel Panhans
Semmering, AUSTRIA

Half Moon Beach Club
Montego Bay, JAMAICA

Mount Irvine Bay Hotel
Scarborough, TOBAGO

Meadowwood Resort & Country Club
St. Helena, CA, USA

Tamarron
Durango, CO, USA

PGA Sheraton Resort
Palm Beach Gardens, FL, USA

Westin Mauna Kea
Kohula Coast Amuea, HI, USA

Sun Valley Lodge
Sun Valley, ID, USA

Chatham Bars Inn & Cottage
Chatham, MA, USA

Pinehurst Hotel & Country Club
Pinehurst, NC, USA

Hanover Inn
Hanover, NH, USA

Sunriver Lodge and Resort
Sunriver, OR, USA

The Woodstock Inn & Resort
Woodstock, VT, USA

Americana Lake Geneva Resort
Lake Geneva, WI, USA

Jackson Hole Racquet Club Resort
Jackson Hole, WY, USA

OUTLET SHOPPING

Quail Lodge
Carmel, CA, USA

Mission Inn Golf & Tennis Resort
Howey-In-The-Hills, FL, USA

Grove Park Inn & Country Club
Ashville, NC, USA

Mount Washington
Bretton Woods, NH, USA

Hotel Hershey & Country Club
Hershey, PA, USA

Shawnee Inn
Shawnee-On-Delaware, PA, USA

Palmetto Dunes Resort
Hilton Head Island, SC, USA

Sheraton Hotel & Country Club
Staunton, VA, USA

Mount Mansfield Resort
Stowe, VT, USA

CASINO

Hotel Panhans
Semmering, AUSTRIA

Paradise Island
Resort & Casino, BAHAMAS

Atlantik Beach Resort
Lucaya, BAHAMAS

Bahamas Princess
Freeport, BAHAMAS

Hotel Cariari
San Jose, COSTA RICA

Jack Tar Village
Puerto Plata, DOMINICAN REPUBLIC

Gentling Highlands Resort
Kuala Lampur, MALAYSIA

Saint Geran Hotel
Poste de Flacq, MAURITIUS

Mullet Bay Resort
St. Maarten, NETHERLANDS ANTILLES

Sun City Resort
Johannesburg, SOUTH AFRICA

Jack Tar Village
Frigate Bay, ST. KITTS

Palmas del Mar
Humacao, PR, USA

Brenner's Park Hotel
D-7570 Baden-Baden, W. GERMANY

─────────── BEACHES ───────────

Sheraton Mirage
Port Douglas, AUSTRALIA

Cotton Bay Club
Eleuthera, BAHAMAS

Divi Bahamas Beach
Resort & Country Club,
Nassau, BAHAMAS

Paradise Island
Resort & Casino, Paradise
Island, BAHAMAS

Atlantik Beach Resort
Lucaya BAHAMAS

Gran Bahama Hotel &
Country Club, BAHAMAS

Bahamas Princess Resort
Freeport, BAHAMAS

Sandy Lane Hotel
St. James, BARBADOS

Southampton Princess
Hamilton, BERMUDA

Marriott's Castle Harbour
Tucker's Town, BERMUDA

**Hyatt Regency Grand
Cayman**
GRAND CAYMAN ISLANDS

Keltic Lodge
Cape Breton Island,
CANADA

Hotel Cariari
San Jose, COSTA RICA

Casa de Campo
La Romana, DOMINICAN
REPÚBLIC

Jack Tar Village
Puerto Plata, DOMINICAN
REPUBLIC

Pacific Harbour Resort
Pacific Harbour, FIJI

Hotel de Chantaco
Saint Jean de Luz,
FRANCE

Discovery Bay Golf Club
Discovery Bay, HONG
KONG

Costa Smeralda Hotels
Costa Smeralda, ITALY

Tryall Beach Club
Hanover, JAMAICA

Half Moon Beach Club
Montego Bay, JAMAICA

Wyndham Rose Hall Hotel
Montego Bay, JAMAICA

Saint Geran Hotel
Poste de Flacq,
MAURITIUS

Jack Tar Village
Nayarit, MEXICO

Las Hadas
Manzanillo, MEXICO

Puerto Azul Beach Hotel
Ternate, PHILIPPINES

Hotel Dona Filipa
Almansil, PORTUGAL

Dom Pedro Golf Hotel
Quarteira, PORTUGAL

Jack Tar Village
Frigate Bay, ST. KITTS

Mount Irvine Bay Hotel
Scarborough, TOBAGO

Amelia Island Plantation
Amelia Island, FL, USA

Boca Raton Hotel & Club
Boca Raton, FL, USA

**South Seas Plantation
Resort**
Captiva Island, FL, USA

Treasure Cay Beach Hotel
Fort Lauderdale, FL, USA

The Diplomat
Hollywood-By-The-Sea, FL,
USA

Longboat Key Club
Longboat Key, FL, USA

The Breakers
Palm Beach, FL, USA

Ponte Vedra Inn & Club
Ponte Vedra Beach, FL,
USA

The Cloister
Sea Island, GA, USA

Mauna Lani Bay Hotel
Kohala Coast, Is. of HI, HI,
USA

Westin Mauna Kea
Kohula Coast Amuea, HI,
USA

Hyatt Regency Maui
Lahaina, Maui, HI, USA

**Kaluakoi Hotel and Golf
Club**
Maunaloa, Molokai, HI,
USA

**Chatham Bars Inn &
Cottage**
Chatham, MA, USA

Broadwater Beach Hotel
Biloxi, MS, USA

Palmas del Mar
Humacao, PR, USA

Salishan Lodge
Gleneden Beach, OR, USA

**Hyatt Regency Cerromar
Beach**
Dorado, PR, USA

Palmetto Dunes Resort
Hilton Head Island, SC,
USA

Sea Pines Resorts
Hilton Head Island, SC,
USA

**Wild Dunes Beach &
Racquet Club**
Isle of Palm, SC, USA

Dunes Village Resort
Myrtle Beach, SC, USA

Myrtle Beach Hilton
Myrtle Beach, SC, USA

**Carambola Beach Resort
Golf Club**
St. Croix, VI, USA

The Buccaneer Hotel
St. Croix, VI, USA

GOLF CAMPS & SCHOOLS

John Jacobs Golf School
Scottsdale, AZ, USA

Tucson National Resort & Spa
Tucson, AZ, USA

The Golf University
Fallbrook, CA, USA

The Broadmoor
Colorado Springs, CO, USA

High Hampton Inn & Country Club
Cashiers, NC, USA

Roland Stafford Golf School
Margaretville, NY, USA

Ben Sutton Golf Schools
Canton, OH, USA

Seabrook Island Resort
Charleston, SC, USA

The Golf School
Mount Snow, VT, USA

Stratton Golf School
Stratton Mountain, VT, USA

AMERICAN PLAN

Banff Spring Hotel
Banff, AB, CANADA

The Alisal
Solvang, CA, USA

The Cloister
Sea Island, GA, USA

Westin Mauna Kea
Kohula Coast Amuea, HI, USA

Hound Ears Club
Blowing Rock, NC, USA

High Hampton Inn & Country Club
Cashiers, NC, USA

Mid Pines Resort
Southern Pines, NC, USA

Balsams Grand Resort Hotel
Dixville Notch, NH, USA

Concord Resort Hotel
Kiamesha Lake, NY, USA

CONFERENCE CENTERS

Bahamas Princess
Freeport, BAHAMAS

Southampton Princess
Hamilton, BERMUDA

Marriott's Castle Harbour
Tucker's Town, BERMUDA

Hyatt Regency
GRAND CAYMAN ISLANDS

Hotel Cariari
San Jose, COSTA RICA

Jack Tar Village
Puerto Plata, DOMINICAN REPUBLIC

Costa Smeralda Hotels
Costa Smeralda, ITALY

Wyndham Rose Hall Hotel
Montego Bay, JAMAICA

Kawana Hotel
Ito City, JAPAN

Pierre Marques
Acapulco, MEXICO

Puerto Azul Beach Hotel
Ternate, PHILIPPINES

Hotel Quinta do Lago
Almancil, PORTUGAL

Dom Pedro Golf Hotel
Quarteira, PORTUGAL

Old Course Golf & CC
Saint Andrews, SCOTLAND

Sun City Resort
Johannesburg, SOUTH AFRICA

Son Vida Sheraton
Palma de Mallorca, SPAIN

Hotel Los Monteros
Marbella, SPAIN

Central Plaza Hotel
Bangkhen, THAILAND

TRANQUIL ATMOSPHERE

Schloss Fuschl
Hof Bei, AUSTRIA

Hotel Panhans
Semmering, AUSTRIA

Keltic Lodge
Cape Breton Island, CANADA

Cazaudehore et la Forestiere
St. Germain en Laye, FRANCE

Les Chevreuils
Lausanne, SWITZERLAND

Dolder Grand Hotel
Zurich, SWITZERLAND

LAKES

Seehotel Werzer Astoria
Portschach am
Worthersee, AUSTRIA

Gray Rocks Inn
St. Jovite, CANADA

Ashford Castle
Cong, IRELAND

Hotel du Golf
SWITZERLAND

MOUNTAINS NEARBY

Hotel Panhans
Semmering, AUSTRIA

Keltic Lodge
Cape Breton Island,
CANADA

Gray Rocks Inn
St. Jovite, CANADA

Hotel du Golf,
SWITZERLAND

Quellenhof Golf Hotel,
SWITZERLAND

Burgenstock Hotels
Burgenstock,
SWITZERLAND

Les Chevreuils
Lausanne, SWITZERLAND

Monchs Posthotel
7506 Bad Herrenalb, W.
GERMANY

Sonnenalp
Sonthofen, W. GERMANY

NATURE CENTERS

La Costa Hotel & Spa
Carlsbad, CA, USA

**Inn & Links at Spanish
Bay**
Pebble Beach, CA, USA

The Broadmoor
Colorado Springs, CO, USA

PGA Sheraton Resort
Palm Beach Gardens, FL,
USA

Sun Valley Lodge
Sun Valley, ID, USA

**Grove Park Inn &
Country Club**
Asheville, NC, USA

**Balsams Grand Resort
Hotel**
Dixville Notch, NH, USA

Sunriver Lodge and Resort
Sunriver, OR, USA

The Buccaneer Hotel
St. Croix, VI, USA

Mount Mansfield Resort
Stowe, VT, USA

HUNTING

Dromoland Castle
IRELAND

Greywalls Hotel
Gullane, SCOTLAND

ECOLOGICAL INTEREST

Keltic Lodge
Cape Breton Island,
CANADA

Kawana Hotel
Ito City, JAPAN

Mount Irvine Bay Hotel
Scarborough, TOBAGO

ESPECIALLY ROMANTIC

The Playa Hotel
Carmel, CA, USA

Sun Valley Lodge
Sun Valley, ID, USA

Samoset Resort
Rockport, ME, USA

**The Lodge at Black Butte
Ranch**
Black Butte Ranch, OR,
USA

Salishan Lodge
Gleneden Beach, OR, USA

Colonial Williamsburg Inn
Williamsburg, VA, USA

WHITEWATER RAFTING NEARBY

The Broadmoor
Colorado Springs, CO, USA

Sheraton Steamboat Springs Resort
Steamboat Springs, CO, USA

Sugarloaf Inn Resort
Carrabassett Valley, ME, USA

Big Sky Resort
Big Sky, MT, USA

The Lodge at Black Butte Ranch
Black Butte Ranch, OR, USA

Sunriver Lodge and Resort
Sunriver, OR, USA

Jackson Hole Racquet Club Resort
Jackson Hole, WY, USA

YACHT HARBOR/MARINA

Sheraton Mirage
Port Douglas, AUSTRALIA

Hotel do Frade
Angra dos Reis, BRAZIL

Hyatt Regency
GRAND CAYMAN ISLANDS

Costa Smeralda Hotels
Costa Smeralda, ITALY

Las Hadas
Manzanillo, MEXICO

Dom Pedro Golf Hotel
Quarteira, PORTUGAL

Grand Hotel
Point Clear, AL, USA

The Diplomat
Hollywood-By-The-Sea, FL, USA

Longboat Key Club
Longboat Key, FL, USA

Stouffer PineIsle Resort
Atlanta, GA, USA

The Cloister
Sea Island, GA, USA

Samoset Resort
Rockport, ME, USA

Lodge of the Four Seasons
Lake Ozark, MO, USA

The Sagamore
At Bolton Landing, NY, USA

Palmas del Mar
Humacao, PR, USA

Sea Pines Resort
Hilton Head Islands, SC, USA

Wild Dunes Beach & Racquet Club
Isle of Palm, SC, USA

Horseshoe Bay Country Club Resort
Horseshoe Bay, TX, USA

Waterwood National Resort & CC
Huntsville, TX, USA

Del Lago Resort & Conf. Center
Montgomery, TX, USA

The Tides Lodge
Irvington, VA, USA

Tides Inn
Irvington, VA, USA

Kingsmill On The James
Williamsburg, VA, USA

Inn at Semiahmoo
Blaine, WA, USA

TO WRITE HOME ABOUT

Divi Bahamas Beach Resort
Nassau, BAHAMAS

Keltic Lodge
Cape Breton Island, CANADA

Pacific Harbour Resort
Pacific Harbour, FIJI

Hotel de Chantaco
Saint Jean de Luz, FRANCE

Bali Handara Kosaido
Country Club, Pancasari, INDONESIA

Dromoland Castle
IRELAND

Costa Smeralda Hotels
Costa Smeralda, ITALY

Half Moon Golf,
Tennis & Beach Club, Montego Bay, JAMAICA

Kawana Hotel
Ito City, JAPAN

Gleneagles Hotel
Tayside, SCOTLAND

Greywalls Hotel
Gullane, SCOTLAND

SPAS

Seehotel Werzer Astoria
Portschach am Worthersee
AUSTRIA

Hotel do Frade
Angra dos Reis, BRAZIL

Casa de Campo
La Romana, DOMINICAN
REPUBLIC

Gentling Highlands Resort
Kuala Lampur, MALAYSIA

Hotel Quinta do Lago
Almancil, PORTUGAL

Turnberry Hotel
Strathclyde, SCOTLAND

Old Course Golf and
Country Club, Saint
Andrews, SCOTLAND

Hotel Byblos Andaluz
Fuengirola, SPAIN

Quellenhof Golf Hotel
SWITZERLAND

Arizona Biltmore
Phoenix, AZ, USA

Hyatt Regency Scottsdale
Scottsdale, AZ, USA

Scottsdale Hilton Villas
Scottsdale, AZ, USA

**Tucson National Resort &
Spa**
Tucson, AZ, USA

**Ventana Canyon Golf &
Racquet Club**
Tucson, AZ, USA

Westin La Paloma
Tucson, AZ, USA

La Costa Hotel & Spa
Carlsbad, CA, USA

**Carmel Valley Ranch
Resort**
Carmel, CA, USA

**Spa Hotel and Mineral
Springs**
Palm Springs, CA, USA

**Inn & Links at Spanish
Bay**
Pebble Beach, CA, USA

Rancho Bernardo Inn
San Diego, CA, USA

Bonaventure Resort & Spa
Fort Lauderdale, FL, USA

**Turnberry Isle Country
Club**
Miami, FL, USA

**Fontainebleau Hilton
Resort**
Miami Beach, FL, USA

**Hyatt Regency Grand
Cypress**
Orlando, FL, USA

The Breakers
Palm Beach, FL, USA

Ponte Vedra Inn & Club
Ponte Vedra Beach, FL,
USA

Innisbrook
Tarpon Springs, FL, USA

**Stouffer Wailea Beach
Resort**
Wailea, Maui, HI, USA

**French Lick Springs Golf
Resort**
French Lick, IN, USA

Sugarloaf Inn Resort
Carrabassett Valley, ME,
USA

Lodge of the Four Seasons
Lake Ozark, MO, USA

Broadwater Beach Hotel
Biloxi, MS, USA

Mount Washington
Bretton Woods, NH, USA

The Sagamore
At Bolton Landing, NY, USA

Concord Resort Hotel
Kiamesha Lake, NY, USA

Sunriver Lodge and Resort
Sunriver, OR, USA

Shawnee Inn
Shawnee-On-Delaware, PA,
USA

Seabrook Island Resort
Charleston, SC, USA

**Del Lago Resort &
Conference Center**
Montgomery, TX, USA

The Homestead
Hot Springs, VA, USA

Colonial Williamsburg Inn
Williamsburg, VA, USA

Kingsmill On The James
Williamsburg, VA, USA

Monchs Posthotel
7506 Bad Herrenalb, W.
GERMANY

Brenner's Park Hotel
D-7570 Baden-Baden, W.
GERMANY

GREAT HIKING

The Alisal
Solvang, CA, USA

Mauna Lani Bay Hotel
Kohala Coast, Is. of HI, HI,
USA

**Elkhorn Resort At Sun
Valley**
Sun Valley, ID, USA

Big Sky Resort
Big Sky, MT, USA

**Grove Park Inn & Country
Club**
Asheville, NC, USA

Mount Washington
Bretton Woods, NH, USA

**Balsams Grand Resort
Hotel**
Dixville Notch, NH, USA

**Fairfield Glade
Conference Center**
Fairfield Glade, TN, USA

HORSEBACK RIDING

Schloss Ernegg
Steinakirchen am Forst,
AUSTRIA

Sandy Lane Hotel
St. James, BARBADOS

Hotel do Frade
Angra dos Reis, BRAZIL

Casa de Campo
La Romana, DOMINICAN
REPUBLIC

Is Molas Golf Hotel
Cagliari, ITALY

Half Moon Beach Cl
Montego Bay, JAMAICA

Hotel Quinta do Lago
Almancil, PORTUGAL

Hotel Dona Filipa
Almansil, PORTUGAL

Hotel Byblos Andaluz
Fuengirola, SPAIN

Hotel Los Monteros
Marbella, SPAIN

Hotel du Golf
SWITZERLAND

Les Chevreuils
Lausanne, SWITZERLAND

Gold Canyon Ranch
Apache Junction, AZ, USA

Boulders Resort
Carefree, AZ, USA

The Wigwam
Litchfield Park, AZ, USA

**Loews Ventana Canyon
Resort**
Tucson, AZ, USA

Furnace Creek Inn
Death Valley, CA, USA

The Alisal
Solvang, CA, USA

**Palm Beach Polo &
Country Club**
W. Palm Beach, FL, USA

Stouffer PineIsle Resort
Atlanta, GA, USA

The Cloister
Sea Island, GA, USA

**French Lick Springs Golf
Resort**
French Lick, IN, USA

Lodge of the Four Seasons
Lake Ozark, MO, USA

Big Sky Resort
Big Sky, MT, USA

Hound Ears Club
Blowing Rock, NC, USA

**Pinehurst Hotel &
Country Club**
Pinehurst, NC, USA

Inn of the Mountain Gods
Mescalero, NM, USA

Rocking Horse Ranch
Highland, NY, USA

**The Lodge at Black Butte
Ranch**
Black Butte Ranch, OR,
USA

Sunriver Lodge and Resort
Sunriver, OR, USA

**Hotel Hershey & Country
Club**
Hershey, PA, USA

Shawnee Inn
Shawnee-On-Delaware, PA,
USA

Palmas del Mar
Humacao, PR, USA

Seabrook Island Resort
Charleston, SC, USA

**Fairfield Glade
Conference Center**
Fairfield Glade, TN, USA

The Homestead
Hot Springs, VA, USA

**Americana Lake Geneva
Resort**
Lake Geneva, WI, USA

PRESERVES & REFUGES

Banff Springs Hotel
Banff, Alberta, CANADA

Grand Hotel
Point Clear, AL, USA

**Loews Ventana Canyon
Resort**
Tucson, AZ, USA

**Carmel Valley Ranch
Resort**
Tucson, AZ, USA

Half Moon Bay Lodge
Half Moon Bay, CA, USA

**The Ritz-Carlton, Rancho
Mirage**
Rancho Mirage, CA, USA

**Grand Cypress Golf Club
& Villas**
Orlando, FL, USA

**Kaluakoi Hotel and Golf
Club**
Maunaloa, Molokai, HI,
USA

Big Sky Resort
Big Sky, MT, USA

**High Hampton Inn &
Country Club**
Cashiers, NC, USA

Marriott's Seaview Resort
Absecon, NJ, USA

Kah-Nee-Ta Hotel Resort
Warm Springs, OR, USA

**Hotel Hershey & Country
Club**
Hershey, PA, USA

Sea Pines Resorts
Hilton Head Island, SC,
USA

Inn at Semiahmoo
Blaine, WA, USA

**Jackson Hole Racquet
Club Resort**
Jackson Hole, WY, USA

──────────────── NOTED FOR WINES & WINE CELLARS ────────────────

Seehotel Werzer Astoria
Portschach am
Worthersee, AUSTRIA
Schloss Ernegg
Steinakirchen am Forst,
AUSTRIA

Schloss Fuschl
Hof Bei, AUSTRIA
Hotel Panhans
Semmering, AUSTRIA
Sandy Lane Hotel
St. James, BARBADOS

**Cazaudehore et la
Forestiere**
St. Germain en Laye,
FRANCE
La Meridiana
Garlenda (SV), ITALY

──────────────── TENNIS—REGULAR ────────────────

**Marriott's Camelback Inn
Resort**
Scottsdale, AZ, USA
La Costa Hotel & Spa
Carlsbad, CA, USA
**Carmel Valley Ranch
Resort**
Carmel Valley, CA, USA
Amelia Island Plantation
Amelia Island, FL, USA

**South Seas Plantation
Resort**
Captiva Island, FL, USA
Longboat Key Club
Longboat Key, FL, USA
**Grove Park Inn & Country
Club**
Asheville, NC, USA

Sea Pines Resorts
Hilton Head Island, SC,
USA
The Homestead
Hot Springs, VA, USA
**Jackson HOle Racquet
Club Resort**
Jackson Hole, WY, USA

──────────────── TENNIS—CELEBRITY TOURNAMENTS ────────────────

Scottsdale Princess Resort
Scottsdale, AZ, USA
**John Gardiner's
Enchantment**
Sedona, AZ, USA
**Loews Ventana Canyon
Resort**
Tucson, AZ, USA
**Sheraton Tucson El
Conquistador**
Tucson, AZ, USA
**Rancho Las Palmas
Resort**
Rancho Mirage, CA, USA

Sandestin Beach Resort
Destin, FL, USA
**Sonesta Senibel Harbour
Resort**
Fort Myers, FL, USA
Kings Bay Resort
Miami, FL, USA
**Naples Bath & Tennis
Club**
Naples, FL, USA
Bluewater Bay
Niceville, FL, USA

PGA Sheraton Resort
Palm Beach Gardens, FL,
USA
**Four Seasons Lodge &
Country Club**
Lake Ozark, MO, USA
Cerromar Beach Hotel
Dorado, PR, USA
Hyatt Dorado Beach Hotel
Dorado, PR, USA
Myrtle Beach Hilton
Myrtle Beach, SC, USA
T Bar M Tennis Ranch
New Braunfels, TX, USA

──────────────── CASTLES ────────────────

Schloss Ernegg
Steinakirchen am Forst,
AUSTRIA
Schloss Fuschl
Hof Bei, AUSTRIA

Manoir Richelieu
Pointe-au-Pic, CANADA
Dromoland Castle
IRELAND

Ashford Castle
Cong, IRELAND
Schlosshotel Kronberg
Kronberg, W. GERMANY

FISHING

Cotton Bay Club
Eleuthera, BAHAMAS

Southampton Princess
Hamilton, BERMUDA

Casa de Campo
La Romana, DOMINICAN
REPUBLIC

Pacific Harbour Resort
Pacific Harbour, FIJI

Dromoland Castle
IRELAND

Waterville Lake Hotel
Waterville, IRELAND

Wyndham Rose Hall Hotel
Montego Bay, JAMAICA

Saint Geran Hotel
Poste de Flacq,
MAURITIUS

Pierre Marques
Acapulco, MEXICO

Las Hadas
Manzanillo, MEXICO

Greywalls Hotel
Gullane, SCOTLAND

Tamarron
Durango, CO, USA

Boca Raton Hotel & Club
Boca Raton, FL, USA

**Turnberry Isle Country
Club**
Miami, FL, USA

PGA Sheraton Resort
Palm Beach Gardens, FL,
USA

Marriott at Sawgrass
Ponte Vedra Beach, FL,
USA

Stouffer PineIsle Resort
Atlanta, GA, USA

Broadwater Beach Hotel
Biloxi, MS, USA

Big Sky Resort
Big Sky, MT, USA

**Balsams Grand Resort
Hotel**
Dixville Notch, NH, USA

Sunriver Lodge and Resort
Sunriver, OR, USA

Sea Pines Resorts
Hilton Head Island, SC,
USA

The Homestead
Hot Springs, VA, USA

**Carambola Beach Resort
Golf Club**
St. Crois, VI, USA

GOURMET DINING

Schloss Ernegg
Steinakirchen am Forst,
AUSTRIA

Keltic Lodge
Cape Breton Island,
CANADA

Pacific Harbour Resort
Pacific Harbour, FIJI

**Cazaudehore et la
Forestiere**
St. Germain en Laye,
FRANCE

Bali Handara Kosaido
Pancasari, INDONESIA

La Meridiana
17033 Garlenda (SV),
ITALY

Costa Smeralda Hotels
Costa Smeralda, ITALY

Tryall Beach Club
Hanover, JAMAICA

Turnberry Hotel
Strathclyde, SCOTLAND

Greywalls Hotel
Gullane, SCOTLAND

Dolder Grand Hotel
Zurich, SWITZERLAND

**Loews Ventana Canyon
Resort**
Tucson, AZ, USA

La Playa Hotel
Carmel, CA, USA

**Ojai Valley Inn and
Country Club**
Ojai, CA, USA

**The Ritz-Carlton, Rancho
Mirage**
Rancho Mirage, CA, USA

**Meadowood Resort &
Country Club**
St. Helena, CA, USA

The Cloister
Sea Island, GA, USA

**Grove Park Inn & Country
Club**
Asheville, NC, USA

The Eseeola Lodge
Linville, NC, USA

Hanover Inn
Hanover, NH, USA

**Carambola Beach Resort
Golf Club**
St. Croix, VI, USA

**The Woodstock Inn &
Resort**
Woodstock, VT, USA

Schlosshotel Kronberg
Kronberg, W. GERMANY

Sonnenalp
Sonthofen, W. GERMANY

OLD & CHARMING

Hotel de Chantaco
Saint Jean de Luz,
FRANCE

Cazaudehore et la Forestiere
St. Germain en Laye,
FRANCE

Quellenhof Golf Hotel
SWITZERLAND
Burgenstock Hotels
Burgenstock,
SWITZERLAND

ESPECIALLY FOR FAMILIES

Grand Hotel
Point Clear, AL, USA
Rancho Bernardo Inn
San Diego, CA, USA
Northstar at Tahoe
Truckee, CA, USA
Charter at Beaver Creek
Beaver Creek, CO, USA
Tamarron
Durango, CO, USA
Grand Cypress Golf Club & Villas
Orlando, FL, USA
Club Med Village of Sandpiper
Port St. Lucie, FL, USA
Callaway Gardens
Pine Mountain, GA, USA

Shanty Creek-Schuss Mountain Resort
Bellaire, MI, USA
Ruttger's Bay Lake Golf Course
Deerwood, MN, USA
Big Sky Resort
Big Sky, MT, USA
Balsams Grand Resort Hotel
Dixville Notch, NH, USA
The Bishop's Lodge
Santa Fe, NM, USA
Sunriver Lodge and Resort
Sunriver, OR, USA
Hotel Hershey & Country Club
Hershey, PA, USA

Tamiment Resort
Tamiment, PA, USA
The Mountain Laurel Resort
White Haven, PA, USA
Seabrook Island Resort
Charleston, SC, USA
Westin Resort Hilton Head
Hilton Head Island, SC, USA
Kingsmill On The James
Williamsburg, VA, USA
The Woodstock Inn & Resort
Woodstock, VT, USA

CHILDREN'S ACTIVITIES

Sheraton Mirage
Port Douglas, AUSTRALIA
Seehotel Werzer Astoria
Portschach am Worthersee, AUSTRIA
Hotel Panhans
Semmering, AUSTRIA
Gray Rocks Inn
St. Jovite, CANADA
Gentling Highlands Resort
Kuala Lampur, MALAYSIA
Sonnenalp
Sonthofen, W. GERMANY
Rancho de los Caballeros
Wickenberg, AZ, USA
Rancho Bernardo Inn
San Diego, CA, USA
The Alisal
Solvang, CA, USA

The Broadmoor
Colorado Springs, CO, USA
Tamarron
Durango, CO, USA
Mission Inn Golf & Tennis Resort
Howey-In-The-Hills, FL, USA
The Breakers
Palm Beach, FL, USA
Stouffer PineIsle Resort
Atlanta, GA, USA
Callaway Gardens
Pine Mountain, GA, USA
Samoset Resort
Rockport, ME, USA
Grove Park Inn & Country Club
Asheville, NC, USA

High Hampton Inn & Country Club
Cashiers, NC, USA
Balsams Grand Resort Hotel
Dixville Notch, NH, USA
The Lodge at Black Butte Ranch
Black Butte Ranch, OR, USA
Seabrook Island Resort
Charleston, SC, USA
Tides Inn
Irvington, VA, USA
The Buccaneer Hotel
St. Croix, VI, USA

HISTORICAL INTEREST

Seehotel Werzer Astoria
Portschach am
Worthersee, AUSTRIA

Casa de Campo
La Romana, DOMINICAN
REPUBLIC

Hotel de Chantaco
Saint Jean de Luz, FRANCE

**Cazaudehore et la
Forestiere**
St. Germain en Laye,
FRANCE

Ashford Castle
Cong, IRELAND

Puerto Azul Beach Hotel
Ternate, PHILIPPINES

Penina Golf Hotel
Portimao Codex,
PORTUGAL

Turnberry Hotel
Strathclyde, SCOTLAND

Old Course Golf and
Country Club, Saint
Andrews, SCOTLAND

Hotel Byblos Andaluz
Fuengirola, SPAIN

Son Vida Sheraton
Palma de Mallorca, SPAIN

Hotel Los Monteros
Marbella, SPAIN

Burgenstock Hotels
Burgenstock,
SWITZERLAND

**Industry Hills & Sheraton
Resort**
City of Industry—L.A., CA,
USA

**Inn & Links at Spanish
Bay**
Pebble Beach, CA, USA

Tamarron
Durango, CO, USA

Amelia Island Plantation
Amelia Island, FL, USA

Eagle Ridge Inn & Resort
Galena, IL, USA

**Marriotts Griffin Gate
Resort**
Lexington, KY, USA

**Grove Park Inn & Country
Club**
Asheville, NC, USA

Kiawah Island Resort
Charleston, SC, USA

Seabrook Island Resort
Charleston, SC, USA

Wild Dunes
Charleston, SC, USA

Tides Inn
Irvington, VA, USA

Ford's Colony
Williamsburg, VA, USA

Colonial Williamsburg Inn
Williamsburg, VA, USA

Kingmill On The James
Williamsburg, VA, USA

SAILING

Bahamas Princess
Freeport, BAHAMAS

Hotel do Frade
Angra dos Reis, BRAZIL

Gray Rocks Inn
St. Jovite, CANADA

Pacific Harbour Resort
Pacific Harbour, FIJI

Is Molas Golf Hotel
Cagliari, ITALY

Costa Smeralda Hotels
Costa Smeralda, ITALY

Las Hadas
Manzanillo, MEXICO

Cherokee Village Golf Club
Cherokee Village, AR, USA

Amelia Island Plantation
Amelia Island, FL, USA

**South Seas Plantation
Resort**
Captiva Island, FL, USA

The Diplomat
Hollywood-By-The-Sea, FL,
USA

**Mission Inn Golf & Tennis
Resort**
Howey-In-The-Hills, FL,
USA

Indian River Plantation
Hutchinson Island, FL, USA

**Grand Cypress Golf Club
& Villas**
Orlando, FL, USA

Maui Prince Hotel
Kihei, Maui, HI, USA

Mauna Lani Bay Hotel
Kohala Coast, Is. of HI, HI,
USA

Westin Mauna Kea
Kohula Coast Amuea, HI,
USA

Samoset Resort
Rockport, ME, USA

**Grand Traverse Resort
Village**
Grand Traverse Village,
MI, USA

Broadwater Beach Hotel
Biloxi, MS, USA

**Pinehurst Hotel &
Country Club**
Pinehurst, NC, USA

The Sagamore
At Bolton Landing, NY, USA

Myrtle Beach Hilton
Myrtle Beach, SC, USA

**Horseshoe Bay Country
Club Resort**
Horseshoe Bay, TX, USA

Inn at Semiahmoo
Blaine, WA, USA

The Resort at Port Ludlow
Port Ludlow, WA, USA

GARDENS

Bali Handara Kosaido
Pancasari, INDONESIA

La Meridiana
17033 Garlenda (SV),
ITALY

Greywalls Hotel
Gullane, SCOTLAND

Hotel Byblos Andaluz
Fuengirola, SPAIN

Boulders Resort
Carefree, AZ, USA

Marriott's Camelback Inn Resort
Scottsdale, AZ, USA

The Broadmoor
Colorado Springs, CO, USA

Innisbrook
Tarpon Springs, FL, USA

Callaway Gardens
Pine Mountain, GA, USA

Westin Mauna Kea
Kohula Coast Amuea, HI, USA

Stouffer Wailea Beach Resort
Wailea, Maui, HI, USA

Grove Park Inn & Country Club
Asheville, NC, USA

High Hampton Inn & Country Club
Cashiers, NC, USA

Hotel Hershey & Country Club
Hershey, PA, USA

Name	City	State	Country
Sheraton Mirage Gold Coast	Port Douglas	Queensland	AUSTRALIA
Seehotel Werzer Astoria	Portschach am Worthersee	Karnten	AUSTRIA
Schloss Ernegg	Steinakirchen am Forst	Nieder-osterreich	AUSTRIA
Schloss Fuschl	Hof Bei	Salzburg	AUSTRIA
Hotel Panhans	Semmering	Semmering	AUSTRIA
Cotton Bay Club	Eleuthera		BAHAMAS
Divi Bahamas Beach Resort	Nassau		BAHAMAS
Atlantik Beach Resort	Lucaya, Grand Bahana Island	Freeport	BAHAMAS
Sandy Lane Hotel and Golf Club	St. James		BARBADOS
Southampton Princess	Hamilton		BERMUDA
Marriott's Castle Harbour Resort	Tucker's Town	Hamilton HM CX	BERMUDA
Hotel do Frade	Angra dos Reis	Rio de Janeiro	BRAZIL
Hyatt Regency Grand Cayman	Grand Cayman		BRITISH WEST INDIES
Banff Springs Hotel	Banff	AB	CANADA
Jasper Park Lodge	Jasper	AB	CANADA
Keltic Lodge	Cape Breton Island	Nova Scotia	CANADA
Manoir Richelieu	Pointe-au-Pic	Quebec	CANADA
Gray Rocks Inn	St. Jovite	Quebec	CANADA
Chung Shan Hot Spring Golf Club	Zhongshan	Guangdong	CHINA
Cariari Hotel and Country Club	San Jose		COSTA RICA
Casa de Campo	La Romana		DOMINICAN REPUBLIC
Jack Tar Village	Puerto Plata		DOMINICAN REPUBLIC
Welcombe Hotel & Golf Course	Stratford-upon-Avon		ENGLAND

Name	City	State	Country
The Belfry	Wishaw	North Warwickshire	ENGLAND
Pacific Harbour International Resort	Pacific Harbour	Deuba	FIJI
Hotel de Chantaco	Saint Jean de Luz		FRANCE
Cazaudehore et la Forestiere	St. Germain en Laye		FRANCE
Discovery Bay Golf Club	Discovery Bay	Lantau Island	HONG KONG
Bali Handara Kosaido Country Club	Pancasari	Bali	INDONESIA
Dromoland Castle		County Clare	IRELAND
Waterville Lake Hotel	Waterville	County Kerry	IRELAND
Ashford Castle	Cong	County Mayo	IRELAND
Caesarea Golf and Resort	Caesarea		ISRAEL
La Meridiana	17033 Garlenda (SV)		ITALY
Is Molas Golf Hotel	Cagliari	Sardinia	ITALY
Costa Smeralda Hotels	Costa Smeralda	Sardinia	ITALY
Tryall Golf, Tennis, & Beach Club	Hanover		JAMAICA
Half Moon Golf, Tennis & Beach Club	Montego Bay		JAMAICA
Wyndham Rose Hall Beach Hotel	Montego Bay		JAMAICA
Runaway Bay H.E.A.R.T. Country Club	Runaway Bay	St. Ann	JAMAICA
Kawana Hotel	Ito City	Shizouka Prefecture	JAPAN
Gentling Highlands Resort	Kuala Lampur	Selangor/Pahang	MALAYSIA
Pierre Marques	Acapulco		MEXICO
Las Hadas	Acapulco		MEXICO
Puerto Azul Beach Hotel	Ternate	Cavite	PHILIPPINES
Hotel Quinta do Lago	Almancil	Algarve	PORTUGAL
Hotel Dona Filipa	Almansil	Algarve	PORTUGAL

Name	City	State	Country
Penina Golf Hotel	Portimao Codex	Algarve	PORTUGAL
Dom Pedro Golf Hotel	Quarteira	Algarve	PORTUGAL
Turnberry Hotel	Strathclyde		SCOTLAND
Greywalls Hotel	Gullane	East Lothian	SCOTLAND
Sun City Resort	Johannesburg		SOUTH AFRICA
Hotel Byblos Andaluz	Fuengirola		SPAIN
Hotel Los Monteros	Marbella	Malaga	SPAIN
Jack Tar Village, St. Kitts	Frigate Bay		ST. KITTS
Hotel du Golf			SWITZERLAND
Quellenhof Golf Hotel			SWITZERLAND
Burgenstock Hotels	Burgenstock		SWITZERLAND
Les Chevreuils	Lausanne		SWITZERLAND
Dolder Grand Hotel	Zurich		SWITZERLAND
Central Plaza Hotel	Bangkhen	Bangkok	THAILAND
Mount Irvine Bay Hotel	Scarborough		TOBAGO
Grand Hotel	Point Clear	AL	U.S.A.
Boulders Resort	Carefree	AZ	U.S.A.
The Wigwam	Litchfield Park	AZ	U.S.A.
Arizona Biltmore	Phoenix	AZ	U.S.A.
Hyatt Regency Scottsdale	Scottsdale	AZ	U.S.A.
Marriott's Camelback Inn Resort	Scottsdale	AZ	U.S.A.
Scottsdale Princess Resort	Scottsdale	AZ	U.S.A.
Loews Ventana Canyon Resort	Tucson	AZ	U.S.A.
Sheraton Tucson El Conquistador	Tucson	AZ	U.S.A.
Tuscon National Resort & Spa	Tucson	AZ	U.S.A.
Westin La Paloma	Tucson	AZ	U.S.A.
Rancho de los Caballeros	Wickenberg	AZ	U.S.A.
La Costa Hotel & Spa	Carlsbad	CA	U.S.A.

Name	City	State	Country
Carmel Valley Ranch Resort	Carmel	CA	U.S.A.
La Playa Hotel	Carmel	CA	U.S.A.
Quail Lodge	Carmel	CA	U.S.A.
Furnace Creek Inn	Death Valley	CA	U.S.A.
La Quinta Hotel Golf Resort	La Quinta	CA	U.S.A.
Silverado Country Club and Resort	Napa	CA	U.S.A.
Ojai Valley Inn and Country Club	Ojai	CA	U.S.A.
Inn & Links at Spanish Bay	Pebble Beach	CA	U.S.A.
Lodge at Pebble Beach	Pebble Beach	CA	U.S.A.
The Ritz-Carlton, Rancho Mirage	Rancho Mirage	CA	U.S.A.
Inn at Rancho Santa Fe	Rancho Santa Fe	CA	U.S.A.
Rancho Bernardo Inn	San Diego	CA	U.S.A.
The Alisal	Solvang	CA	U.S.A.
Meadowood Resort & Country Club	St. Helena	CA	U.S.A.
The Broadmoor	Colorado Springs	CO	U.S.A.
Tamarron	Durango	CO	U.S.A.
Sheraton Steamboat Springs Resort	Steamboat Springs	CO	U.S.A.
Amelia Island Plantation	Amelia Island	FL	U.S.A.
Boca Raton Hotel & Club	Boca Raton	FL	U.S.A.
South Seas Plantation Resort	Captiva Island	FL	U.S.A.
Grenelefe Resort	Grenelefe	FL	U.S.A.
The Diplomat	Hollywood-By-The-Sea	FL	U.S.A.
Mission Inn Golf & Tennis Resort	Howey-In-The-Hills	FL	U.S.A.
Indian River Plantation	Hutchinson Island	FL	U.S.A.
Longboat Key Club	Longboat Key	FL	U.S.A.
The Doral Hotel & Country Club	Miami	FL	U.S.A.

Name	City	State	Country
Turnberry Isle Country Club	Miami	FL	U.S.A.
Grand Cypress Golf Club & Villas	Orlando	FL	U.S.A.
The Breakers	Palm Beach	FL	U.S.A.
PGA Sheraton Resort	Palm Beach Gardens	FL	U.S.A.
Palm Aire Hotel & Spa	Pompano Beach	FL	U.S.A.
Marriott at Sawgrass	Ponte Vedra Beach	FL	U.S.A.
Burnt Store Marina Resort	Puta Gorda	FL	U.S.A.
Innisbrook	Tarpon Springs	FL	U.S.A.
Palm Beach Polo & Country Club	W.Palm Beach	FL	U.S.A.
Saddlebrook Golf & Tennis Resort	Wesley Chapel (Tampa)	FL	U.S.A.
Stouffer PineIsle Resort	Atlanta	GA	U.S.A.
Callaway Gardens	Pine Mountain	GA	U.S.A.
The Cloister	Sea Island	GA	U.S.A.
Kapalua Bay Hotel & Villas	Kapalua, Maui	HI	U.S.A.
Maui Prince Hotel	Kihei, Maui	HI	U.S.A.
Mauna Lani Bay Hotel	Kohala Coast, Is. of HI	HI	U.S.A.
Westin Mauna Kea	Kohula Coast Amuea	HI	U.S.A.
Kiahuna Plantation Resort	Koloa, Kauai	HI	U.S.A.
Hyatt Regency Maui	Lahaina, Maui	HI	U.S.A.
The Westin Kauai, Kauai Lagoons	Lihue	HI	U.S.A.
Sheraton Makaha Resort	Makaha, Oahu	HI	U.S.A.
Kaluakoi Hotel and Golf Club	Maunaloa, Molokai	HI	U.S.A.
Sheraton Mirage Princeville Hotel	Princeville	HI	U.S.A.
Elkhorn Resort At Sun Valley	Sun Valley	ID	U.S.A.
Sun Valley Lodge	Sun Valley	ID	U.S.A.

Name	City	State	Country
Eagle Ridge Inn & Resort	Galena	IL	U.S.A.
French Lick Springs Golf Resort	French Lick	IN	U.S.A.
Marriotts Griffin Gate Resort	Lexington	KY	U.S.A.
Chatham Bars Inn & Cottage	Chatham	MA	U.S.A.
New Seabury Cape Cod	New Seabury	MA	U.S.A.
Sugarloaf Inn Resort	Carrabassett Valley	ME	U.S.A.
Samoset Resort	Rockport	ME	U.S.A.
Shanty Creek-Schuss Mtn. Resort	Bellaire	MI	U.S.A.
Grand Traverse Resort Village	Grand Traverse Village	MI	U.S.A.
Boyne Highlands Resort	Harbor Springs	MI	U.S.A.
Lodge of the Four Seasons	Lake Ozark	MO	U.S.A.
Marriott's Tan-Tar-A Resort	Osage Beach	MO	U.S.A.
Broadwater Beach Hotel	Biloxi	MS	U.S.A.
Big Sky Resort	Big Sky	MT	U.S.A.
Grove Park Inn & Country Club	Asheville	NC	U.S.A.
Hound Ears Club	Blowing Rock	NC	U.S.A.
High Hampton Inn & Country Club	Cashiers	NC	U.S.A.
Etowah Valley Country Club	Hendersonville	NC	U.S.A.
The Eseeola Lodge	Linville	NC	U.S.A.
Pinehurst Hotel & Country Club	Pinehurst	NC	U.S.A.
Mid Pines Resort	Southern Pines	NC	U.S.A.
Mount Washington	Bretton Woods	NH	U.S.A.
Balsams Grand Resort Hotel	Dixville Notch	NH	U.S.A.
Hanover Inn	Hanover	NH	U.S.A.
Marriott's Seaview Resort	Absecon	NJ	U.S.A.
Inn of the Mountain Gods	Mescalero	NM	U.S.A.

Name	City	State	Country
Desert Inn Hotel and Casino	Las Vegas	NV	U.S.A.
The Sagamore	At Bolton Landing	NY	U.S.A.
Nevele Country Club	Ellenville	NY	U.S.A.
The Lodge at Black Butte Ranch	Black Butte Ranch	OR	U.S.A.
Salishan Lodge	Gleneden Beach	OR	U.S.A.
Sunriver Lodge and Resort	Sunriver	OR	U.S.A.
Avalon Lakes Golf Course & Inn	Warren	OH	U.S.A.
Shawnee Inn	Shawnee-On-Delaware	PA	U.S.A.
Hyatt Regency Cerromar Beach	Dorado	PR	U.S.A.
Palmas del Mar	Humacao	PR	U.S.A.
Kiawah Island Resort	Charleston	SC	U.S.A.
Seabrook Island Resort	Charleston	SC	U.S.A.
Marriott's Hilton Head Resort	Hilton Head Island	SC	U.S.A.
Palmetto Dunes Resort	Hilton Head Island	SC	U.S.A.
Sea Pines Resorts	Hilton Head Island	SC	U.S.A.
Westin Resort Hilton Head	Hilton Head Island	SC	U.S.A.
Wild Dunes Beach & Racquet Club	Isle of Palm	SC	U.S.A.
Myrtle Beach Hilton	Myrtle Beach	SC	U.S.A.
Fairfield Glade Conference Center	Fairfield Glade	TN	U.S.A.
Hyatt Regency DFW	DFW Airport	TX	U.S.A.
Horseshoe Bay Country Club Resort	Horseshoe Bay	TX	U.S.A.
Waterwood National Resort & CC	Huntsville	TX	U.S.A.
Walden on Lake Conroe	Montgomery	TX	U.S.A.
Woodlands Inn Resort & Conf. Ctr.	The Woodlands	TX	U.S.A.
The Homestead	Hot Springs	VA	U.S.A.

Name	City	State	Country
The Tides Lodge	Irvington	VA	U.S.A.
Tides Inn	Irvington	VA	U.S.A.
Colonial Williamsburg Inn	Williamsburg	VA	U.S.A.
Ford's Colony	Williamsburg	VA	U.S.A.
Kingsmill On The James	Williamsburg	VA	U.S.A.
Carambola Beach Resort Golf Club	St. Croix	VI	U.S.A.
The Buccaneer Hotel	St. Croix	VI	U.S.A.
Mount Mansfield Resort	Stowe	VT	U.S.A.
Sugarbush Inn	Warren	VT	U.S.A.
The Woodstock Inn & Resort	Woodstock	VT	U.S.A.
Inn at Semiahmoo	Blaine	WA	U.S.A.
The Resort at Port Ludlow	Port Ludlow	WA	U.S.A.
The American Club	Kohler	WI	U.S.A.
Olympia Village Conference Center & Spa	Oconomowoc	WI	U.S.A.
The Greenbrier	White Sulphur Springs	WV	U.S.A.
Jackson Hole Racquet Club Resort	Jackson Hole	WY	U.S.A.
Monchs Posthotel	7506 Bad Herrenalb		W. GERMANY
Schlosshotel Kronberg	Kronberg		W. GERMANY

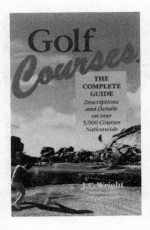
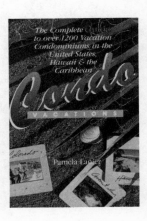

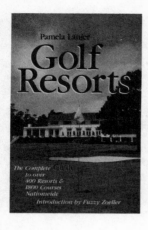

Golf Resorts
The Complete Guide

The first ever comprehensive guide to over 500 golf resorts coast to coast. Includes complete details of each resort facility and golf course particulars. As an added bonus, there is a guide within the guide of over 1,800 public golf courses with full details. Introduction by Fuzzy Zoeller.

Elegant Small Hotels
A Connoiseur's Guide

This selective guide for discriminating travelers describes over 200 of America's finest characterized by exquisite rooms, fine dining, and perfect service par excellence. Introduction by Peter Duchin.
"Elegant Small Hotels makes a seductive volume for window shopping."
—Chicago Sun Times.

All-Suite Hotel Guide
The Definitive Directory

The only guide to the all suite hotel industry features over 800 hotels nationwide and abroad. There is a special bonus list of temporary office facilities. A perfect choice fr business travellers and much appreciated by families who enjoy the additional privacy provided by two rooms.

AVAILABLE IN BOOK STORES EVERYWHERE

Travel Books from
LANIER GUIDES

ORDER FORM

QTY	TITLE	EACH	TOTAL
	All-Suite Hotel Guide	$14.95	
	Condo Vacations — The Complete Guide	$12.95	
	Golf Courses — The Complete Guide	$14.95	
	Golf Resorts — The Complete Guide	$14.95	
	Golf Resorts International	$19.95	
	Elegant Small Hotels	$14.95	
	Sub-Total		$
	Shipping		$ 2.00 each
	TOTAL ENCLOSED		$

Send your order to:

TEN SPEED PRESS
P.O. Box 7123
Berkeley, California 94707
Allow 3 to 4 weeks for delivery

- -

Please send my order to:

NAME _____

ADDRESS _____

CITY _____ STATE _____ ZIP _____

Travel Notes

Travel Notes

Travel Notes

Travel Notes

Travel Notes

Travel Notes

Travel Notes

Travel Notes

Travel Notes

Travel Notes

Travel Notes